Library of
Davidson College

Order and Might

SUNY Series in Philosophy
Robert Cummings Neville, Editor

Order and Might

Nathan Rotenstreich

State University of New York Press

Published by
State University of New York Press, Albany

© 1988 State University of New York

All rights reserved

Printed in the United States of America

No part of this book may be used or reproduced
in any manner whatsoever without written permission
except in the case of brief quotations embodied in
critical articles and reviews.

For information, address State University of New York
Press, State University Plaza, Albany, N.Y., 12246

Library Congress Cataloging in Publication Data

Rotenstreich, Nathan, 1914-
    Order and might.

    (SUNY series in philosophy)
    Includes index.
    1. Power (Social science) 2. State, The.
3. Human rights. 4. Political obligations. I. Title.
II. Series.
JC330.R673 1988   303.3'3   87-9980
ISBN 0-88706-628-3
ISBN 0-88706-630-5 (pbk.)

Contents

Author's Note

PART ONE: THE DOMAIN

		Page
Chapter One	Modes and Forms	3
Chapter Two	The State and Order	21
Chapter Three	Manifestations of Power	37

PART TWO: ACTION

Chapter Four	Of Politics	57
Chapter Five	Politics and History	71
Chapter Six	Politics and Morality	83

PART THREE: PRINCIPLES

Chapter Seven	Of Justice	107
Chapter Eight	Of Freedom	135
Chapter Nine	Of Equality	185
Chapter Ten	Of Rights and Duties	209
Chapter Eleven	Presuppositions and Some Consequences	223
Index of Proper Names		233
Subject Index		235

Author's Note

The present book is an attempt to explore the structure of the socio-political existence. The assumption is that there is no genetic explanation to the factual presence of that existence within the scope of reality and within the realm of the variety of human activities. The shift towards a phenomenological exploration is the positive side of the lack of a genetic one.

The "Gestalt" of the socio-political existence as a conjunction of order and might and the continuous effort to mold the realm presupposes attitudes or human intentionalities against the background of history, practice, and its diverse experiences. Some of the aspects of these components have been dealt with in the author's previous books.

I wish to thank my friend Professor Berel Lang for his support and to express my gratitude to Ms. Judith Block and the staff at SUNY Albany Press for the care and attention they gave to the manuscript.

Jerusalem, 1987   N.R.

PART ONE

The Domain

Chapter One

Modes and Forms

I

Examination of problems pertaining to society and to man's social reality is a partial attempt at self-knowledge; within that reality we exist. As our existence is characterized by consciousness and behavior, the examination is in certain respects analogous to one of epistemology and ethics. Therefore, we shall follow the methodology often used in epistemological and moral enquiry. Our point of departure is the world of experience, and our first step will be to chart the spheres which constitute that world. The nature of the subject matter warrants this procedure. If one undertakes to examine a datum whose meaning is somehow familiar to all on the basis of day-by-day experience, the task is to isolate it from other data and resolve it into component elements. So we begin with a morphological analysis of social reality, as it presents itself to us. The second step, parallel and complementary, is what may be called a *regressive* analysis to determine the preconditions of significant phenomena revealed by the first.

The subject matter of our examination is familiar to us. Thus we will start by indicating what we mean when we say "society" or "state", by tracing its essential characteristics. At this early stage, it is not possible to propose a comprehensive definition; indeed, no such definition is to be found. The way to define it is progressively to expound its major distinguishing features. We do not intend to offer the abstract definition of society as a vague compound of atomic particles, which assumes that a society of men represents a species of the genus of compound entities resolvable into their constituents. Our concern is with a human society to which we are related and of which we already have an incipient understanding, however imprecise. By restricting the universe of discourse to society in this sense, we have circumscribed the first area of our investigation.

II

We proceed from what may tentatively be called the totality of the forms and modes of concerted human life and action. By forms, we mean the patterns of interrelatedness, such as the family, the agricultural community, the city, and the state, which display varying degrees of organization, occasionally formulated in rules and regulations. By modes, we mean the broad diversity of corporate relations and activities which resist pigeonholing in patterns, including, for example, the bonds established between individuals who share a common evanescent interest, either theoretical or practical, or the collusion of the members of a theatre audience or a cafe clientele. The distinction between forms and modes provides no information whether, for instance, they are long-lived or short-lived, inclusive or partial, involving the participation of all the inhabitants of a particular territory or the absence of comprehensive membership. The diverse forms of corporate life and action cannot be reduced to a common denominator. Thus, for example, there are significant differences between the form of family and of state life; society is a pattern of living and acting in concert constituted by manifold and diverse modes and forms. Within it, one finds not only the family and the theatre audience but also, let us say, groups of friends and agricultural communities. This view implies that the state itself is included in society as one of its many forms. From another point of view, the state differs and is separate from society: it differs precisely because it is one form among many and is separate because its mode of existence and operation is distinguishable from society's. Because society includes manifold modes and forms of corporate life, its features are vaguer, less definite, more difficult to specify and classify by pattern and rule. The state, being a special form, has a higher degree of determination, formulated or not, and a more clearly structured order; it is an institution. Society contains institutions but is not itself one. This description is deliberately drafted in terms of degree, of "more" and "less" marked determination and order. There is no way of drawing a sharp line between society and state, as if there were two distinct realms—one void of order and patterned conduct, the other characterized by determinate patterns and order, and as if the transition from one to the other presupposes a leap. On the basis of this mode of comparison and grading, it may be said that the state is a mode not only of corporate human life but also one which has taken on form, namely, one featuring institutionality and order, and, within certain limits, lending itself to definition. But to say that the state is an institution and an ordered form is not enough. Among the diverse forms included in society as an all-embracing whole, the state is the most sweeping, being a form of comprehensive order and organization. Like society, it is inclusive and comprehensive; unlike society, it is one form among many, whereas society is a whole composed of many subordinate forms. The state is comprehensive as form and organization; society is comprehensive as a totality.

III

What is meant by "an organization of human beings"? It originates in, and is constituted by, corporate life and action. By its very nature, it sets bounds to the conduct of human life and action in concert. In the modern state, the limits thus set are very obvious, in the bounds between citizen and alien, between an "insider" of the organization and an "outsider," between adults with rights and minors without them, and so on. Organization, as such, does not create the bounds *ex nihilo*. Limitation of conduct is operative at all levels and stages of life. Even friendly human relations set limits, for friendship implies a state of affairs in which it is justifiable to expect a certain type of conduct between a person and his friend, and which involves obligation, permission, and prohibition, though not defined by a canon; if the expected conduct is not forthcoming, the friendship is evidently null and void. Limits exist in the family sphere as well. Even the collusion between the members of the theatre audience tacitly circumscribes conduct. But in the state, organization is explicit; the state expressly curbs conduct. Every organization circumscribes conduct within fixed bounds. At times, the circumscription assumes a legal form, written or unwritten. If the state functions as an overt manifestation of latent limitation, it is but a crystallization or accentuation of the ways of corporate life inherent in the diverse modes and forms of society. Every organization is a crystallization; and, as an organization, the state is one too. Family bounds are drawn by genealogy: descendants of forefathers are insiders, persons of other extraction are outsiders. In the state, bounds are drawn by an act of organization, and the state itself is the product of an act of that kind.

Patterns of corporate life, other than the state, which are likely to be fluid in mode or form—like friendship or family—emerge in the organization of the state. Organization is not an absolute beginning but an overt accentuation of the preexisting orders. Accordingly, it may be said that the state is to the shifting and indeterminate patterns of the conduct of society what every expression is to its indeterminate matter. A similar transition from vagueness to explicity is that from naive knowledge to science and from folklore to the craft of fiction. Science is not the invention of knowledge but its deliberate expression and cultivation; it isolates knowledge from the total body of activities of man's daily life and frees it from the diverse spheres of doing. The same with fiction and folklore: the art of fiction is not a part of the total network of human activities as a fable is woven into the web of relations between father and son; it is rather a conscious creation and, in that respect, a singling out and bringing into relief of what is already present in the fable. Wherever we find a projection of a given factor, for example, bounds-circumscription in the state or deliberate knowledge in science, we set a transformation from vagueness and enmeshment to structure. The purpose of this analogy is to show that, as accentuation, the element of organization typifying the state as a form is parallel to the element of activity operative—e.g., in science and literary art. It is that element, and not the element of power, which is the first aspect to disclose itself in an analysis of the place of the state in relation to the modes and forms of corporate life which make society.

IV

The modes and forms of the behavior of men who live and act in concert are not dictated by the order of the cosmos or of nature as are the patterns of conduct of atoms in the laws of physics. Yet, at the same time, they are not altogether arbitrary or entirely contingent upon the voluntary choice which directs us to different courses of action. Socio-political life is neither as natural as the course of physical or biological nature nor as arbitrary as the joining of a club. It occupies a position between compulsion and arbitrariness. We are members of society by virtue of our diverse modes of conduct; in this respect, the state accentuates and renders prominent the fact of our membership in society by demarcating the bounds of the society to which we belong, in terms, for example, of political and geographical limits. It is possible to break off a friendship, but the breach always abides within the realm of society. The status of the state gives overt expression to factual membership in society by changing it from a mere factuality to a compulsion. Consequently, in the state, an element of coercion is added to that of factual membership. Accentuation through organization emerges as an accentuation through compulsion.

This coercion or necessity is never tantamount to natural necessity, lacking, as it does, the force of the laws of nature. The coercive force of the state is a necessity within the limits of society, not within the limits of the cosmos. Attention must be called to yet another distinguishing feature of the state as a form among forms. It is distinguished from other forms included in society as a total form of forms not only by its peculiar intermediate status between compulsion and arbitrariness, but also by the power accruing to its organization to impose demands upon human beings and to force man to subject his modes of conduct to its rules. It exerts influence by the very fact that it circumscribes conduct; its influential aspect becomes its coercive aspect. As the element of organization in the state does not represent a creation *ex nihilo,* so too, that of coercion is not introduced by a *tour de force.* There is latent force at other levels and stages of social life. Every human encounter, every confrontation of X with the fact of Y's existence if a confrontation with a limit or curb to X's field of activity. Inherent in the very fact of Y's existence is a restraining factor, which can also represent a claim worth X's consideration, whether to be rendered spontaneously on his part or forced upon him by the inescapable fact of Y's existence. In the state, that element, latent in corporate life, is made manifest. It is deliberately isolated, as it were, from the tissue of corporate life, and deliberately and openly maintained, for the deliberate purpose of subjecting us to its influence. In this respect as well, the state does not represent a novel factor; as wielding power, it is not a metamorphosis of an earlier apolitical phase of corporate life.

If the power accruing to political organizaiton is but one manifestation of the latent force of social life, then the state, as organization, does not occupy an entirely independent position in relation to society. Just as science represents the quintessence of naive knowledge, so the state represents the quintessence of the multifarious modes and forms constitutive of social or corporate life. The broad diversity of social relations does not cease to exist within the comprehensive framework of the state-forms; and it is only owing to the continued existence of this diversity that the state-form is one of the many forms of social life; that society, through statehood, is vouchsafed new channels and patterns of corporate life.

The process of crystallizing accentuation whereby society passes into statehood accounts for the mode of existence peculiar to the state. Occupying a median position between coercion and arbitrariness, the state could not exist were it not to be acknowledged as a state and were men not to direct themselves towards it as towards a form of organization accompanied by power. The state is not a part of nature whose existence is independent of the activity of men who direct themselves towards it. For a state to be maintained, it is necessary to maintain not only the inclusive organization but also those modes and forms of corporate life and action which alone render the state meaningful as a structure of compact organization.

V

It is now necessary to examine the concept of order, which has bearing upon additional aspects of the nature of the state. The meaning of the notion of the state as order, or of the concept of political order, can be clarified by analysis of different connotations of the concept of order in general. That its primary sense is not confined to the political universe of discourse is attested by our speaking, for example, of the order of cardinal numbers, or of nature. If we have recourse to the concept of order in a social or political context, it is solely because of its relevance to other, broader, contexts, and because its essential ambiguity is not cancelled when it is transferred to a political universe of discourse. Thus, for example, within the context of mediaeval philosophy and Christian theology, it connotes the state of earthly or mundane existence in preparation for the Kingdom of Heaven. It was possible to give it this meaning because, at bottom, it stands for the allocation of things in their allotted place or places. To earthly existence was assigned the place of preparation for the Kingdom of Heaven. In this significance, the idea of order pertains to a relation between mundane and extramundane realms of being. The ordering factor accordingly represents a relation between parts of being. But the idea of ordering things or assigning places can also connote allocation in accordance with a principle or rule within a single realm. The term 'order' is employed within the context of the cardinal numbers, where order represents a series or sequence in which each succeeding number is larger by one unit than the one preceding it.

There is yet another, more general, sense in which the term 'order' is employed. In this, it means a network of interrelationships and linked correspondences between sounds or colors or even ideas, as when we speak of orderly systematic thought. Here, although there is neither a rule of allocation as in the context of cardinal numbers nor a metaphysical topography as in the mediaeval idea of order, it is still customary to designate such linked entities by the term 'order.'

In the political usage of the concept of order, one usually refers to the following principal connotations:

1. The concept of political order in the general sense of a framework or structure of life in concert composed of many component factors, that is, of many human beings. In this sense, 'political order' stands for an organization or cohesion.

2. The concept in the sense of a disposition subservient to some definite end, say, disposition for the sake of self-sufficiency in the Aristotelian sense, or for the sake of preservation of life, as understood by Hobbes, or for the sake of realizing justice, as proposed by various philosophical schools and social movements. The order of the state is controlled by a principle of allocation which is not composed of the totality of interrelationships within it, but is a destination towards which it is directed. The analogy here is between the mediaeval concept of order and the concept of political order.

3. At times, political order serves to denote the allocation of things in their proper places, the determination of fields of conduct, the dictation

of permissible and prohibited, the definition of the character and hierarchy of political authority. In that sense, it may be regarded as assigning places to things when by things one means the modes of conduct of men in society. The concept may be so used even when we have no rule for arranging things in their places as we have in arranging a sequence of cardinal numbers, or, more circumspectly, even when we employ a variety of rules for determining the relative places of things and do not possess a well-defined principle such as the one employed by mathematicians.

Finding that the concept of political order is employed in several different senses, we are led to the conclusion that no single connotation can be said to exhaust the complex meaning of it. Not even the order of family life can be reduced to any single connotation: it consists not merely of biological or genealogical ties between parents and offspring but also of economic relations, patterns of etiquette, and the like. This is all the more true of the political order. One implication of crystallized complexity is the ambivalence, duality and, at times, even clash between order as disposition designed for a purpose and order as allotment of places to things. A tension exists, for instance, between power, which guarantees compliance with the state's idea of how component factors are to be disposed in their respective places, and justice for all irrespective of allotted position. The variety and complexity of factors constitutive of the state illuminate both its place in relation to other forms of corporate life and the inner structure of the state-form itself as an accentuation of many diverse subsidiary structures.

Because the political order is, in every instance, a crystallization or accentuation, the political domain remains a public domain, and the political order a public order proper. Its very essence stands to be open and, only because it is open, it constitutes the most comprehensive order of corporate life. Being common to society as a whole, it must be public. A state which is not public is a contradiction in terms. No matter what goes on in the state, it is always public, at least as a matter of principle, even in connection with secret deliberations which serve the public—i.e., open—sphere.

The nature of the political order can also be illumined by comparing it with what may be called the biological order of corporate life—like the order existing in the kingdom of the bees. A biological order serves one purpose; for example, the production of honey with bees, or the survival and propagation of the species in the animal kingdom. It is always an order of the species, never of its individual members. Unlike the biological, the political is not an order of the species, as the empirical fact that no one single political order exists for the human species as a whole makes clear. Even supposing that a universal human state might be established, it would probably include many different subsidiary orders. But what really matters is this: granting that the one and only purpose in the political order is to guarantee and promote the survival of the human race, what is meant is survival not through propagation or reproduction, but, at most, through the instrumentality of the organization and the protection that it affords. The structure of the political order, unlike that of the biological, is not a system of biological functions serving biological ends but, at best, a system of nonbiological means invented to safeguard biological existence. Even conceding biological teleology, one would still have to admit that the manifest functions of the political order subserve many other ends which cannot be accounted for by the protective theory, in terms of protection from aggressive individuals or aggressive groups. Even a spokesman for the protective theory, who would hold these other functions to be secondary, would admit that they have become independent and, in fact, filling the expanse of the social reality, they command the response of individuals. Thus functional manifestations of the political order, such as the determination of structures of conduct or the guaranteeing of equality, can in no wise be identified with the function of protecting life, in the primary sense of that concept, let alone with the assurance of the survival of the species.

Nor can the political order be identified with, or reduced to, the disposition and maintenance of the division of labor among men, either in the sense proposed by Plato, who considered it the good of the political order, or in the sense proposed by Marx, who considered it the evil. Underlying both approaches is the assumption that the political order is based upon the inherent difference between men and their mutual interdependence, which, owing to the creation of the diversity of wants, can only be satisfied through reciprocal aid. This view, however, overlooks the fact that the political order implies reciprocal dependence against the background not only of diversity but also of equality. Men who differ still acknowledge each other because, as human beings, they share something, and because the political organization crystallizes this common factor and brings it into relief, even though it does not thereby cancel the diversity. Diversity in itself cannot account for the nature of the political order as a common order. Nor can interdependence against the background of reciprocal accommodation of wants be identified with the acknowledgement of the common order, even assuming that this common order sanctions and protects diversity. For, even allowing the validity of the theory that the political order is based on diversity, one would still have to recognize the allocation of places to people as a function of it. That allocation, as the correlate of order, is not a ramification of diversity and division. Allocation or disposition is controlled by a principle which is not in itself equivalent to diversity and division, even though they might constitute its content. As a dispositional function, political order implies not only them but also the allocation of each and every constituent to a proper sphere; the circumscription of individual realms inherent in it indicates that the fact of human diversity in life in concert, of men seeking cohesion in diversity, is not the ultimate orgin of it. The origin must be sought elsewhere, and the first step towards its disclosure has already been taken. Our examination of the characteristic features of social and political organization showed that the political order is distinguished from the natural by both a vulnerability to infraction and its constitution by deliberate acts of accentuation and crystallization. Acknowledgement of its real existence and authority does not exclude the possibility of a real infringement of its laws. It is possible, then, to recognize the yoke of political authority, and yet not submit to it, by deviating from the rut into which submission directs us. In this respect, the political order is distinguished from the order of the numbers as well. For, were one to stray from the groove established by the order of numbers by saying that the number two follows the number three, one would fall into a contradiction, whereas a breach of the political order involves no inner contradiction. The political order is not comparable to that of a chess game from which we can withdraw by simply refusing to play. It is a public order, and it it impossible to subsist outside its realm.

To say that the political is not a natural order is to say, among other things, that it does not exist physically. But it does have physical anchorage; it is an order in space, it occupies a geographical or territorial position. Yet it does not so hold unless we are perpetually ordering it. There is no political order without acts of directedness and intentionality, none in the acknowledgement of order as a certain meaning, or even as an idea. Men must live and act in concert for the expression to exist. The existence of political order is rooted in human reality; if it has the status of a reality, it is only because the human beings who constitute and maintain it are real. It is a plain expression of what is called 'integration,' and, without men who direct themselves towards that, integration is nonexistent.

No phase of man's existence is void of order as disposition or placement and circumscription of realms. Were there no order, there would be no existence. Existence, as a fact, implies circumscription of realms and, in itself, confronts us as a limiting factor that prevents us from levitation in empty space. As a limiting and restraining function, every circumscription of realms determines patterns of conduct. In that way, every realm or bound suggests regulation and—what may be called—factual normativity, not of values such as the good or the beautiful, but normativity nevertheless. It is a normativity stemming from the fact that the circumscription of bounds compels us to take given conditions into consideration and to respond to them accordingly. In an existence whose realms are charted, our attitudes and actions are not unregulated; for existence, as such a circumscription, is regulative. Man's relation to that part of the world in which he exists—whose factuality he acknowledges and whose bounds delimit his sphere of life and activity—is a regulated one, regulated by his relation to the factuality of his fellow's existence, whether as an individual or as a group.

VI

From this point of view, one may aver that the question related to the first origin of the political order is meaningless. There exists only a transition from one order to another, from a factual order to one constituted from and by an intentionality directed to constituting it—or else from fragmentary orders to a more comprehensive order. We could say that the political order is established by preformation, as the biologists call it, by development from one initial form to another. We must not disregard the question whether the existence of the state as order and organization is by nature, that is, whether or not man is a political being by nature. In the preceding analysis, we sought to place the state between arbitrariness and necessity. Now we shall place man, in terms of the state or the political order, between contract and necessity by nature.

We must first enquire into the meanings of nature and its applicability to the political order. We may perhaps distinguish in the context between four meanings of nature and natural.

1. 'Nature' or 'natural' connotes a situation or feature which is fundamental or primary. The natural order would be the one lacking a prior origin, as with the war of all against all, a situation which, in this view, is the primary and thus the natural one.

2. 'Nature' connotes a status or essence: that which is part of the essence of the thing or entity under consideration, is natural; for example, man is a political being in terms of his essence. To say this is not to say that he is factually, a political being from the dawn of time; it means that, by his very essence, he is a political being. To put it negatively, so long as man's political essence has not been realized, his essence as man is unrealized. This concept of nature warrants the claim that man may be a political creature by nature even if the political order is constituted by contract.

3. The third connotation is akin to the second but analytically distinguishable from it. Here, 'nature' stands for a standard or norm, a state of affairs, by which human activity ought to be regulated. It is not just an essence realized as a matter of course but one worthy of realization. For example, it can be said—and has been said by Kant—that while man's essence implies both sociability and unsociability, sociability is implied by his normative essence and must be preferred to the unsociability which is

also present. This meaning of 'nature' underlies the observation that man is aggressive in fact but civilized by norms and that the norm is preferable to the fact.

4. 'Nature' can also be employed to signify that which man has not created. When something is so said to exist by nature, its existence is held to be independent of intentional human effort, as distinguished from the existence of things which man himself creates—his tools, for instance. It is this sense that underlies the distinction drawn between natural and historical reality, contrasting the automatic process of nature, which does not presuppose human endeavor, with the process of history, which does. A second distinction is that drawn between natural and artificial objects and states, when 'artificial' denotes what is created by intentional effort. Here again, 'nature' means the primordial or primary, but emphasis has been shifted from temporal priority to priority of character or essence.

We may now consider the validity of the assumption that the political order exists by nature or that man is a political creature by nature. Even at first glance, it is clear that the assumption is based upon the concept of nature in the twofold sense of aboriginality and essentiality. Since no phase of human existence is void of order, the existence of order may be said to be natural, as being aboriginal, ultimate, or underivable. It might be permissible to add that even Hobbes's idea of the state of nature is not incompatible with the idea of an aboriginal order, except that, according to him, the natural or primordial order is unstable, insecure, and fraught with danger because it harbors the omnipresent threat of violent death inflicted by the individuals. In human reality order exists by nature, provided one understands nature in the sense of an aboriginal state, but not that the order of human reality exists by nature in the sense of independence of man's creative effort and activity.

The Aristotelian doctrine concerning man as a political creature by nature is based upon the third connotation, the idea of nature as a normative essence. For that matter, in the Aristotelian philosophy as a whole, nature generally connotes the entelechy of teleological essence, so that it is understandable that man is said to have realized his essence or *telos*—at least from the point of view of his practical life—once he has realized it as a political creature. But the assumption that man finds his realization in the political order is open to question. Indeed, the question which inevitably arises is implicit in Aristotle's further assumption that man's ability to maintain the political order presupposes, and is planted in, his nature as a thinking and speaking creature. This second assumption can be developed in a direction which diverges from Aristotle's line of reasoning by correlating it with the idea that the political order owes its existence to our directedness towards it, as well as our endeavors to maintain it. The two ideas, taken in conjunction, justify the assertion that the existence of the political order presupposes the existence of men who understand it and relate themselves to it on the basis of their understanding. This understanding need not necessarily be explicit. Human activity within the circumscribed limits of order, and in keeping with its prescriptions, presupposes and manifests understanding, active or actual. That I refrain from seizing the space occupied by my fellow renders my conduct concordant with the demands implicit in the bounds circumscribed by his existence; bounds which, to be respected, must be understood.

Thus, to posit the existence of the political order, we must presuppose the existence of men endowed with understanding. To assume the existence of a common order is to assume the existence of human beings possessed of common understanding. Understanding cannot warrantably be identified with the understanding of the political order, or, for that matter, of any specific state of affairs. Neither understanding in itself nor understanding-guided activity is confined to, or exhausted in, the political domain. Both belong to the essence of man, and that is manifest in different ways and in different spheres of existence. Understanding always points to a relatedness founded in discernment and alertness, and whose nucleus is theoretical. Being practical, political activity within a network of relations controlled by the political order does not exhaust the essence of human activity. When we say that man acts in keeping with this ordered network of relationships—we say that man, who is not merely practical, is capable of being practical, that is, political. Man is an understanding creature by nature, and, as such, is capable of being a political creature. Integration, as the *conditio sine qua non* of political order, presupposes understanding, which is not exhausted in integrative activities. Hence man's nature, as his essence, is not to be equated with his character as a political creature.

One possibility of human nature is realized in the political domain, but that does not use up its other immanent possibilities, nor is it even independent of them. The life of the political order is not sustained by political acts alone. It is impossible to derive that life from man's nature or essence as a creature endowed with understanding, just as it is generally impossible to derive actuality from potentiality. Nevertheless, if we take the existence of the political order as our factual point of departure and enquire into the conditions of its possibility, we find that it presupposes human nature as endowed with understanding. Thus Aristotle's tenet that man is a rational creature does not warrant his conclusion that man is a political creature by nature.

A further questioning of Aristotle, again on Aristotelian grounds, reveals that while his correlation of man as a linguistic with man as a political creature is acceptable, the inference which he makes is not. In itself, the correlation is upheld by two principal features of language—its function as the vehicle of intersubjective communication and its essence as a realm demanding understanding, whether on the part of the speaker or the auditor. Language is not a chaotic conglomeration of sounds welling up in our throats at a given instant. It is an order obtaining between meaningful sounds arranged in well-defined places. Were language the vehicle of personal emotions only, it could not transmit them, let alone be intelligible, to people who do not share those which it articulates. It is precisely by occupying a semiobjective or intersubjective position that it is capable of serving as a vehicle for personal emotions and is rendered an initial realization of both understanding and order. Furthermore, its structure is not a given fact, that is, is not implicit in the factual existence of a multiplicity of human beings; it is a created structure. If the notions of man as a political and as a linguistic creature are correlative, it is because language is at once the primary reflection of understanding, that is, of the essential attribute of human nature, and the primary realization of an order open to human understanding. The political order is, accordingly, only one manifestation or realization of order in general, of created, intelligible, order; it is not primary, if only because the order of language must accompany us at all times and because our nature as political creatures presupposes our nature as creatures of speech.

Consequently, the conclusion that the political order exists by nature—in the sense of an essential attribute of human existence—cannot be accepted without reservation, especially when essence is assigned normative value. If the political order is just one realization of human nature, there is all the more reason for challenging the assumption that it is its supreme realization. The political order is related to man's ability to understand and, consequently, to his ability to orientate himself to existence by means of his understanding, to create structures of understanding and to circumscribe his existence within those self-same structures. That being so, what obliges us to give priority to understanding realized over understanding in itself? The belief that manifest realizations of understanding are preferable to understanding as such is derived from a specific Aristotelian theory whose axial assumption is that actualization is preferable to potentiality, or realization to possiblity. Even conceding the validity of this assumption, the question still to be answered is this: Are there sufficient grounds for assuming that understanding is, in itself, a mere potentiality which is realized or actualized only in the public spheres of, let us say, language and the state? It seems that the answer is no. Understanding is a realization in itself, although it is also realized outside, in the public domain. But there is one realization of it which can never appear in public, namely, reflexive understanding or understanding of understanding. This, as a matter of principle, cannot be realized save within understanding itself and can, therefore, establish no public domain. As creatures endowed with understanding, men are creatures who understand their understanding. Understood understanding is not a bond between men; by its very nature it is a interiorized bond which never appears in public and is never institutionalized. The objection to the view that the political order exists by nature in the sense that it comprises a normative essence is thus twofold: first, that it manifests but one aspect or possibility of man's essence; second, that there is one aspect of man's nature, as a creature endowed with understanding, to wit, his reflexive understanding, that can never be realized in it. It is, therefore, unjustifiable to present it as the norm or standard of man's essence. That essence does not have to be actualized, because it is in a state of actuality by its very nature.

If this is so, man is not only a suprapolitical creature—and, as such, potentially a political one—but also an extrapolitical one. The understanding of understanding, or the consciousness of consciousness, is the unique possession of the individual, whose realization is neither in the public nor in the semi-objective order, political or linguistic. Consciousness as alertness, as discernment stemming from alertness, and as self-examination of alertness is the specific distinguishing feature of the individual. Man's position in the universe is linked to the fact that none of his creations, neither the political order nor language, is conscious of itself. In so far as any human creation has consciousness, it is the consciousness of the individuals who direct themselves towards it. No matter how much greater than their creators men's creations may be—and this applies to the works of individual creators too, such as works of art—the creations lack self-consciousness, simply because they are created and exist in the sphere which is separated from that of their creators. Endowed as he is with self-consciousness, the individual does not find his exhaustive realization in the political order. Nor is the political order simply a continuation of the individual; it is his creation, and, because it is, it does not mirror its creator faithfully. The gulf and incommensurability between creator and creation make a conflict of norms conceivable. There can be a clash between the norms of the individual, as a creature who understands his understanding, and of social organization as set in integrative and ordering functions that do not, of themselves, turn towards the inner world of the individual.

The individual is also distinguished from his creations by his status as a physical existent. Precisely because man's creations, such as the state, do not possess that status, they are incommensurable with individuals, who alone possess it. The political order is not a physical reality. Accompanying that status of the individual is his consciousness of self, or understood understanding. The existence of this difference between the individual, possessing a physical status accompanied by self-conscious consciousness, and the state, which possesses neither quality, bars any attempt to treat the political order as an unqualified continuation of man or a simple realization of his essence. It leads us to observe that there is a certain distance between man and the political order as a crystallization of only one aspect of his nature. The possibility of subjecting the individual to the coercive power of the political order turns on this difference. Coercion has its source in the distance brought about between one individual and another, and is an attempt to overcome it within its own limits; the distance between the individual and the political order and the resultant coercion prompt us to question the Aristotelian theory and to doubt that man's rational nature finds its full realization in the political domain. Indeed, we are led to hold that it is not in the political order that the most faithful or noble expressions or realizations of man's essence are to be sought.

Our regressive analysis of the political order designed to disclose the conditions of its possibility, has shown that its existence presupposes a previous order. The analysis can regress no further. The chain of ordering functions is not logically derivable from, or referable to, man's nature as a creature endowed with reason. His rationality does, to be sure, *enable* him to be a political creature, but it does not, *of necessity*, propel him towards political existence.

That the political order is not inevitably an explication or realization but, more often than not, a limitation of man's essential potentialities can be established on empirical grounds as well.

1. Within that order, there is reciprocal subordination of men to each other and submission to the political order. That order is riddled with tension, and, confronted with them, man acts as a creature endowed with understanding. But tension does not spring from the nature of understanding: it springs from the contact between men, and also from the distance between them.

2. To admit that a certain aspect of man's rational nature is realized in the political domain is not to deny that the domain, as an actual entity, is made up of factors which neither continue nor explain rational potentiality. Thus, for example, the domain is situated in a certain area of the globe: the political order exists between certain human beings and renders them insiders and others outsiders; it implies a particular attitude towards those who inhabit realms beyond its bounds. These are empirical facts and cannot be traced to rational potentiality as their source.

VII

The palpable difference between man as endowed with rational potentiality and the empirical conditions of his existence has a bearing upon the problem of whether, and in what sense, the political order may be said to exist by nature. We noted that order as such cannot be said to exist by nature if by nature one means an aboriginal situation. Is this assertion valid when by nature a standard or norm is meant? Is it justifiable to maintain that the existence of the state is natural in the sense that it constitutes a norm for man? To say "yes" is to imply that the political order is a norm for the rational potentiality with which man is endowed. But this cannot be so, since that potentiality, as a spontaneous factor, possesses an intrinsic norm of its own. Rational spontaneity is regulated by intentionality towards whatever is its object, and intentionality implies spontaneous submission to, or acknowledgement of, the regulative authority of the object about to be known. Thus objectivity, and not the political order, is the norm of rational potentiality. We would go so far as to say that the objectivity, as the norm of intellectual power, is the *conditio sine qua non* of man's ability to constitute a political order; because, first of all, objectivity controls the intellectual activity not of A or B or C but of A and B and C together, and so forms the meeting ground of multiplicity of men. It is his acknowledgement of, and submission to, the regulative control of an existence transcending his own that underlies man's acceptance of the political order as a public order which he is obliged to respect by acting in accordance with the demands that it makes upon him. There is thus a certain parallelism between the norms of objectivity and of order.

The political order is not a norm for intellectual capacity, nor does it represent an adequate substitute for the norm of objectivity. There are two further reasons for rejecting the assumption that it can serve as the standard of intellectual power. The first is that, by virtue of that power of his, man adopts an attitude towards the political order, examines it, judges it, criticizes it, and acts upon findings of his examination and critique. This implies that intellectual capacity is not regulated by its creation, qua the political order. The other reason is that the political order, as a norm, is necessarily partial, as is the norm of every other partial domain. On the other hand, rational capacity creates a comprehensive realm which is not partial, whose norm, that of objectivity, is inclusive and not exclusive or partial.

So much for the assumption that the political order exists by nature as representing a norm of man's nature. Let us now examine the bearing of the fundamental difference between rationality and the existing political order upon the fourth, and last, sense in which at existence is said to be natural. It is customary to distinguish between nature and history on the ground that whereas the existence of nature does not depend upon the man's creative efforts, that of history does. This distinction and the meaning of nature upon which it rests shed light upon a significant aspect of the political order, one which sets it apart from every other human, and, in this respect, every other historical creation. It is ubiquitous in time, immanent in the very concept of men. It is not, then, the fruit of individual creative endeavor, as are, for example, works of art or literature or philosophy. It is anonymous and, as such, akin to language, which is also a kind of order. As compared with individual creations, it is to be regarded as primordial, as inevitable or as ultimate as is language. This does not render it immune to criticism. From this point of view, one can say that its existence is natural, that is, void of arbitrariness; this means that even though it is not given automatically by nature or by the species, it is still a permanent and constant factor within the limits of human history. Though the particular forms or manifestations of the political order are evidently subject to change, one must differentiate between historical change—as operative, say, in the transition or mutation from a monarchical to a republican regime—and the existence of the political order, which as such, is not exposed to mutations.

It is because the political order is a constant factor inside historical reality that it is characterized by anonymity. It is coeval with mankind. As the organized structure of mankind's existence in concert, it pervades the human domain and is related to the individuals who are its texture as the whole is related to its parts. It owes its existence not to any one group of individuals, let alone to any single individual, but to the human race as a whole. Historically regarded, it has no birthday. Only those human creations can celebrate birthdays which owe their existence to the creative power of individuals, and which are piecemeal, fragmentary, fruits of human endeavor. The nucleus of begotten works is specific, and their existence depends on the relation between the creator and his creation. But the creating individual is never submerged in the work that he has created. In both these respects, the political order is a unique artifact: related to no one creator, either individual or group, it encompasses all those who contribute to its creation. The existence of particular historical creations is transcended by that of their creators, whereas the existence of the political order engulfs that of its creators, and they create, sustain, elaborate, and promote the structure of their life in concert from within.

The existence of the political order occupies a point midway between nature and history. The political order is at once historical and nonhistorical: historical because its existence is sustained and perpetuated by the creative endeavors of men, generation after generation; nonhistorical because its birth cannot be dated or confined within any historical epoch. The most that one can say is that a particular form of political order—such as a given state— is begotten or constituted at a definite historical hour or period, provided one bears in mind that this begetting or constitution is only the transplantation of a preexistent form from one place to another and an accentuated crystallization of a preexistent structure of life in concert. Compared with, and in relation to, other historical creations, the existence of the political order may be regarded as nonhistorical or natural—an ultimate limit. Every creation of men, such as works of art or scientific theories or philosophical systems, emerges from potentiality to actuality within the limits of the existing political order, even though its content may have no direct bearing upon it. Similarly, every literary creation of men is born and exists within the inviolable limits of the order of language.

In relation to its individual members, therefore, the political order represents an unbegotten inclusive structure; its status is fundamental and its power overriding. It is that creation of mankind within whose historical limits men endeavor to create relational structures invested with regulative authority and even the coercive force which normally accrues to the order of nature and not to order made by man. The demands laid upon us by the order of nature must be complied with, on pain of death. The demands of the political order, man-made though that order be, must be complied with as if they were nature's, as if they possessed the same pressure of coercive force that nature wields over its denizens.

This is not to say that the coercive force of the political order is equal to that of the order of nature. The penalty, so to speak, for violating the laws and order of nature is implicit in the violation itself. You cannot break a natural law. Try to walk on air and down you must fall. But you can violate the laws of the political order, whose coercive force is implicit in the penalty that you will probably pay for the violation, but not in any physical or automatic impossibility of violation. Because of this inequality of coercive forces, the political order is historical in comparison with natural existence, and nonhistorical in comparison with other historical existents.

NOTES

1. On this, see R. Smend: *Verfassung und Verfassungsrecht*, Duncker & Humblot, München 1928.

2. The systematic aspects related to the broad issue of reflection and action are explored in the present author's book *Reflection and Action*, Martinus Nijhoff, Dordrecht 1984.

CHAPTER TWO

The State and Order

I

The methodological premise of our analysis is that there can be no comprehensive definition of the essence of the state. We can only approach a definition by a cumulative series of partial descriptions in which each step includes, and is grounded upon, what has been ascertained by the preceding one. As one of the prominent features of the political order is its institutionalized structure, an analysis of the concept of institution will be an apt starting point.

Of all modes and forms of human coactivity, the political order presents the most institutionalized structure. The concept of institution, for the social anthropologist, connotes a constant pattern of conduct whose constituent elements can be enumerated and defined, as well as a structure of corporate human activity.[1] The study of institutional forms does not, then, include the individuals but is restricted to the common area of men's corporate activities. If all modes of human togetherness which display a more or less determinate structure are institutional forms, then even the family can be regarded as an institution, for by its very nature it is a patterned mode of interrelationship. 'Sonhood,' for example, is a determinable or definable relationship, as is 'fatherhood,' and the rules and codes of conduct governing the first differ from those governing the second.

Compared with other institutional forms of corporate activity, the state is the most standardized. Because it is composed of fixed or constant patterns of conduct, the political order reveals a standard or average structure. It is characterized by a higher degree of invariability and a greater conformity to well-defined patterns of conduct than other modes or forms of corporate life and activity. The state can, accordingly, be regarded as a social institution *par excellence*.

What specific characteristics make the institutional nature of the political order so salient?

1. The structure implies both unity and order. Every order fulfills a unifying function in relation to its component elements; the political order is a unifier *par excellence*, because it absorbs the entire manifold within its bounds. That the political unity is inclusive as regards its members is attested, say, by the fact that even the member who would rather not be posited in his proper place—and, as we have seen, order implies allocation or placement—is nevertheless so placed. The state is an institution *par excellence* in part because its order is palpably coercive. The political order operates not by a spontaneous but by a calculated or designed and deliberate arrangement. The ordering agency of the order itself, namely, of the laws and institutions of the state, prescribes the order in conformity to a pattern; patterned order emerges where there is no guarantee that order will be generated spontaneously.

2. The state is the most comprehensive sphere of interhuman encounter within the limits of a given society, and so it is marked by a higher degree of publicity than any other structure of corporate life and activity. The inclusiveness of the political order stands out in unison with its coerciveness and its publicity. This renders intelligible the relative invariability of its patterns of conduct, which makes it again an institution *par excellence*. We may generalize: the more comprehensive and relatively inviolable the order, the broader, the more patterned, formalized, and standardized are the codes of conduct to which its constituent factors conform.

3. It is also by reason of relative stability or invariability that the political order can be regarded again as an institution *par excellence.* That fixity is lodged not only in a comprehensive and coercive inclusiveness, not only in a comprehensive publicity, but also in a relative insensitivity to shifts or changes in its elements. This can be seen by contrasting the political order with a less stable mode of institutionalized togetherness—the family. Alterations in the structure of familial togetherness occur with the passing of the generations, and as members choose to build their own families outside the original familial complex. The political structure is not exposed to such direct and obvious effects from alterations due to the passage of generations.

Being the most comprehensive and so the most institutionalized order within the limits of a given society, the state can be said to embrace other more partial institutions within its domain. This quality is sometimes given legal expression, for instance, in the formulation of the relationships between local authorities and the central government; this is not always so, as witness the relations between the embracing state-institution and the embraced family-institution. Therefore, it may be said that, its comprehensiveness notwithstanding, the state is still, here, a particular or partial mode of togetherness, for the comprehensiveness is bounded by the limits of the particular society in which it obtains, and all particular societies are partial. Even the political order is thus only *a* togetherness, not *the* togetherness, a particular and partial, not a universal and total, form of human togetherness. Even were a global structure of organization or togetherness established, the particularity and partiality of the manifold societies would not be expunged, and a way would have probably to be found of reconciling the totality of such a structure with the particularity of the societies that it embraces.

The factual inclusiveness of the political order gives substance to the view that the state has a normative as well as a factual status and is the most comprehensive form of togetherness, exercising hierarchically the supreme regulative authority. The factual premise of comprehensiveness is taken as sufficient to warrant the nonfactual conclusion that the whole is preferable or superior to its parts. This amounts to an unjustifiable identification of facts and ideologies. To affirm the preferability of an inclusive structure, one must add an ideological premise, pertaining to the preferability of totality, to the factual and, *per se*, nonideological premise that a relative totality exists. It goes without saying that a man who considers himself a member of a church, and not merely, or primarily, a member of the state, need not necessarily admit the supremacy of the political pattern of togetherness even when he admits its inclusiveness within the limits of a given society.

II

One empirical manifestation of the political order's comprehensiveness is its connection with a territory. All institutional forms of corporate life and activity operate within a territorial orbit for the simple reason that their members lead their lives on earth. But, unlike other institutional structures of togetherness, such as the family or the church, the state subsists and functions within territorial bounds and upon a territorial basis, not merely because it is a mode of order or interrelationship between earthly creatures, but also, and primarily, because connection with a territory belongs to its very definition. One cannot overemphasize the significance of the correlation between the institutional structure of the state and a given territory as its necessary substratum. A political structure presupposes here an intrinsically apolitical foundation as the precondition of its existence and agency. The territorial base of it is in itself apolitical, because it exists by nature as a natural datum which becomes politically meaningful only by virtue of the political structure built upon it. The peculiar link between the political order and territory as an apolitical factor corresponds to the status of the existence of the political order as circumscribed between the existence of the order of nature, independent of men's ordering activity, and that of the order of history, dependent upon the said activity. As the existence of the state is between nature and history, so its essence is an integration of a formalized or institutionalized pattern of conduct, historical and man-made, and a territorial base given by nature.

The essential connection between the state and its territorial substratum is not intrinsically a formalized relation expressed in legal terms, as is that of property-ownership, though it does involve a certain aspect of legality. Even when the connection preconditions legalized relationships of property-ownership, it is not reducible or equatable to them. The territoriality of the political order is to be regarded as a concrete expression of the limit-circumscription characterizing order as such. The fact that order implies limit-circumscription is manifest, in this particular instance, in the territorial boundaries drawn by the political order. Just as the quasi-natural mode of existence of the political order is, at times, put forward as an argument for assigning it a normative status, so the prejuridical or ajuridical nature of the state-institution's relation to its territory is occasionally interpreted as an indication of its superiority over other institutional forms of men's life and action in concert. Antelegal ownership of territory is taken to justify assertion of the state's priority over those institutions whose property-ownership is formulated in legal terms. The fallacy of this interpretation is that the relation to a territory characterizing the essence of the state structure does not endow the state with the extrapolitical and hence ajuridical nature of its territory. On the contrary, by its connection with the political institution, the territory is transposed, as it were, from the natural to the historical plane of existence. Consequently, the ownership relation between the state-institution and its territory is potentially juridical even if it has not been actually formulated in explicit legal language. Because legality is implicit in the political order as a formalized, public, and inclusive structure, it is likewise implicit in that order's ownership of its territory. Formalization or legalization is rendered possible, and even necessary, by the existence of the state-institution.

Here, once again, is evidence that the state cannot be said to exist "by nature" in the unqualified sense of that notion. As an institution *par excellence*, the state could not exist without men's deliberate acts of integration and formalization. Formalization is not an automatic process. It presupposes conscious design as well as intentional realization of design by a conscious process of abstraction; every formalization is the outcome of abstraction, and no abstraction exists automatically or "by nature." Without a formalized relation to the world, we would not be able to maintain the state as a vehicle of formalized and legalized patterns of interrelationship and codes of conduct. As man's rational nature is the *conditio sine qua non* of the existence of the political order, so his capacity for abstraction or formalization is the necessary condition of the formalized or institutionalized essence of it.

Being a formalized structure centred in man's formalizing power, the state does not include the original act whereby it is constituted from within its embracing domain. It owes its constitution to formal modes of directedness within itself, and they, in turn, are rendered possible by its containing structure. As an institutional form, it does not owe its existence to a "prime mover"; it undergoes a perpetual process of self-constitution operative in different phases of men's life and action in concert and contained by its own product.

III

Let us now consider another constituent of the essence of the political order, namely, the power-factor. In some political discussions, "power" is used in the sense of "government." Yet government is only one institutionalized manifestation of power. Existence, we said, as a circumscription of limits defining modes of relationship and conduct, implies order, and this order is coercive. Power, then, is latent in reality itself as order or limit-circumscription. The basic fact that we cannot move about freely within a given territory, simply because it is populated by men and women and occupied by objects and governed by the laws of nature, reflects the coerciveness laid upon us by reality. It is partly because facts are imbued with power that we acknowledge them; we say "partly," because in certain instances the acknowledgement is not merely a response but also a conscious act of consideration. Collision with coercive facts can be accompanied by a conscious acknowledgement of their power to curb us. This applies to our acknowledgement of our fellow, too; acknowledging the fact that his existence stands over and against our own, we *ipso facto* acknowledge the element of power latent in the fact that he exists. In the state, the power latent in the factual network of interhuman relationships is made manifest. The state possesses power incommensurable with the sum total of "power-quanta" possessed by its individual members as factual existents; the state is a manifest expression of the power latent in togetherness, and not the sum total of fragmented energy possessed by each individual in isolation. The factual corporate existence or togetherness of human beings is transmuted into explicit power by the instrumentality of the comprehensive or inclusive and institutionalized form of the political order.

The first step towards constituting the state as a manifest power is taken when men acknowledge the existence of their togetherness as well as the coercive force which accrues to it from its very existence. Were men to adopt a nominalistic view of reality and be incapable of discerning the real existence of "universals," they would not maintain a corporate form of interhuman relationship, much less an explicit expression of cohesion in the form of state-power. The constitution of the state may be deemed men's endeavor to endow that power, which owes its existence to their directedness towards it, with the real or concrete massiveness. Power, as such, lacks it because it does not occupy a place in space. The legal coerciveness of the state is one of the most palpable expressions of that endeavor; if power is the active manifestation of the existence of togetherness, legal coercion is the active manifestation of power. Because the state owes its existence to the power rendered unto it by men's togetherness, and because its reality presupposes the rendering of power, it is inevitably—and perpetually—concerned for its own preservation. Its reality is a borrowed one, not given by nature, so it must be on guard constantly least the investment of power, essential to its existence, be denied. As a manifest expression of togetherness for togetherness' sake, state-power is by its very nature self-centered.

Thus constituted and maintained, the state as power occupies a paradoxical position. Deprive it of men's intentionality towards order and of their endeavors to express order manifestly, and you render it null and void. Because its existence is borrowed, it is concerned to free itself of dependence upon the lenders and their intentional "loans" of manifest power, and to achieve the security of a self-maintaining entity. Yet, were it not for men's purposive relation towards the political order, were it not for their aim to transmute the power latent in togetherness into manifest power and channel it then into concrete and specific moulds and activities, the existence of the state would be impossible.

There are many forms of standardized organization reflecting men's endeavor to create well-defined structures of corporate activity subservient to specific and determinate corporate goals, and governed by formal codes of conduct. These structures include not only organizations geared to a single, particular end, such as chess clubs, but also complex organizations serving more complex, less specified, ends, such as schools, townships, or municipalities. In contradistinction to such partial instrumental structures, the political structure cannot be correlated with any determinate purpose, no matter how complex, even though its formalized and code-controlled pattern might seem to imply such a correlation. Unlike other institutions, the formalized structure of the state is not intimately bound up with, or subservient to, any well-defined aim; this is not a contingent feature of it, but signifies something integral to its very essence. Just as togetherness subserves no single and readily definable end, but is a complex reticulation of interrelationships, so the state, emanated or projected from and by togetherness, subserves none which might be understood as defining its function.

Nevertheless one might venture to define the purpose or *raison d'etre* of the state as threefold.

1. The state functions as a formalized or standardized, comprehensive, and territory-tied expression of the fundamental situation of human togetherness.

2. It is subservient to its own interests of self-preservation, aiming at the perpetuation of the fundamental situation of which it is a revealed and active manifestation or, negatively, at the prevention of its nullification. In the interests of this objective, the state may be wielded—in the name of self-preservation—against the very society and/or individual members upon whose gift of power its existence depends.

3. Within the fundamental situation of togetherness by and for whose sake it is created, state-power is channelled with a view to achieving such specific ends as safeguarding the physical existence of society (which may be regarded as a ramification of the state's concern for its own self-preservation), public hygiene, housing projects welfare, and education.

Whereas the first two aspects of this threefold *raison d'etre*—revealed manifestation of the existence and power of togetherness and self-preservation—represent fixed features of the political structure, invariable in themselves though achieved by variable means, the third—subservience to, and instrumentality for, specific ends—is in itself variable and relative to shifting historical circumstances. The specific aims to be achieved by the instrumentality of the state are contingent upon, and vary with, men's changing notions of their own nature and objectives. of what they seek in, and expect from, their togetherness, and of which of the results that they want to produce by channelling the power of their togetherness they have put at their own disposal. Taken not in isolation but as interactive in a whole, the three functions can be said to constitute the peculiar end of the state as a formalized instrumental organization with differentiates it from other forms of human organization and order, including the form of society.

IV

We turn now to the examination of some of the functions of power on the empirical plane of human reality.

One is to accentuate the limit-circumscription fulfilled by the order of corporate human existence. The public sphere of human existence may be described as the locus or point of intersection of men's individual lines of conduct. Those lines, which have their start in the private domain of each individual, terminate in the public domain, where their junction must be so arranged as to permit their coexistence. There is no phase of corporate human existence empty of consideration for one's fellow, if only as the tracer of one line of action among many. The inevitable concern for, or acknowledgement of, him is itself an active manifestation of the order latent in, and implied by, existence in general and human existence in particular. The inevitability of order and its active manifestation are not to be presented as a sort of impenetrable container in which we are all, so to speak, imprisoned. The inevitable order is actively manifest in our conducting ourselves in conformity with that follows from the essence of corporate existence, that is, of existence within a common structure or network of interrelationships. Acting within and conforming to the containing order, we acknowledge its regulative power. An order which does not fulfil a regulative function for its individual *relata* is no order. As regulative, order is necessarily a power-factor. Order and power are two sides of the same coin; order is a situation of which power is the active manifestation; power is order in action. So manifest, political power may be described as the order of society in action directed towards its own very maintenance.

Political power, as the order of society in action, is an additional dimension of order superimposed upon the order of society; it is social order, plus an explicit call to order vested with power to render the call effective. Owing to the existence of the state, the active intervention of power in the doings of society becomes both possible and actual. Political power intervenes in the social domain; this is exemplified, for example, by the translation of order into formalized patterns and codes possessed of the authority of law, by the potential coercion with guarantees the observance of legalized patterns and codes, and by institutions whose essence consists in a crystallization of power for power's sake. The constitution of the formalized order of the state is in itself an indication that the people who constitute it do not rely upon the power of the preexisting order to maintain itself. Therefore, they endeavor to guarantee its continuance and to establish channels for harnessing and regulating its power. The instability of the social order is thus the premise of the constituted political order. The order of society stands on the self-cirsumscripton of each one and all of its individual members. Underlying it is an encounter of all with all, transcending the isolated and particular encounters between individuals, and setting further limits to men's action. Above and beyond the isolated acts of acknowledgement by isolated individuals of the curbing capacity of other isolated individuals, there is the universal acknowledgement by all of the curbing or confining power of all towards each and of each towards all. The state, as manifest power, represents a projection of the limit-consciousness underlying interhuman relationships.

The extent to which the state as power manifests the factual existence of order is the extent of its constituting a limiting factor for the individual members of society who maintain the order. The circumscribing power of the state transcends the curbing capacity of man's encounter with his fellow. On the factual plane of life in concert, men encounter but a few occupants of the social space. Here, the sphere of intersecting lines of human activity extends no further than the area of everyday experience. By contrast, the state crystallizes and accentuates the existence of social space as transcending the partial empirical spheres of men's daily lives. One function of the state is to confront men with the existence of society as overreaching the limits of individual and partial experience, and subsisting in the form of a universal—and, as such, an abstract—body. By rendering latent limits manifest, the state renders the abstract existence of social space explicit and gives it a quasi-concrete reality within the partial sphere of individual experiences.

The curbing capacity of our fellow is inherent in his existence as a physical fact. As such, he occupies a place in space, and that place represents a stubborn facutal limit which refuses to be disregarded. Contrariwise, society, as an abstract universal, occupies no place in space. Its spatiality is borrowed; it belongs only to the particular and concrete individuals living and acting within it. The state as power is to society what physical spatiality is to its individual members. Were men not to wield their power of formalizing abstraction so as to conceive of their corporate existence as a universal and comprehensive containing structure, were they not to translate that conception into a political mould of projected power, the state, as power, would not exist.

The act of detachment of individuals from their own individual modes of existence is at the same time an act of integration. In this case, the integrative activity is designed, by imbuing it with coercive force, to release integration from its initial dependence upon the spontaneous activity of the individuals who bring it into being. Whereas we are forced to acknowledge our fellow by his very place in space and by the limit which that place appoints, acknowledgement of the state as the projected power of society is not so forced upon us. That is why we endow that state with coercive force and place it in a position of a universal limit, analogous to that occupied by concrete individuals in their capacity as partial physical limits. Evidently the authority of the universal body-politic over its individual members is greater than that of the particular physical limit inherent in the encounter between any two individuals or groups. Nevertheless, this greater authority would be nonexistent were it not for our propensity to acknowledge it and our power of abstraction, which enables us to transcend physical limits and direct ourselves to an abstract but power-endowed entity that has no foundation of its presence in physical reality.

V

The ascription of power to the state seems to dwell in the suprapersonal or impersonal nature of the state's limiting power and in men's willingness to compensate their initial togetherness for its lack of physical reality. Our acknowledgement of a fellowman, as forced upon us instantly by the very fact of his existence or by the restrictive power of his place in space, is in itself no guide to how we are to act. After all, it might very well take the form of an aggressive desire to remove the intractable physical limit. In itself, our fellow's limiting power presents a problem, not a precept. It is because I cannot help acknowledging his existence as a limit to my own sphere of activity that I am faced with the problem of what I am to do about this limit or how to give practical expression to my acknowledgement of it. In this respect, it may be said that the existence of the state as power guarantees a certain minimum of action in conformity to the nonaggressive possibilities implied in this acknowledgement. Thus, for example, the function of political power is to see to it that I pursue not the possible course of attempting to remove the limit from my path but the alternative course of respecting my fellow's existence. From this angle, the function can be described either as the protection of existence (Hobbes's conception) or as the mediation which it effects between the conflicting interests of its members (Locke's conception). The intervention of state-power in the empirical sphere of interhuman relationships guarantees our active and constructive, or at least nondestructive, acknowledgement of our fellow. That acknowledgment is not only negative in the sense of refraining from attempts to remove him from our path, or even in that of reciprocal nonaggression stemming from reciprocal fear; it is also positive in the sense of recognizing his right to exist as implicit in his very existence. Insofar as it functions to evoke that positive recognition, the state can absorb and render effective such abstract principles of conduct as justice or equality.

The question that we must now answer is this: Granting that the function of state-power is, in theory, to guarantee positive expressions or our acknowledgement of our fellow's factual restraints, what grounds are there to assume that it will be able to do so in practice? The answer seems to be that, because it is projected not by isolated individuals or partial groups but by the inclusive and abstract cohesion of togetherness, the power of the state is suprapersonal or impersonal. Owing its existence to none of its constituents, the political order cannot be equated with or reduced to, any prior specific interest or aim, but serves to guarantee the realization of many diverse interests and aims within togetherness. The state represents the interests of togetherness and not the interests of any isolated constituent. It is by virtue of its suprapersonal or impersonal nature that the state may be said to occupy an independent, or semi-independent, position. Hence it can fulfil in practice its function of intervening in the social order for the sake of protection, mediation, and—at times—the realization of abstract moral principles.

VI

Because state-power is our product or projection, we can calculate, measure, and even predict its effects and mode of operation. Having assigned certain functions to an instrumental structure that we ourselves have made, and having empowered it to fulfil them, we know—at least to some extent—how this instrument will be wielded and what is to be expected of it. We expect, for example, to be protected from aggression, or obliged to take each other into consideration, or to have abstract principles (e.g., justice) realized, because we have created the state as a means of doing these things. There is a paradox or a circle at the core of the state's essence; created by togetherness for togetherness' sake, it uses its borrowed power to compel its creators, to continue the act of creation upon which their existence hinges. In actual fact, state-power occupies a certain normative status in relation to us, a status present in its very factuality, constituted and abstract though this factuality is. But does this factual normativity which accrues to power warrant the conclusion, drawn, for example, by Machiavelli, that power represents an independent and hence primary norm, or does the constituted essence of power indicate that it is a derivative and hence a secondary norm? For the present, it is enough to note the intrinsically problematic nature of state-power as a projection of togetherness for togetherness' sake.

We can now circumscribe the position of the state within the broader framework of society by reviewing the three analytically distinct dimensions or planes of order composing the public sphere of human reality. On the most basic plane of men's life in concert, order subsists by virtue of the very fact of their cohesion or togetherness. Seeking to preserve their togetherness, men create a second plane of order and give it the power of "calling them to order"; to guarantee the effectiveness of their projected power, they create a third plane, by actualizing the abstract power of togetherness through semiconcrete channels of intervention within the concrete realm of social existence.

A distinction should be introduced between 'power' and 'government.' Power is that abstract entity projected by the 'body-politic' and accordingly impersonal. Government is abstract power expressed semiconcretely: wielded or effected by concrete human beings, it is an empirical and not an abstract entity. Metamorphosed into government, the projected power of togetherness, itself an abstraction, has become fixed in the empirical reality from which it was originally projected or abstracted. Set in an act of crystallizing and projecting a preexistent order, the position of power is derivative. Set in an act of channelling and embodying this projected power in semiconcrete moulds, government is doubly derivative. As power is the abstract representation of the abstract entity called the 'body-politic,' so government is an empirical representation of an abstract power. In this respect, empirical government is not only distinct from, but even incompatible with, abstract power. Power exists in society as a whole, government exists in certain parts of this whole and not in others. Hence there are no grounds for assuming the identity of power and goverment. They are as incommensurate as are abstract and empirical entitites, inclusive wholes and exclusive parts. Just as the relation between political power and social togetherness is problematic, so is that between government and power.

It is necessary to isolate power from other constituents of social reality; yet its analytical distinctness must not be mistaken for real independence. We are dealing with a factor derivative by its very nature, and owing its existence to acts of integration on a more primary plan of human existence. If the existence of political power is not sustained by men's integrative activities on the social plane of their life in concert, then, *ex hypothesi*, power is not political. The correlativity of political power and social integration is manifest in the day-to-day course of political life. One need only reflect upon the implications of the situation in many new states. Here is a striking example of what happens when a political order is established in the absence of a foundation in preexistent social cohesion. For one thing, the lack of integration or togetherness on the social plane must be offset by assigning to the state the integrative function which normally brings the political order into existence; that is, the state is expected to create the fundamental situation of togetherness from which it ought to have been projected and crystallized in the first instance. For another, owing to the assignment to the political order of functions fulfilled by society, the balance between social cohesion and political power is shaky, so that political power not only fails to realize its integrative aims but actually aggravates the preexistent dissolution, undermining rather than sustaining the cohesion whereon it depends for its existence.

Bearing in mind that the isolation of the power-factor is valid only for the purpose of analysing its essence, we may best begin with a brief survey of a few classical definitions of power. In the twenty-eighth paragraph of his *Critique of Judgment*, Kant defines power or might as follows: "*Might* is that which is superior to great hindrances. It is called *dominion* if it is superior to the resistance of that which possesses might."[2] This definition recurs, in various guises, throughout the subsequent history of political theory. But Kant himself was not considering political questions when he proposed dealing with that aspect of nature whereby it is said to be sublime. The heading of the paragraph is, "Of Nature Considered as Might." Nevertheless, one can show the political bearing of the definition, without undue deviation from his original meaning, by understanding the hindrances of which he speaks as obstacles within the social order, and political might as that which is superior to them. Perhaps Hegel was interpreting Kant in the manner when he defined might as "the power to exist and to safeguard existence within the negativity of self."[3] Hegel understood "hindrance" as "negativity"; "superiority to hindrance," which constitutes might, is the power to exist by resisting negativity. But he has introduced a new element by stressing the antithetical correlation between might and what must be resisted. Another variation on the Kantian theme is Bertrand Russell's definition of might as the power to produce desired results;[4] although he does not specify what he means by "results," it would not be out of keeping with his general theory to surmise that he had social results in mind.

As to power in the strictly political sense, it may be defined as the superiority to hindrances manifest in the capacity to impose and sustain state-legislation, that is, the power to sustain the state, or the political power itself. In that sense, power is primarily self-sustaining or self-preserving; political power is the self-preservation of the state *ex definitione*. That is why legislation is considered its primary manifestation,[5] and why sociologists frequently define power as that which facilitates the achievement of results desirable to those who have collective interests or aims.[6]

Our purpose is not to take issue with post-Kantian definitions but to call attention to the theoretical presuppositions which, explicitly or implictly, underlie them. One such presupposition is the assumption that the power-factor can be uprooted from the broader context of social order and presented as an entity capable of self-determination. As concerns social and political power, the assumption that power is either self-generating or self-determining is invalid. That political power is incommensurable with the existential factors to which it owes its generation does not nullify that indebtedness. Power can sustain order in existence but cannot bring it into existence. It is superior to hindrances but cannot create them. By its nature, it lacks the factual massiveness possessed by the factual structures on the concrete plane of social existence, to which it is superior in might but not mass. For example, political power does not create those family bonds which may, from its point of view, at times constitute hindrances, or those sentiments, opinions, or interest which may very well be incompatible with its own. Even when it is said to be superior to the hindrance of subversive or antisocial leanings, this only means that it has reinforced the opposing tendency operative on the social plane. Were the disruptive elements not to be resisted on the social plane by social forces of order, there would be no political power with which to resist them. Political power is at once the guarantee and the product of social order or integration.

The reciprocity of society and state is but one expression of the fundamental structure of existence. All modes of existence are complex fabrics of interrelated factors and spheres whose interaction does not cancel the difference between them. Just as the political plane presupposes the social plane, so, for example, the plane of historical existence presupposes that of biological existence. And just as the living organism when biologically regarded is said to exemplify laws other than those it exemplifies when chemically regarded, so the body-politic exemplifies other laws regarded from an historian's or from a political theorists' point of view. The principle of interrelatedness is as basic as that of specification or differentiation. You can and must isolate biological from physical processes in the laboratory. Do so in actual fact, and neither the physical nor the biological processes remain. You can isolate political power from the social order for the sake of theoretical analysis. Yet take away the social order in actual fact, and you are left without political power.

Through there is no philosophical ground for questioning the consciously abstract and methodologically restricted definitions of political power, it is imperative to note the fallacy of misplaced autonomy.

NOTES

1. S. F. Nadel defines an institution as "a standardized mode of co-activities" in *The Foundations of Social Anthropology*, London 1951, Cohen & West, p. 108.

2. *Critique of Judgment*, tr. J. H. Bernard, Macmillam, London 1931, p. 123.

3. **Aesthetik**, Aufban Verlag, Berlin 1955, p. 202.

4. *Power, A New Social Analysis*, London 1939, p. 35: Allen & Unwin, "Power may be defined as the production of intended effects."

5. Paul Tillich, *Love, Power, and Justice*, Oxford University Press, London 1954, p. 15.

6. Talcott Parsons, "The Distribution of Power in American Society," *World Politics*, X (1957/1958), pp. 123-143.

7. The instrumental aspect in the essence of state is present in Robert Nozick in spite of his reservations. It appears as "a protective agency dominant in a territory." *Anarchy, State and Utopia*, Basil Blackwell, Oxford 1974, p. 11i9.

CHAPTER THREE

Manifestations of Power

I

After examining the conditions that render the existence of political power possible and actual, one might perhaps be expected to explain why it is necessary. It is possible because force is latent in the structure of men's togetherness, actual because men project the force latent in their togetherness into crystallized institutional forms. The question might be asked whether, as a crystallized form emanating from a preexistent order of society, it is necessary, and, if so, why. If the (efficient) cause of its existence is a process of power-projection and crystallization nurtured by the activities constitutive of men's life in concert, what, then, is its reason, or ground, or final end? To attempt an adequate answer would be as futile as attempting to explain why any particular crystallized form or structure or order is as it is and not otherwise. We can no more put our finger on the logical or ontological *raison d'etre* of the state than on the ontological reason why phrenological features are such and not otherwise, or why the laws of nature are such and not otherwise.

By denying the possibility of explaining why crystallized forms are necessary, one questions the Aristotelian identification of form and *telos*, that is, of form as factual shape or structure and as conceptual essence. "Form" is equivocal. It may mean shape or limiting structure in contradistinction to amorphous, indeterminate, unlimited "matter." And it may mean essence, or even perfection, in contradistinction to what is nonessential, accidental, indeterminate, and, as such, imperfect. Though it is unjustifiable to understand institutional forms, social or political, in the second Aristotelian sense, they may be, and frequently are, understood in the first. Thus, today, "form" is often employed in the sense of a delimiting crystallized pattern or a manifest structure functioning as a limit. And, indeed, there is a sense in which forms such as, for instance, actual phrenological features, particular natural laws, or specific linguistic structures function so. For that reason they cannot be conceived as "perfect."

In the present analysis, "form" will be used in the sense of typical shape, and the political order, as institutional form, is conceived as the shape of the social order. The state is, as it were, the mirror of society in which the body-social is at once reflected and transformed. The state is to society as form is to matter, manifest or actual limit to latent or potential limiting capacity. In this respect, its status is analogous to that of other crystallized forms or images; it is one among many concrete manifestations of a rhythm swinging from spontaneity to settled structure, from expansive impulse to crystallized limit. From the viewpoint of this rhythm, political power is to the social order a limiting crystallization. The shift from order-generating activity to formed power implies a distance between the two poles, and the emanation is not a simple continuation of its own fountainhead. As the ground of the existence of crystallized political power, the crystallizing rhythm is at the same time the ground of a duality between the crystallized effect and the relatively amorphous cause by which it is generated. To abolish political power would amount to establishing men's togetherness upon a foundation relatively free of limits. To abolish the social order out of which power is generated would amount to establishing all human order upon brute force divorced from the relationships and activities that make up social cohesion or togetherness. Thus the correlativity of order and power bars the possibility of both limit-abrogating chaos and unchecked coercion.

What, then, are the concrete manifestations of the swing from the amorphous energy latent in social cohesion to the crystallized and formalized power manifest in the political order? One is the conduct of society's individual members. Once power is projected out of the social order into institutionalized patterns of conduct, the individual need no longer rely entirely upon his own judgment when it comes to deciding upon courses of action terminating in the public sphere or involving him in the web of interhuman relationships.[1] The individual conforms to the patterns and codes of conduct he finds at hand, partly because he hesitates to depend wholly upon his own discretion as a sure guide, and partly because he is sometimes perplexed as to how he must act in the given circumstances. The given pattern liberates him from indecision and from the necessity to make, and act upon, decisions for which he alone is responsible. Codes of conduct relieve him of a burden by affording him the guidance and support of fixed moulds for those activities of his which enmesh him in a network of relationships with his fellows. The state sets a fairly detailed code of conduct before the individual, prescribing the mode of behavior appropriate to a wide variety of occasions, at least such as may confront him in the public domain. A code of this sort saves people the trouble of puzzling out problems that pertain, for example, to the relation between the individual and the community, or between social groups and society at large. But every given political code or pattern is partial, and it is applicable only to such situations as lend themselves to stereotyped responses, which may, accordingly, be prescribed beforehand. The limits of patterns of conduct are evident, for example, in these phases of life's cycle, dark or bright, mournful or joyous, which men mark by ritual action. Confronted with death or birth, the individual may know how he must behave, because his behavior then is regulated by ritual. Yet no ritual can regulate, let alone prescribe, man's emotional response to these occasions or anticipate or control the undercurrent of feeling that will accompany his execution of the rite.

II

Another feature of the transformation in question is the establishment of new modes of interrelationship within society. The superimposition of the political order upon the order of society means new relations not only between the body-social and the body-politic but also (and consequently) among the individual members of the body-social. The major innovation is the relationship of subordination. One does not find this in Rousseau's political thought, which is only understandable in the light of the fact that he believed social cohesion to be self-maintaining and based upon a general will to which society's individual members are related not by subordination but by participation. The power-factor, as projected out of social cohesion, is distinct from, and incommensurable with this primary mode of togetherness; there is no guarantee that togetherness will maintain itself in existence. Precisely the vulnerability of its existence warrants the projection of power ot secure it. It follows, then, that political power, namely, power to impose cohesion from above and to subordinate, is a distinct and independent factor. Its projection out of the realm of social togetherness to preserve that realm implies and presupposes acts of interference within the empirical order of society and the complex of human relations. Though designed to secure the unity of the body-social, the projection of political power splits it into the power-wielding arm of government and the members subordinated by government, into active instruments of power and passive fields of operation controlled by them. The relation between the individual members of society at the prepolitical level of order may be described as one of subordination only in the sense of reciprocal subordination, or such subordination as is implied by the mutual limitation of individuals occupying here and now their mutually exclusive places in space. Political subordination is not a reciprocal relation but a nonreflexive one creating a hierarchy of superiors and inferiors. Social subordination is, so to speak, horizontal; political subordination is vertical. On the horizontal—social—plane, the direction of subordination as limitation is reversible; on the vertical—political—plane, it is not. On the social plane, both I and my fellow may respect the limits circumscribed by each other because both of us are confronted with the force of a physical fact. On the politcal plane, we respect the limits set by the representatives of projected power, because they control this power and we do not. In view of the new mode of subordination engendered by the projection of power out of the body-social into the body-politic's arm of government, one may describe the socio-political complex as a weft whose warp comprises horizontal threads fashioning the individual members of society into a reversible pattern of subordination, and whose woof comprises vertical threads binding society at large and political power as government into a pattern of irreversible subordination.

III

The third manifestation of the swing was alluded to in the preceding chapter, where we considered the concrete purposes to which power is subservient. We observed that power serves two primary purposes, the one self-centered—designed to safeguard its own existence—and the other focussed upon the social sphere and designed to facilitate the attainment of a variety of social and human ends. There are two further expressions of power. One might be called power-centric and comprises the institutions and operations subserving the maintenance of government, that is, of subordination, the smoothly functioning political machine, conditions allowing for political decision and action. The other comprises all those material interests to be served by government once its efficient functioning is secured, that is, once it creates the conditions rendering possible the realization of its projects.

The power-centric manifestation of the swing expresses the fact that the process of power-projection is endless. As living and acting in cooperation, we feed a twofold creative process whose two products are the latent order of our togetherness and the manifest political form into which that latent order is projected. But once it is emanated from social togetherness or order, political power turns towards its source; it entertains plans, designs, and purposes affecting its source; it manifests concern for its order; and it cares whether it is structured or chaotic, whether men are, or are not, woven together into a fabric of horizontal subordination.

IV

The power-centric manifestation of the crystallization of energy latent in togetherness may be formulated in terms of what in modern times is called the sovereignty of the state. A state is definable as sovereign when it manifests the power to maintain itself in existence. But state-sovereignty is not always so understood. According to one view, a state is sovereign if it monopolizes the power to declare a state of emergency. This theory, whose leading proponent is Carl Schmitt, correlates the existence of the political order with that of states of emergency, such as war. It is based upon the notion that authentic situations are extreme ones. In the sphere of the individual, an authentic situation is fraught with fear, whether the determinate fear of death or the indeterminate, vague, feeling of emptiness and anxiety. In the realm of society, an authentic situation is one of war. That the theory is untenable is clear, if only because the manifestation of political sovereignty is not centrifugal but centripetal, not primarily directed outwards—that is, towards another body-politic in an extreme situation of military emergency—but inwards, towards the body-politic itself. The primary manifestation of sovereign political power is not belligerence but self-preservation, not an extreme but precisely a normal state of affairs, a state of perpetual carrying into effect of the state's power-centric purpose. The state's very existence is its sovereignty. And its sovereignty endures because and as long as the process of power-projection endures. Were this power-generating process to end, the state would change from a living operating body into an outdated relic. The primary limits to sovereignty are set not by the existence of other states, as sovereign as the state under consideration, but by the nature of political sovereignty as a specific crystallized form of social cohesion. A form is sovereign because it is vested with the crystallized power of the body-social, and it is limited in its sovereignty because it cannot create the source of its own power.

V

Another concrete manifestation of the state as crystallized power is in the relation between political power and law. Law may be loosely defined as a principle of relationship, to which conformity renders the relationship regular, fixed, or necessary. In this regard, there is a certain analogy between the laws of nature and the laws of the state. The laws of nature denote the necessity of identical consequences following upon identical antecedents in identical circumstances; they define the character, govern the regularity, and constitute the necessity of the relationships between antecedent conditions and subsequent results. Whereas, in the political domain, the law defines and governs the regular relationships obtaining in identical circumstances either among the individual members of society or between the individual and the state. In the realm of nature, the behavior of biological organisms is said to conform to law if it is predictable; in the socio-political realm, the behavior of human beings is said to conform if it fulfils predetermined expectations and is predictable. For example, a law-abiding relationship of fatherhood implies that the individual exemplifying it can be expected to provide for the education of his son, and a law-abiding relationship of citizenship implies that all "eligible" citizens exemplifying it can be expected, for example, to serve in the army. In either case, the regularity of the relationship and of the conduct exemplifying it, which constitutes the ground for our expectation or prediction, is defined and controlled by law. The regularity or law-abidingness of the relationship between human beings and their socio-political environment is analogous to what it is in the relationship between organisms and their natural environment. In a sense, law establishes not only the predictability but also the necessity of human conduct. The existence of law makes it necessary that individuals do certain things, for instance, serve in the army or educate their children by sending them to school; and not do others, for instance, injure their fellow-men or provoke public disturbance. As regulator of necessary conduct, law is a further manifestation of crystallized power; whereas political power is a crystallization imposing subordination to order, law is a set of rules regulating order. But if we disregard analytical distinctions, then, in actual fact, conformity to law is subordination to power. The body of political law is manifest and underlined order regarded from the angle of content; the state is that self-same order regarded from an institutional angle. In functional terms, the state is not prior to law or law to the state. Together, they represent two sides of the crystallized form.

The question might here arise: If, in actual fact and function, political power and law represent two sides of the same coin, why do we, nevertheless, distinguish between them? It is because the correlativity of power and law does not imply their identity. Their nonidentity directs law not only towards society but also towards power itself. Law endows power with authority and prestige, attributes by whose virtue it wins the respect of men. By virtue of law, political power becomes not only might but also right. Backed by law, government becomes first in the order of both authority and power. Law elevates power from the position of a brute-fact to that of a value-charged fact. As if in requital for the gift of authority as meaningfulness, power invests law with authority as coercive force. In itself, law cannot enforce the prohibitions that it dictates, but, backed by power, it can enforce compliance with them by penalizing their violation. For example, were it not subject to penalty, theft might not constitute a binding or inviolable prohibition in the eyes of a would-be thief, though it would be a criminal offense in the law's eyes. Law grants power a meaningful status of authority and power grants law a factual foundation of enforcement. The reciprocity of the power-law relationship dwels in the character of the *relata*: as a body of rules of conduct, law constitutes content; as coercive limitation crystallized power constitutes a brute-fact. Thus each partner can bestow on the other that, and only that, which it possesses "by nature."

This reciprocity is also manifested in political power being, among other things, the power to legislate laws, and in its legislating, it invests itself with legislative authority. The existence and implementation of power are authorized by laws where power itself legislates. Here we have further evidence of the power-centric nature of political sovereignty. The factual sovereignty or self-preservation of power finds legal expression in its authority to adopt self-preserving measures. We come across a circle.

But, as the state not only seeks self-preservation but also directs itself towards the social sphere, so law not only authorizes power-centric purposes but also regulates human relationships in the social sphere. True, the conjunction of power and law precludes the possibility of translating all patterns of human conduct and relationship into legal language. Like its partner, an institutionalized or standardized form-law is likewise standardized. Some phases of human life resist standardization. It can now be said that some human relationships resist channelling into legal or standardized moulds. For example, although it is possible for the state to legislate and enforce laws guaranteeing a child his father's protection, it is impossible for the state to legislate, or at least to enforce, laws that guarantee a child his father's love. To be sure, there is no fixed criterion for determining the nature of those phases of human life subject to legalized channelling. What does and what does not lend itself to legalisation is a question which has been, and no doubt will be, given many different answers in the course of mankind's historical process and in response to the changing circumstances which that process creates. All the same, it seems certain that for all its diverse and varying historical applications, the distinction between matters within the reach of legislation and those beyond it remains constant. Thus, at one historical period, freedom from economic want is not guaranteed by law; at another, with the limits of legislation expanded, it is. Still, expanding though it be, the circumference of the sphere subject to legalization or standardization will never be all-encompassing; law will always be confronted with an "out-of-bounds" realm of relationships which resist all "card-indexing."

That the reach of law is not boundless follows from its character as a code of conduct. That its authority is not immune to criticism and questioning follows from its nature as a body of meaning or content. Men approach that particular content as they do any other—as rational creatures approach rational objects, with the aid of instruments of reflection, analysis, question, criticism, and doubt. Since it is law which invests power with authority, there will always be room to ask what invests authority with authority. Legalized authority is not, then, infallible authority. It is never exempt from questions as to the ground or justification of its authority. And it is no answer that law as such is the ground of authority, since this is precisely what the questions are about. Now, no one would contest the warrant for the legalized authority of power, in the sense of its bestowal by legal procedure. But that, obviously, is not the only sense in which justification can be understood and demanded. To ask whether authority is justified is also to ask whether, besides being legal, it is also right, when the measure of right and wrong is a matter not of procedure but of moral or religious principle. For example, in a given state, the death penalty might be demanded by a law that is justifiable as having been legislated in conformity to the procedure of an authroized legislative body, such as a House of Representatives. Yet for all its legal correctness, it might be morally wrong, and it is possible to question the authority of its justification by confronting it with other, moral or religious, authorities.

Right and wrong being matters of principle as well as of legal procedure, the partnership between power as brute-fact and law as content is neither autonomous nor impeccable. Authorized power or power-backed law is open to question from other quarters, in the name of other measures beyond the ken of the partnership. It is always permissible to assume that beyond law which delivers authority to political power there exists another law, natural or religious, for example, based upon another meaning of just and unjust. When he questions the authority of a particular procedure backed by the power-law complex in the name of other authorities, the individual stands in a relationship of certain insubordination to the law which he is challenging.

So, not even law can guarantee to power the inalienable security which it is so anxious to achieve; it actually inhibits the full realization of the political order's power-centric purpose. By virtue of its partnership with law, power is not only invested with authority but also directed into fixed channels and thus transformed from unmanageable brute force into manageable government. The price paid by power for the authority of law is its own subordination to it. Law implies limit, and legalized power is limited power. As a standardized body of contents regulating the structure and functioning of the socio-political complex, law establishes a state of affairs in which men can foresee and calculate the effects of their conduct in the public domain. Because the political order is a legalized one, the individual can anticipate the future, take it into account, plan for it, predict it. By establishing fixed channels, law introduces regularity, and thereby rationality, into the public domain. Power invested with legal authority is stabilized power, whose operations are rational and predictable.

Not that power derives no advantage from its legal confinement to fixed channels: it is thereby afforded the means of self-generation and of self-entrenchment in ordered structures. Since it is an emanation of order, that generation shows that law is the partner not only of power but of order as well. As partner of order, law transplants the principle of order—that is, the principle of placement and dispensation towards given ends—from the realm of power-projecting order to the realm of projected-power. By diverting power into fixed channels—say, into the regular channels of legislative procedure—it restrains power's expansive impulse, keeps it within bounds, prevents it from misdirection. As the authorized expression of and curb to power, law plays a double role in socio-political reality. It is as the partner of order that it keeps power within limits. Ordered power is power subordinated to structures differing from the nature of power as force. Power is confined within two limits: on the one side is the social order from which it is generated and on the other the legalized political order into which it is directed. This implies that whereas power may be said to occupy the position of an extreme when regarded from the viewpoint of its relation to the order by which it is projected, it may also be said to occupy the position of a mean when considered from the viewpoint of its relation to law. From the second angle, it subsists between the order of society and the standardized order of law, between the order by which it is generated and the order that facilitates and secures its enduring generation.

VI

The combination of power as force and of law as content does not reduce law to a chattel of authority-seeking power, but affords it the means of directing itself towards the creation of human relationships, and even of objective conditions which do not obtain there *ab initio*. Law can fulfil socio-centric as well as power-centric functions, and it can effect those designs of the political order that appertain not to its own self-preservation but to society at large. Law might be instrumental in the realization of such ends as political or economic equality, the distribution of national income, or old-age security. In that capacity, the specific law can function not only as rubber stamp of the existing power-factor and of the measures that it adopts to secure its own survival, but also as creator of a new order. The specific spirit and letter of the particular innovating laws are historical, that is, contingent upon and relative to fluctuations and shifts in the march of the generations. Yet a constant feature of law, as socio-centric, is that it need not necessarily be an image of the old, preexisting order, but may at times foreshadow, anticipate, or preenact a novel order to come. In that case, the specific law re-creates the body-social in its own image. For example, the principle of equality was brought into being by legislation which sowed a seed that would take ages to come to fruition. Here the novel ordering principle was not projected from below, that is, from the preexistent pattern of social togetherness, but from above, by the legislative or legal arm of the body-politic, like the Supreme Court of the United States. In view of the possibility of anticipating a novel pattern of social relationships, so-called advancement in the socio-political sphere may be described as a crystallized projection of men's hopes, aims, and desires into the domain of law. To the extent that law not only rubber-stamps existing structures but also creates novel patterns, it may be described as an objectivization of men's desires. This objectivization need not necessarily reflect a general desire, but it might be projected from the hearts of individuals who are capable of taking advantage of the machinery put at their disposal by crystallized power to inject into the body-social those principles which will evoke or awaken spiritual stirrings in other hearts. It is because it emerges under, and in response to, specific historical conditions, and is projected by the desires of individuals, that law in its innovating capacity is historical.

One could describe the partnership of power and law as a relationship of mutual "sanction," power being sanctioned through legal justification, and law by the power to impose penalties upon its trespassers. Law invests power with authority to manifest itself as a penalizing machine. The normative status of law as a body of meanings is no guarantee that men will respect or acknowledge it by conforming to the decrees which it authorizes in practice. Enforcement of laws presupposes a factual and instrumental mediator with the power to compel men to submit to meanings. That role is played by political power, that is, by the state and its institutions. Sanctioned law is power-backed law, which is in a coercive position analogous—to a certain extent—to the coercive status of the laws of nature; it is in the position of a law that cannot be broken with impunity. Were it not for the physical force provided by the political framework, the law—for its authority of content—could not be sure of the opportunity of being put into effect. Thus, to impose penalties is to enforce law. Yet, deprived of legal sanction or justification, there would be nothing to distinguish law enforcement from brute force. Thus the partnership of power and law permits law to tame its mate in one of two ways: by effecting a complete metamorphosis of brute force into legalized or authorized power—thus rendering submission to government as physical coercion equivalent to righteous conformance to law as meaning; or, at least, by minimizing the grosser aspects of brute force through its reduction to the subservient status of a mediator whose justification lies in its function as an agent of a normative body of meaning, namely, of law. Metamorphosis of power into law is a constant feature of social utopias, and confinement of brute force within the functional limits of authorized power is a constant feature of political reality.

That power and law sanction each other as a matter of fact does not imply that they justify each other as a matter of principle. The authroity of law does not equal the instrumentality of power; and the acknowledgement of law as meaningful does not imply subordination to the power-sanction. From the standpoint of the philosophical tradition, this means that it is impossible to accept Hegel's identification of law-abiding conduct (or conformity to power-sanctioned law) with rationality. Hegel's line of reasoning is as follows. The individual's rational will is identical with the will of the whole body-politic. Thus, an individual's conduct is rational, that is, controlled by his rational will, when, and only when, it is controlled by the universal-rational will. Thus, the use of power to enforce law, that is, to enforce the universal and rational will, is itself rational, since it forces individuals to be rational. This argument fails to distinguish between two essentially incompatible factors, reason and force, and their respective authorities. The authority of reason is ideal; it is the authority of meanings justified by rational persuasion. The authority of power is factual; it lies in physical might. Even granting that power-sanctioned law is a manifestation of a universal will and, as such, rational and right or justified, it is evident that one cannot deny that it is, at the same time, a manifestation of force. Even when it is a "servant" of reason, power is physically coercive and opposed to rational and persuasive modes of effecting subordination to law. We obey the prescription of rational men because we are persuaded that they are right. We obey the decrees of government because we are sometimes afraid to declare that they are wrong by violating them, since they will surely declare that they are right by punishing us. It can be maintained that there is no gap between rational conduct and the rational principle to which it conforms, but cannot be held that there is no gap between conduct under compulsion and the power-factor to which it submits. The distance between the coerced individual and the coercing force would remain, even were it possible to justify coercion as the instrument of imposing "rational" conduct upon occasionally irrational individuals by penalizing irrational conduct. Furthermore, even were we to acknowledge that the authority of law implies its authority to invest power with authority, we would thereby be acknowledging only a general principle and leaving its particular applications open to question. One can allow that law invests power with authority, and thus makes might right, yet protest at the same time that a particular power-backed law or group of laws is wrong.

Because men are persuaded that social integration is desirable and/or justified, law is imbued with real authority to effect integration through the instrumentality of power. But integration is in no wise an unequivocal notion, and many historical illustrations testify that it lends itself to many different interpretations. The idea of integration does not indicate—to take one telling example—whether the integrating principle will be a principle of equality or of inequality. It is clear that the principle controlling specific courses of integrating policital action is contingent upon, and varies with, the points of view of the men who formulate it. The status of politics is based upon the possibility of interpreting social integration in more ways than one, since one of the functions of politics is to interpret social integration and to translate the interpretation into legal forms. Another phenomenon, whose status can be traced to the indeterminate nature of social integration as lending itself to diverse interpretations, is what is known as revolution in the political sphere. It involves the subversion of a particular political structure, established in conformity to particular laws governed by a particular interpretation of integration, for the purpose of setting up a new political structure governed by a new interpretation of integration. Though there are, of course, many types of political revolution, at least one may be described as an attempt to establish a novel mode of social integration, involving subversion of the laws regulating the prevailing order. Such a revolution expresses a theoretical negation of a particular existing interpretation of social integration by undermining, in practice, the legal forms into which it has been translated.

The possibility of interpreting social integration in more ways than one is also behind the distinction between positive law as a particular expression and interpretation of social integration, and natural law as an immutable norm of all modes of integration; since it is underivable from any historical integrative nexus, it constitutes a permanent principle regulating men's interrelationships. The premise of our analysis is that man, as a rational creature, is the creator of the political domain; we are, therefore, led to the conclusion that the purpose of natural law is to uphold this status and to determine the relation and mutual adjustment between it and the demands of social integration as expressed in positive laws sanctioned by power. Various matters comprehended by the positive laws legislated in a state bear witness to their double role as subservient to power-centric purposes and also as assimilating contents related to man as a rational creature worthy of consideration. As assimilating contents related to men, positive law is designed to guarantee man's right to be taken into consideration as a rational creature, his right to self-realization under the sponsorship of (for example) educational institutions, his right to defend his person and his privacy, and so on. The authority or justification of natural law is in its relation to man's prepolitical and presocial essence; the authority of positive law is in its relation to processes of social integration and power-generation. That both types draw their authority from distinct spheres of human reality is evidence that there is no preestablished harmony between them and that a conflict between them is possible. Thus—to take a salient example— whereas natural law declares the equality of men as rational creatures, positive law might sanction inequality as expedient for the efficient functioning of the state, and then the rights defended by natural law, for man's sake, are overridden by positive law, for the state's. But why is it that power— although it shares the authority of its partner—must resort to coercion? Perhaps power must so resort because men are liable to withhold in practice the acknowledgement which they extend to its authority in theory. Or perhaps because men's acknowledgement of the authority of legalized power does not necessarily imply their acknowledgement of its particular decrees. Men might admit the justifiability of state interference in the economic sphere and in the same breath deny the justifiability of one or other aspect of the state's economic policy. Or, to take a more radical argument, the state might suspect that not only the authority of a particular policy but even the authority of the political apparatus as a whole was being covertly denied in men's hearts, though overtly acknowledged in their actions. The reason for the use of force in totalitarian regimes is, from this point of view, the reverse of the reason for its use in relatively liberal ones. In the second instance, it is wielded to guarantee that the acknowledgement forthcoming as a matter of principle and in theory will be reflected in practice; in the first, to guarantee that the open show of subordination in practice will be accompanied by an attitude of acceptance or acknowledgement in theory or spirit. Still, it must be observed that, no matter what the reason, minor or major, the use of force never extends to all aspects of human life and activity. Even totalitarian regimes recognize the existence of a margin of spontaneity beyond the reach of coercive measures. That they do not transgress the limits of this margin might be attributed to their assumption, conscious or unconscious, that once a sufficient degree of pressure has been exerted, men will respond to it, spontaneously as it were, with terror converted into awe, coupling their negative abstention from protest with the positive acknowledgement of might, if not as right, then at least as awe-inspiring. It might be said that the coercive policy of totalitarian regimes is based upon the assumption that man is not only stricken with physical terror in his confrontation with overwhelming political might, but he is also inspired with a sense for sublimity. The tacit anticipation, even on the part of totalitarian regimes, that the individual's negative submission to power will be accompanied by positive acknowledgement or awe is a tribute—voluntary or involuntary—to the real impact of the norm of authority.

VII

No matter, then, what the source of acknowledgement, whether recognition of the value of integration or admission of the sublimity of might, the gulf between the concrete individual and authorized power can not be bridged. The mutual distinctiveness of concrete individuals and the crystallized power which they themselves have projected obtains even when the value or authority of the crystallized projection is recognized. The irrevocability of this divorce follows not only from power's mode of existence as projected over and against its creators, but also from its paradoxical essence as at once the crystallized expression of integrated society and the agent of social division. As we noted, one of the major concrete effects of power-projection and crystallization is the splitting-up of society into government embodied in concrete representatives and subordination to government on the part of concrete individuals. The horizontal plane of social integration through reversible subordination is bisected by the vertical ladder of political dominion through irreversible subordination. Though theoretically a projected-image of the body-social, power in actual fact is incarnated in only one member of that body, to wit, in the "right hand of power." The total nexus of social integration from which power emanates is interpreted in a necessarily partial fashion by a partial group of concrete individuals representing power incarnate, that is, power as government. This implies that abstract power is no more identifiable with concrete government than any abstract entity is identifiable with any concrete one. One implication of this general incommensurability of the abstract and the concrete is the untenability of the political theory which would identify ideal wholes with their concrete representatives. Plato and Marx are the chief proponents of this theory, and it might be appropriate to use their views to illustrate what may be called the fallacy of misplaced totality. Marx's assumption that it is possible to realize an identification of an empirical body-social or of one of its parts—namely, the proletariat—with the total idea of humanity is fallacious even on his own premises. For he allows that there is a difference between the proletariat as a concrete historical reality and the idea of human brotherhood. Furthermore—and still on his own premises—there is a difference in content between the total idea and its historical representative, besides the difference in mode of being, the one ideal, the other real. The proletariat exists not only in the dimension of the future, where the ideal of humanity is to be realized, but also in the present, where a particular class of human beings endeavors to realize particular aims, such as the improvement of its standard of living. There is no need to assume an identity of content between particular ends pursued in the present and the supposedly universal ideal of humanity on the horizon of the future.

Plato embodies the total image of the body-politic in the partial class of philosopher-kings, working on the assumption that the incommensurability of the concrete part and the abstract whole does not apply to his rulers, who, in virtue of their power of philosophic or synoptic vision, are free of the taint of partiality. As incarnate in philosophers, faithful servants of the synoptic vision, governing is likewise synoptic. But the difference between concrete philosopher-kings and their abstract philosophic vision comprehending society as a whole is apparent on Plato's own premises. For, even granting the impartiality of the philosopher-kings by virtue of his synoptic vision, the trouble is that it is precisely because of their contemplative function that they are barred from actual participation in the diversity of activities constitutive of the whole which they contemplate. But if, in practice, the rulers do not participate in those activities and so do not share the interests of the artisans and guardians of Plato's *Republic,* how can they possibly entertain an adequate or synoptic vision of the totality constituted by the interaction of those interests? There is a difference between a synoptic vision, which discerns the respective places of diverse interests, activities, and roles in the political whole, and an assessment of political reality grounded in practical experience. Thus the vision contemplated by the philosopher-kings of the *Republic* is not synoptic in the sense of being implanted in and reflecting "the fertile depth of political experience." It is, at best, a synoptic vision from the point of view of the detached observer, and, as such, it is bound to be partial since it excludes the point of view of the implicated agent. It follows that one can be either a ruler or a philosopher; the practical dominion of the one, and the theoretical contemplation of the other, are mutually exclusive. Hence, the vision of the rulers, philosophers though they may also be, is vitiated by the partiality of all concrete activities. This applies *a fortiori* to the vision of those who, from the outset, are barred from filling the role of the representatives or agents of power. No matter what the abstract entity—whether humanity or society synoptically envisaged, or power as the projected image of social togetherness—and no matter who its concrete agents—whether isolated individuals or a class of individuals or so-called public servants—there is no exception to the general principle that every actualization or incarnation is a limitation.

VIII

So much for the paradox of projected-power as being ideally an image of social togetherness and actually an agent of social division. Power embodied in government cannot possibly represent the society at large. What is even graver, power embodied in government and subservient not to socio-centric, or even anthropocentric, but to power-centric purposes is all too likely to entertain projects fraught with danger for society and its members. The dangers of concentrated and self-centered power, once a matter for theoretical misgiving, are today all too palpable as concrete fact. Power's insatiable will to power has led it, over the past decades, to seek conquests beyond its native socio-political bounds even in outer space, beyond the earth from which men—with the aid of power—derive the means of physical survival. It is almost as if power will not be satisfied until it has established its dominion over the entire cosmos. There seems to be good cause to call this illegitimate adventure of projected power a case of cosmic imperialism. Sovereignty, hitherto a political concept, may be taking on a cosmic meaning, on the tacit assumption that only by cosmic conquests can the survival of political power on earth be secured.

The suppressed premise of power's cosmic campaign is that the cosmos constitutes territory. But there is no conceivable sense—literal or metaphorical—in which the term 'territory' can be applied beyond the limits of our planet. It denotes a tract of land, that is, a region of the earth, inhabited by human beings whose very lives depend upon their intimate bond with it. Biologically, man is a land animal which extracts the means requisite for life's processes from the earth and from the enveloping air. Historically and politically, man is confined to no specific tract of land, but may make his home almost anywhere on the surface of the earth. The entire earth is his territory, at least potentially. In extending his dominion over larger and larger expanses of earth, he alters the denotation of the term. In seeking to extend his dominion beyond the earth and its atmosphere, to outer space, he alters its connotation. All territory is terrestrial, not only because the dictionary tells us that the term comes from the root *terra*, but also because man is a terrestrial creature by nature and, therefore, cannot survive in extraterrestrial regions, unless, like a snail, he carries his earthly abode with him in the form of a n hermetically sealed container provided with the comforts of home—oxygen, for example. Since he carries his means of survival with him, because he knows that he will not find them in the cosmic spaces which he invades, the cosmic nomad, unlike his earthly brother, is not extending the limits of his so-called territory in quest of means of survival. If this is so, the question is: Why invade the cosmos at all, as there is nothing to be gained so far as the struggle for human survival is concerned? And the no less obvious answer is that the cosmic campaign is in many cases a military campaign which, like other such campaigns, calculates profit and loss in terms not of human life but of strategic bases conquered.

This amounts to cosmic imperialism; however, it is unjustifiable not only on rational grounds (as based upon a self-contradictory concept of "territory") or on utilitarian grounds (as profitless for human survival), but also, and especially, on moral grounds, (as an illegitimate usurpation of power all too likely to recoil upon the ultimate source of political power, namely, man as a rational creature). That the ultimate end of cosmic imperialism is invulnerable dominion over mankind, on earth, is clear. That there is no justification for it is just as clear. The anthropocentric purposes of power are justified by natural law, its socio-centric purposes by men's desire to secure social integration, and its power-centric purposes by the assumption that only political sovereignty can secure impregnable social integration. The only ground of cosmic conquest is the lust for power which regards human beings at best as means and at worst as hindrances. Since the very existence of political power would be impossible were it not to be generated and regenerated perpetually by human and diversion activity, the legitimate or authorized limits of power can extend no further than the legitimation implied by its very generation. Legitimate power is power emanated from society and directed back towards it, either in the form of law or through the agency of legal machinery. Legitimate political power is confined within the limits of human society and to that portion of the earth inhabited by men. Obviously, the primary purpose of cosmic usurpation or cosmic imperialism is not to open man's horizon to the farthest reaches of the universe and thus make him a citizen of the cosmos, as the Stoics put it, or inspire him with the cosmic loyalty of which Whitehead speaks, but to give dominion the upper hand in its war with often insubordinate individuals by providing it with cosmic military bases.

Permit the quest for dominion to proceed unchecked in the cosmic direction and you open the door to dominion unchecked in the human. Just as physical science has made it possible to invade outer space, so chemical science and psychology have made it possible to invade man's inner self, with drugs or by brainwashing, for instance. Both invasions are morally wrong, if survival of man as a rational creature, and not dominion, is the ultimate moral standard. Even were we not to discern, through critical reflection, that military conquest of cosmic "territory" is logically absurd and profitless, as well as morally wrong, our concern with self-preservation ought to warn us that such aggressive flouting of cosmic limits is dangerous, not to the immortal stars but to mortal man.

Do the relationships of subordination and government obtain only in the political domain, or can they be found in other realms of human reality as well? It might be suggested that the relationship of submission to expert advice, say, of a doctor, or even the relationship of compliance with the guidance of a reliable person as involving acknowledgement of authority, represents nonpolitical exemplifications of the relationship of subordination to authoritative ruling. There are, however, several reasons which make it necessary to distinguish between acknowledgement of authority in general and subordination to government as the authorized representative of power in particular. For one thing, submission to expert advice or guidance implies acknowledgement of authority founded on experience or knowledge; submission to political power as government implies acknowledgement of authority founded on the projective position of power. In the second case, the object of acknowledgement is the authority not of experience or regulative knowledge, but of the status or position in which power is placed as a result of social integration. For another thing, submission to expert guidance or advice is an empirical relation between concrete and individual *relata* subsisting on the same plane of existence even though occupying different positions (of adviser and advised) as dictated by the mode of their encounter. By contrast, subordination to authoritative power is an abstract relationship between all members of society on the one hand, and, on the other, an abstract entity which they interpret as invested with authority, but which lacks such authority in itself. Finally, although it may be regarded as a mode of subordination, submission to the authority of an expert can always be interpreted as directed towards the good of the advised, guaranteeing him health or longevity, for example. Subordination to the state cannot be interpreted as directed purely towards the good of the subordinates, since it guarantees acknowledgement of the independent status and crystallization of society as a whole. Hence, it would be more accurate to define expert advice as a mode of administration rather than of coercion, even though it does imply subordination; and to describe the authority of political power as a mode of coercion rather than of administration, even though it is, in part, based upon administrative factors. Though all subordination to administration is subordination to authority, not all subordination to authority—and acknowledgement of political power is a case in point—is submission to administration.

NOTE

1. Arnold Gehlen, "Mensch und Institutionen," in *Anthropologische Forschung*, Rowohlt, Hamburg 1961, pp. 69ff.

PART TWO

Action

CHAPTER FOUR

Of Politics

I

The term 'politics' is used in two primary senses: either as the analytic and comparative study of the state as power and organization, which includes a philosophical analysis of its position within human reality, or as the type of human activity that concerns the state. The subject matter of the previous analysis can be described as politics in the first sense; the present discussion will consider politics in the second. It may be remarked that guidance for government in the Machiavellian sense concerns politics as an activity, even though it presupposes, as its point of departure, certain assumptions as to the essence of the state.

II

On turning to consider the nature of political activity, one is faced with the question of whether it is characterized by distinguishing marks not relative to the particular socio-historical circumstances in which it is conducted. Does it feature patterns governed by determinate ends and dictated by no particular technique or theory? Discussion of politics generally deal with techniques and even with the rules which control them. For example, the definition of politics as the "art of the possible" usually implies that the nature of political activity is relative to particular circumstances and consists in an assessment of the line of action possible in given circumstances; correlated to this is an abandonment of projects whose realization is impossible in them. Politics in the technical sense may be approached as an activity governed by the principle of "muddling through," that is, of getting things moving with no long-range end in view and without making any radical decision involving a breach between the parties. The essential characteristics and status of politics are determined by the nature of power. Since the existence of power is not self-sustaining, but depends upon the process of power-projection, its maintenance calls for activities directed towards assuring that process. In this respect, politics might be understood as the activities directed towards power-generation. But, in a narrower sense, it is distinguished from men's spontaneous and perpetual activities of power-projection. What distinguishes it from the process of power-generation is that, whereas that process is a situation and not a deliberate act, politics, as activity conducted by and in the constituted state and designed to maintain the process prerequisite to its existence, involves deliberate decisions. Accordingly, one may define it, in that narrow sense, as an activity consciously directed towards power and engendered by the political order's inability to count upon automatic constitution, administration, and organization of the state.

III

The political domain being brought into, and maintained in, existence through an activity of integration, conscious or unconscious, politics may be described as an activity whose purpose is to promote integration or to activate the social forces making it and to direct them towards power, or as a regulative activity related to the process of integration and designed to secure its character. In that sense, it is connected neither with parties nor with groups; it represents a deliberately sponsored and maintained process whereby men constitute their collective power and the achievement of definite purposes through that power. It is, therefore, the activation and regulation of integrative activities and also their concrete, empirical expression.

This accounts for the essentially dialectical nature of political activity. Though directed towards collective power, it is always conducted by particular persons and, in that regard, is a partial activity; its aim is collective, its agents are partial. The transition from general directedness towards power, in the regulated concrete and empirical activities wherein that directedness is manifest, makes for differences of opinion as to the factors that actually bring about integration. The result is a diversification of politics into partial activities through the agency of partial groups or individuals seeking to unite into groups. When refracted through the prism of concrete individuals acting in concrete circumstances and entertaining certain opinions concerning themselves and their situations, directedness towards the general and collective, is transformed into a partial activity reflecting the partial design of persons who represent but a part of the body-politic. It is necessary, therefore, to distinguish between two aspects of politics: the collective aim of maintaining power and the rhythm of the process. This distinction leads to the differentiation of that aim from a diversity of partial intentions.

Not all collective aims are necessarily so diversified when it comes to realizing them in practice. To take an extrapolitical example: a trend towards collectivity is at work in the scientific domain, where it is regarded as a sum total of findings and methods in the service of the achievement of knowledge, that is, of a common knowledge, one belonging to no particular individual or group. The community wrought by science is a product of the de-personalization of knowledge and knowing. The methods of scientific research are deliberately designed to guarantee the independence of its findings from the desires or views of the individual observer. The political domain, even though it features certain impersonal structures such as legal and institutional moulds, does not lend itself to thoroughgoing de-personalization. The limited degree possible there is due to the existence of that domain as depending upon directedness towards its maintenance by concrete individuals who compose it. Again, this is not so with the scientific domain, since the body of scientific findings exists even when we, as concrete human beings, give it no thought, as well as when we are unaware of its existence. Collective political power would not exist if we did not direct ourselves towards keeping it alive.

IV

Politics is a teleological activity which furthers the given end of maintaining the state as projected power, characterized by the features analyzed. While the purpose of political activity is given and even determined from the outset, its service of that purpose brings it to men's concrete existence, with a view to shaping it. Politics is the regulative activity conducted by particular human beings within the limits of their state. It shapes not only men's general directedness towards the state but also their natural, geographic, demographic, and even historical environment from the state's position. For the very reason that they are directed towards a predetermined purpose, the processes through which politics is executed vary with the shifting circumstances—physical, personal, and historical—of men's lives in concert. Thus, there is a difference between the processes that are conducted by and directed towards people habituated to organization and sharing the habitual modes of acknowledging their collective framework, and those that are conducted by and directed towards people not so habituated. The political domain rests upon a vacillating balance between the process of power-projection and the deliberate maintenance of power which does not rely upon spontaneity; the nature of its processes is relative to the existence or nonexistence of that balance. A society whose spontaneity does not tend towards antisocial or antipolitical manifestations calls for a different mode of political activity from that whose spontaneity is likely to dissolve or atomize cohesion. Hence, the state as power is constantly on guard if the maintenance of order is to be guaranteed.

The transition from general directedness towards the collective end to a diversified variety of concrete processes, whereby it is realized in practice, renders politics subservient to other human purposes such as defense, protection of life and limb, and education. In that capacity, it aims not only at constituting power and maintaining its existence, but also at maintaining the shape of the order of society itself. From this angle, it reflects the reciprocity and tension that characterize the relationship between power and order. As subservient to socio-centric purposes, it is an activity directed towards interference in the order of society through the instrumentality of power. It is necessary to extend the definition of politics and describe it as a teleological activity aiming at the twofold purpose maintaining the form and shaping the content of the socio-political apparatus. Its formal purpose is to guarantee that partial groups of human beings will not splinter the cohesion manifest and realized in power. Its material purpose is to tighten the bonds which constitute the social order and, by interfering in it, secure its support for power, if only because of the repercussions in the social order that failure to maintain power entails. This seems to be what Althusius had in mind when he defined politics as the art of joining or combining together.[1] To enlarge upon his definition, one might describe politics as the art of joining together for the sake of either generating power or of utilizing it to attain certain ends. It is, then, a two-faced activity proceeding from order to power on the one side, and from power to order on the other. Through politics, the social order shapes power and yokes it to purposes transcending its aim of self-preservation, purposes such as defense and social security. And, through politics, power shapes the social order, imposing upon it patterns such as equality before the law, economic equality, or information channels.

V

Proceeding in two opposite directions, whose mutual adjustment is not safeguarded let alone preestablished, politics can be seen as an activity designed to establish a *modus vivendi* between the factors operative within the social order and the existence of power. From this position, politics is manifested in the attainment of agreement or adjustment within the social order for the sake of power, that is, in an arrangement securing the acknowledgement of the existnce of power by individuals and groups as well as the expression of that acknowledgement in practice, namely, in active conformity to its demands. This aspect is morphological, not historical, for it belongs to the nature of society and state, not to particular and variable historical circumstances. The consequence of directedness towards power and the creation of conditions favorable to its maintenance is the use of power. In the final analysis, politics serves power so as to take advantage of it. For it is not a contemplative activity which leaves its object unaltered, but a practical one, seeking to use its object —power—for the realization of its projects as they are determined by the directions of its agents. Accordingly, the partial directedness of particular persons towards the collective ends of maintaining power in existence and exploiting it in practice is directedness towards transforming the partial will of particular persons into a general will; that is, towards incarnating power in the contents projected by partial will. Thus, particular individuals might aim at attaining equality and endeavor to harness collective power to their purpose with the aid of legislation or court decisions or information and instruction provided by the state, its insititutions, and its representatives. Within so-called democratic purviews, political activity aims at winning general agreement upon its purposes. "General" agreement may imply either the general ratification of a specific content by all individuals or groups, or general agreement upon a common principle, in which case not all agree, for example, upon nationalization of industry, but all acknowledge the authority of the state, regulated by majority decision, to nationalize by law. Because the maintenance of political power is not automatic but an achievement, and since there is no guarantee that the agreement requisite for its achievement will be forthcoming, politics must authorize coercion. Underlying politics is the paradoxical assumption that coercion can play the part, or take the place, of agreement; the tension between agreement and coercion essential to the domain of the state is the primary premise of all politics.

The existence of directedness towards power or coercion invites the ever-present possibility, or even risk, that human beings who live in the state measure themselves and all their activities from the point of view of whether or not their actions contribute to the maintenance of power. Social order, thus regarded, will be conceived as a compound of groups of human beings of which each possesses partial power. As for men's opinions and beliefs, they too will be approached from this angle: Do they support or undermine the cohesion upon which power depends? Viewed in that light, politics is directed not only towards a collective power-centric purpose, not only towards the employment of collective power for socio-centric purposes, but also towards the creation of power cells within the periphery of collective power. In that sense, political activity presupposes that power can be activated by power and not by activities conducted by individuals banding themselves together spontaneously. Relying upon that presupposition, it creates partial organizations within the body-social with a view to regulating collective power not only by opinions and beliefs but also by subsidiary organs of collective power. Because the domain of the state is penetrated by the factor of power, we notice emerge organizations exerting influence, pressure, and power within the spheres of which the state is made up. As a result, the state stamps its features upon the social order, and that order, as the creator, is shaped in the image of its creature. Conversely, the character of these partial organizations is conditioned by the nature of the integrating forces in operation in the body-social. This cohesion is produced by the acknowledgement of the authority of collective power in its integrative capacity. Given acknowledgement of the state's collective authority in and for itself, society can be divided into heterogeneous elements depending upon religious, ethnic, or ideological composition. By contrast, in societies where that acknowledgement is not conceded, the security of political cohesion may call for the creation of a primary basis of social solidarity by homogenizing many—for example, religious or ideological—factors which shape the social structure. This implies the somewhat paradoxical conclusion that the more men acknowledge the authority of the political factor in itself, the less their politics entails comprehensive politicization of society. Conversely, the less it can count upon general acknowledgement, the more the state shapes society in its own image by promoting those social factors—such as religion or convention—which make for social solidarity and, consequently, for political cohesion.

Another purpose of political activity is implicit in the assertion that politics is a struggle for power. Partial warrant for the assertion are the attempts of particular persons to implement collective power as incarnate in government. From that angle, political activity may be described as seeking a share in power and as struggling for it. This aspect is in Althusius's mind when he defines politics as mutual participation in the life of the collectivity or as action and exercise in society.[2]

VI

There is a familiar view that politics does not call for regulative principles but is regulated by the history of the society in which they operate. It is expounded, for example, in the writings of Michael Oakeshott.[3] What obliges us to take issue with that view is not an ideology other than the one which it tacitly assumes, but a morphological analysis of the position of politics. The analysis yields the conclusion that political reality is characterized by a tension between order and might underlying the perpetual attempt to establish mutual adjustment between the two permanent elements of social reality. Oakeshott does not go so far as to advocate the abandonment of conscious directedness. What he proposes is, as it were, a conscious abandonment of conscious directedness and a submission to the guidance of historical patterns regarded as if they were reliable guides at all times just as they are; as if they themselves called for no interpretation. But if we consider the fundamental dialectics of politics as a partial activity deliberately directed towards a collective end or seeking to transmute its partial projects into collective ends, we must point out that politics is bound up with men's interpretations of their own partiality and of those matters common to all. One cannot excise politics from the position of concrete individuals subsisting in the present and regard the present merely as the shadow cast by past generations. For all his professed pessimism regarding the possiblity of altering man's way, Oakeshott's tone, when discussing politics, is optimistic, perhaps overoptimistic. His position is based upon the assumption that it is possible to overcome the tensions at the heart of political reality. Furthermore, because politics involves interference in the course of events, operating as it does between the poles of order and might, it *ipso facto* implies regulation or shaping of the course of events. It cannot, therefore, be reduced to the almost passive activity of swimming with the stream of events as it flows from past to present.

VII

From this point of view, politics may be said to subserve formal purposes. We speak of purposes in the plural because politics relates to diverse phases of human existence and requires a diversity of ends to be realized by political activity. Let us, then, examine some of these formal purposes.

If the existence of the state is the necessary condition of politics, then one can say that the existence of its creator—man—is a primary and, in this respect, a prepolitical purpose. The state as "purpose" may, accordingly, be regarded as the ultimate condition of politics as an "activity." Given the existence of the state as power, the purpose of politics is the participation of concrete human beings—collectively or partially—in government as the expression and representative of power. Moreover, in its capacity as an activity directed towards participation in government, politics aims at regulating government in conformity to the demands of order. The second purpose can engender alternative courses of political action: either the maintaining of the given order with the aid of power as government, or the creating of a new order by the instrumentality of government. Thus the establishment of a relationship between power and order is a primary purpose subserved by all kinds of political activity.

Power itself is transformed and regulated by the endeavor of politics to effect an encounter between power and order. Henceforth, politics may be said to serve the purpose of curbing power, either by subordinating it to the existing order or by activating it for the creation of new one. In itself, the effort to bring power and order together circumscribes power within a field of factors and, dialectically, transforms the power to which we are subordinated into a factor itself subordinated to regulation. There is, accordingly, no such phenomenon as "pure politics", in the sense of an activity subservient to the exclusive purpose of maintaining the state in and for itself. Politics represents a complex mode of activity constituted by the interaction of numerous factors and implicated in manifold fields, and is, therefore, irreducible to the purely "political" component of that complex. The state is a permanent objective of politics because its existence is never self-sufficient, never achieved once and for all, never crystallized and entrenched in its own domain in such a way as to be independent of perpetual directedness towards itself. For a created entity, undergoing the process of creation can always occupy the position of a purpose, at least from the point of view of the human beings who conceive it not as a bird in the hand, so to speak, but as one in the bush, and know that, were it in the hand, it would not a living bird but a fossil. The second purpose of politics, shaping the state as power in conformity to order, is not contingent upon variable conditions, and certainly not upon the arbitrary desires of particular individuals. In this service, politics appoaches power and the state as the handmaiden of order. If one examines history, and especially the turn that it has taken in modern time, from the point of view of this distinction between the two purposes of politics, one observes that the conception of power as subservient to purposes is a change for the better in the historical process. And, although power is still an end in itself, its implementation as a means testifies that men have not as yet correlated their ends, individual and social-related, with political processes. Either people let the established order alone, just as it is, regarding power as its guardian, or, at best, assign to power only the human meaning of form-construction and not the social content of "concerning itself with human beings in concert." This induces them to consider power itself as their highest end and places them in a position of dependence upon, and commitment to, power, which offers them nothing in return so far as concerns their nonformal interests, such as raising their standard of living, or child welfare, or old-age and employment security. Orientation towards two purposive projects—maintaining the state as a form and shaping it—implies still another purpose of politics, that of charting a middle course between the two, or guiding men towards a decision which is to be pursued at the expense of the other if no middle way can be found. The bearing of this upon the relationship between politics and morality will be considered presently.

It is in the sphere of foreign relations that the formal orientation of politics is brought into sharp relief, since politics is not confined there to the relationships between power and order within the limits of power, but is concerned with interpower, that is, with interstate relationships. As a rule, the primary purpose in this sphere is to secure the existence of the state against the background of interstate relationships. Yet, even here, one witnesses the interference of order in power and the regulation of interstate relationships in conformity to economic, social, religious, and other guiding factors. Thus the tension between the maintenance of power and its regulation obtains also in the domain of interstate relationships, regulating foreign, as it regulates domestic, politics.

VIII

Let us return to the relation and tension between the existence of collective integrating power and the partial will directed towards maintaining it in existence. We are not in a better position to determine why is it that a tension of this sort exists in the political realm. A partial and tentative answer has already been suggested, namely, that collective cohesion subsists in actual fact, or empirically, only as refracted through the prism of partial and concrete persons acting in partial and concrete circumstances. Dependence upon particular circumstances and persons is by the same token dependence upon partial motivation. There is, perhaps, another reason. Even though political cohesion is never achieved once and for all, there is, nevertheless, a difference between the maintenance of cohesion and the purposes with which it is imbued. In practice, political activity assumes that there is no difference of opinion concerning the need to maintain the political order itself: in other words, that the existence of the political order is not a purpose subject to "prismatic" refraction, and that this refraction, or difference of opinion, pertains to its meaning and effects. Consequently, although politics proceeds on the assumption that political cohesion is a bird in the bush, it must still be regarded as if it were one in the hand, and the center of gravity of its interest shifts to the specific and partial relationships between power and order. Only at definite, critical, historical moments—say, in wartime emergencies or under the threat of invasion—does the integrating purpose of cohesion come explicitly to the fore. When it swings into focus on problems of shaping the political order, political activity works on the assumption that, if formal cohesion is to have real bearing upon the concrete lives of men who direct themselves towards it, it must be a shaped, given content. One can say, for example, that, were there no justice in the state, the state itself would be nonexistent, even though, in principle, it is possible to distinguish between the state as crystallized cohesion and justice as the content with which that cohesion is invested. Hence, one might add that the more grounds a man has for owing allegiance to the political form, the more he owes allegiance not only the the status but also to the contents of formal cohesion; likewise, the stronger will be his allegiance to the state as a whole, the more highly will he esteem it, and the richer will be his modes of directedness towards it.

Our distinction between the two purposive projects to which politics is orientated may be regarded as a variation on the Aristotelian motif that the state comes into existence for the sake of mere life but exists for the sake of the good life. The more men are persuaded that the good life is possible only in and through the state, the more secure—internally—is the state's existence. Historical experience attests that the stronger the socio-centric and anthropocentric character of the state, the more patriotic its citizens, that is, the stronger their allegiance to the state. There is a danger, here, of distortion and poltical phraseology, of making it appear that the state is steeped in human contents, while in reality it is not.

Seeing that politics serves formal purposes, and that it must always grapple with the problems of the relationship between power and order or of the shaping of power in conformity to order, it may be concluded that there is and can be no politics without contents. By maintaining the relationship between power and order, politics invests power with the content, e.g., of protecting private property or abolishing it, of promoting aspirations towards equality or suppressing them. Because there is no directedness without content, political activity is confronted with the problem not only of defining the relationship between the elements of content but also of determining the principle in conformity to which relationship is defined. In view of the fact that the activity is orientated to a content and fills the formal factor—that is, political power—with it, there is no evading the question of the norm to which the encounter between power and order must conform. In itself, political activity implies an answer to tacit or express questions such as, "Is equality worthy of being realized or not?" and "Do liberty and propery go hand and hand, or are they independent of each other?" These questions are matters of principle implicated in, and regulating, the establishment of a relationship between the content-constituents of order and power. The two permanent purposes of political activity, maintaining power in existence and shaping it by investing it with content, compel politics to determine which of them is preferable. Witness, for example, the debates on issues such as this: Should the mere existence of human or political life be guarded without troubling to consider the nature of the most desirable regime, or should the existence of the regime be protected even at the expense of life itself? Underlying issues of this type are ethical problems whose scope transcends political limits but whose nature emerges in the political domain as through a magnifying glass. The subservience of politics to more than one purpose is likely to entail conflicts of purposes; and in that event, merely to recognize the conflicting factors will not do. This is the fundamental problem of the norm which we follow in overcoming the conflict, deciding which purpose is preferable, and adopting a particular line of action on the basis of our decision.

The term 'politics' can be employed not only in the comprehensive sense of directedness towards the state but also in the partial one of directedness towards institutions such as banks or universities. Yet, even in that partial sense, it denotes an activity which serves two basic purposes, namely, the maintenance of a form, whether of a bank or a university, and its shaping in conformity to specific purposes, such as financial investments or emphasis on particular fields of studies. Thus, both primary constituents of politics— with due allowance for appropriate changes—are discernible in partial contexts as well, except what the content of the formal constituent, is different because the form to be maintained in existence is not political power but a particular institution. There is however, one common distinguishing mark: just as the state functions as a framework, so does the institution. Just as the maintenance of the state's apparatus is the controlling purpose of politics in the comprehensive sense, so the maintenance of the institution's apparatus is the controlling purpose of politics in the partial one.

To conclude, political activity always implies directedness towards the maintenance of a formal apparatus, which, no matter how rich in content, is never all-encompassing. Not even where the cultivation of science constitutes a purpose of politics is scientific activity transformed into political. Even as content-orientated, politics serves the purpose of creating the environments within which these and other human contents are realized, or, more generally, in which men live their lives and enrich their experiences. For example, even when political activity aims at guaranteeing equality, the concrete individual's real, empirical, encounter with the world and his fellow-man inevitably lies beyond its reach. Being directed towards the apparatus of the state, it remains formal even when it invests that comprehensive framework with content: whatever politics touches is turned into a framework, and no framework can replace content as the medium in which the real lives of real men are led. So that the distinction between them and the state remains tangible, even when they direct themselves towards the state—and they cannot help doing that—or the state occupies itself with its own directedness towards them.

IX

By transferring human ends to the domain of political power, politics seeks to render them permanent, proceeding on the assumption that power occupies a permanent position, at least in comparison to other factors. Yet, if it were not regarded as a purpose, the object of perpetual directedness, power itself would not exist. Consequently, human ends can never attain that degree of permanence with which politics, by merging them with political power, seeks to endow them. To be sure, totalitarianism represents an attempt to achieve this end by effecting a total identification of political power with the particular purpose to which it is harnessed. Totalitarian politics seeks to invest purpose with power and, by so doing, to make power itself appear as if it were a definite social objective with a definite social content. This hasty identification of two distinct spheres of political activity produces those human repercussions known to us from the totalitarian politics which our age has experienced. Beneath totalitarian politics is the assumption that to affirm power is to affirm the particular content with which it has been invested and to warrant the use of the coercive force of political power for the sake of zealous and thorough protection of the end that has been merged with power. Any deviation from this purpose in thought, speech, or action is as an injury inflicted upon political power and the body-politic. Totalitarian politics protects power as if it were all-in-all of human content and of political purposes alike; and it protects the human content that has been merged with power as if it were identical with political power.

Yet, there is no such thing as totalitarian politics, since politics lends itself to formal definition as an activity only in relation to, and against the background of, the tension between the content of order and the purpose of maintaining power in existence. Hence, in totalitarian regimes, political cohesion cannot be interpreted in more ways than one, cannot be refracted through the variegating prisms of partial organziations within the all-encompassing state. Totalitarianism stands upon the uniformity of the interpretation of cohesion, that is, upon the doctrine that the one and only valid, legitimate, and conceivable interpretaion, in both principle and practice, is that dictated by the government. From this it follows that in totalitarian regimes there are no politics in the sense of an activity conducted by men directed towards the purposes of power and of content. What we have is merely the adminstration of the state by its rulers. To identify politics with the state as an expression of state-power, rather than with dynamics as an activity directed towards state-power, is, of course, to empty it of all content. Another aspect of the phenomenon of totalitarian politics is the yoking of political power to a particular purpose and the subordination of all other human ends to that. Thus, for one example, it is yoked to the project of guaranteeing employment for all, freeing all from fear of unemployment, and rewarding all for their labors, or of guaranteeing that there will be no private ownership of the means of production. Such projects are conceived as the only human prupose for whose sake all — or at least some — of the other purposes may be disregarded, deemed secondary, or dismissed as illusory. Applying power to an exclusive or unique purpose obviously entails identifying the purpose with the political sphere or looking upon other purposes either as transferable to the state or as insignificant. And as far as concrete human beings are concerned, it entails the demand — more often than not covert — that they renounce their diverse aims and evaluations in return for, let us say, freedom from fear of unemployment of the assurance that there shall be no more private property. Identification of power with a single specific human purpose devalues all purposes which resist absorption into the domain of poltical power.

Hence, a morphological analysis of the essence of politics is important not only because it profides the descriptive-conceptual basis for philosophical inquiry; such an approach to the essence of political activity, its intrinsic polarities, and its place in human reality is important also because it affords the touchstone for distinguishing between those elements which are susceptible of institutionalization in power and those which are not.

NOTES

1. *Grundbegriffe der Politik* (*Politica methodice digesta* 1603), V. Klosterman, Frankfurt a/M 1948, p. 13.

2. Ibid., p. 14 ($Κοινοπραξία$).

3. See, for example, his *Political Education* Bower & Bower, Cambridge 1951; see also the present author's critical analysis included in his book *Philosophy, History And Politics, Studies In The Contemporary English Philosophy of History*, Martinus Nijholf, The Hague 1975, pp. iii ff.

CHAPTER FIVE

Politics and History

I

Borne by real human beings acting here and now, political directedness occurs within the nexus of historical conditions. In the present discussion, the term 'history' will accordingly by employed in the conventional sense of the occurrences of human existence in time and the activity of human beings in and through it. From this angle, historical conditions figure in the assembly of the conditions whence politics emerges.

Another aspect of the relationship between political reality and history is brought to light by historical discussions of politics. Take the familiar saying that history is the politics of the past, meaning that historical research is concerned with the political events of the past. As it stands, this statement cannot be accepted as exhausting the complex of factors constituting history as the object of research. Because it scrutinizes the traces left by them upon present data, the research treats of past events in general, and accordingly is defined not by matters of content but by the dimension of time. So it can be, and is, open to all past events and their diverse vestiges — political, economic, and ideological. Since it is impossible to assume that the relationship between historical research and political reality is either necessary or self-evident, one can only establish its existence by a more thorough analysis of the specific position which politics occupies in relation to the historical domain. The purpose of the analysis is not to correlate politics and historical research but to seek an answer to the question of the bearing of political activity upon the historical course of events and upon historical consciousness, including its scholarly manifestations.

II

The answer must take into account the structure of history in its twofold capacity as the understanding of events proceeding from the past to the present and the shaping of events proceeding from the present to the future. The contemplative directedness towards the past and the formative-constitutive directedness towards the future constitute the background of political activity. Yet, as an integrative activity of actual human beings directed towards power-constitution, or as reflecting men's wish to constitute power and perpetuate its existence, political activity looks ahead and forward to power's existence hereafter in a given moment, and over a span of time. Hence it is directed towards the future. As the future is a dimension of historical occurrences, political activity must be related to that same dimension.

As the understanding of events that have already occurred and as directedness towards the past, history exercises a restraint on political activity. For, in this sense, history can be said to determine the conditions of political acts and also to provide opportunities for courses of political action against the background of given circumstances which, in part at least, have been created by history. History created the relations between Britain and France, between the United States and the Soviet Union, between the Soviet Union and China, and between the State of Israel and the Arab States. It is within the nexus of relations given by history that political activity—as involving intervention in the course of events proceeding from the present to the future—is conducted.

This does not imply that all the conditions of political activity in the present are the fruit of history. For geography or meteorology do not owe their existence to history as a chain of occurrences produced by the acts of real human beings. But men do, by their historical activities, thread conditions not of their own making into the texture of their lives and works. Because men fashion means of sheltering themselves from the climate or even synchronize the rhythm of their lives with the seasons, climate has to be regarded not merely from a meteorological but also from a human point of view, and it has to be conceived as related to man as a factor to which he relates himself. In other words, climate is of historical significance even though it is not an event of history.

When we examine the relation between politics and the historical future, the first thing to observe is that the purpose of politics does not exhaust the future as the dimension in which purposes are to be realized. In the historical future, there are other purposes besides the political one, and in relation to them men engage in artistic, scientific, and religious activities which likewise contribute, in differing measures, to the making of the future.

As the span of time, the future is total. No content of human activity, and no purpose, can exhaust the expanse of the time-dimensions. Moreover, there is no way of knowing what prints our activity will leave. We cannot foresee whether the future repercussions of, for example, our religious activity will affect mankind or a part of it. It is not only as occupying a part and no more of the expanse of the future-dimension that the political future—as shaped by the purpose and practice of politics—is restricted. Restriction is also implicit in the circumstances of political integration being effected through the agency of human beings acting in determinate circumstances and entertaining this purpose at all times. Men would like to see the success of their directedness towards power. They want to see power brought into, and kept in, being within the horizon not only of future generations but also their own. If men invest their capital and savings, they can anticipate dividends to be enjoyed in the distant future, even in the future of their children and grandchildren. Or if men relate themselves to the world in a religious manner, shaping their ways of life conformably, the traces of their religious attitude can be left to the course of events, and it is not for them to finish the job. But, in the political domain, although men do direct themselves towards the existence of power even beyond the biographical reach of their own lifespan, they also direct themselves towards its existence within their own present reach.

The political domain being that of power possessing coercive force, its coercion has to be revealed in the present and not only in the future, near or distant. It seeks both to perpetuate itself beyond the experience of men and to experienced by them. So, it is a matter not for generations unborn, let alone for the Millennium, but for present directedness towards a purpose at hand. That is why it is possible to define the purpose of politics—in the sense of transcending the mere existence of power—in a more restrictive and determinate manner, however diversified its determination be. Thus peace, war, abolition or prevention of unemployment, or compensation in the event of unemployment, and the building of educational institutions—are purposes conceivably within the reach of the actual experience of actual and active human beings. When a man makes a political decision, he expects to experience its consequences himself, at least those which pertain to the very existence of power and its shaping. Hence the political future is a relatively near one. Measured in years, the distance between the political present and future is short—a matter of five-year and ten-year plans.

III

Thus far, the relationship between man in history and political activity has been explored from the formal point of view of dimensions of time.

Now—to put forward a more comprehensive thesis—it may be asserted that political activity is historical activity *par excellence*. One way of verifying this is to consider the difference between history and biography. What distinguishes the course of an individual's life from that of history is, among other things, the public character of history in occurrence and in understanding. A matter that concerns all, or at least many—and a minority of many is never one—is historical. Relatedness to the public domain is an aspect common to history as a whole and to the political sphere. The state is the most prominent public domain because it is both the formal expression of social togetherness and the securing agent for the existence of togetherness. Politics is an activity for power's sake, that is, for the sake of the public domain as a whole. No other human activity—artistic, scientific, or religious—is as directly and prominently related to the public domain as the political is. The purpose of scientific activity is to discover truth; that of artistic activity is to shape matter or language. The purpose of political activity alone is identical with its field of operation, so that it not only leaves historical traces but also serves as the adjutant of history in the sense of the public domain or of the most comprehensive public domain. In this respect, politics differs not only from scientific and artistic but from economic activity as well. Here we must take issue with the well-known theory that assigns primary historical import to economic activity. It is true that economic activity is conducted in the public domain. In and through it, men come into mutual contact regulated by the division of labor; through it, they have recourse to markets, institutions, organizations, arrangements, and state-intervention. Nevertheless, the public character of the operations and works notwithstanding, economic activity is subservient to the individual and its purpose is to satisfy his wants, to provide him with goods, to foster his biological existence and so on; and all wants are individual, even when the single individual has recourse to the many. Even though it is conducted within the realm of togetherness, what is crystallized through economic activity in the economic domain is not social togetherness but the standing of each individual in his particular place, and his endeavor to bring the products of this activity from the public domain to his own private sphere. Economic activity is moved by the final causality of the individual's private domain, whereas political activity not only moves in the public domain as its field of operation but is also moved by it as its final cause or *raison d'etre*. In so far as history is occurrence within the public domain, as well as the shaping of it, and in so far as political activity is the perpetual creation of the public domain, that is, of history or the historical domain, political activity is the basic historical activity.

It is possible for economic activity to serve as the instrument of political power or to be directed to power-centric ends; the position of power can be fixed in, among other things, the economic relationships obtaining within society. Thus, in a given society, the existence of economic order and a level of production and consumption may be taken to indicate that social togetherness has found political expression. Historical experience shows that the more active men's participation is in the activity of production and consumption, the more comprehensive is their political activity. It can be shown that when economic goods are the portion of the many and not merely of the few, the many become a factor contributing to political shaping; for through their part in economic togetherness, they come to share in the political. The connection between democratic institutions and a people's level of economic development reflects this correlativity. For that level is an index of the many's level of activity and initiative which are requisite for the establishment and functioning of democratic institutions based upon a minimum remove between the people subordinated to government and government itself.

Yet, even though it makes for conditions congenial to the maintenance of political activity, the relation of economic activity to power is not causal but instrumental. Whether it operates as the instrument of consumption or of power-constitution, economic activity in itself creates neither the state as an emanation of order nor the position of quasi-independence occupied by it in relation to the social order. The state can be used by the social order, including the economic elements thereof, and the order can be used by the state. But the state is one thing, the economic network another. Regarded analytically, the state as a domain is distinct from politics as an activity. On the other hand, no economic entity is projected from economic activity; and, consequently, in economic activity, the aspect of domain is hardly distinguishable from that of activity as is the case in the domain of state and politics.

The difference between economic and political activity implied in the relation between the state, politics, and history can be clarified differently. In conceptual terms, the constitution and shaping of power are the elements of all political activity. Yet, even though the political domain possesses an essential aspect of its own, in point of fact there is neither a state without political activity nor political activity outside concrete action in historical time. The purpose of political activity is realized within history and occupies no position save the one that it builds for itself through the mediation of the historical process. This is not true of economic activity, which rests on given grounds, on the physical existence of man. Even when it overreaches physical existence in the direction of luxuries and finery, it is still attached to its point of departure, that is, the physically existing consumer-person. In that sense, it may be said to serve a prehistorical and even extrahistorical purpose, whereas political activity serves an intrahistorical one and has no hold outside the historical process. Of course, in history, the wants of men are subject to change; and history does, indeed, entail a constant redefinition of wants or, at least of their variations. But the fundamental situation of want is not created by history, and its extrahistorical status is presupposed by economic activity, whose historical variations stem from its efforts to adapt itself to consumer-man or him to itself. This is not so with political activity which is, as it were, enclosed within history and sustained by intrahistorical sources solely.

There is yet a further aspect of the historical nature of political activity. The political entity—power or might—is an abstract one ever in need of men's directedness towards it. It is crystallized neither in the physical domain nor in that of artificial products, while economic activity, at least to a certain extent, is crystallized in objects, commodities, so that it may be said to have a hold in physical crystallizations, though certain services—such as insurance—cannot be regarded as objects for all their economic import. Having regard to the crystallizations in the economic domain, the product of economic activity cannot be described as merely projective, in the sense that the product of political activity can. At this juncture, there emerges a paradoxical difference between political and economic activity. Not being crystallized in objects, political activity entails a distance between men and their product, a distance manifest in actual fact in the authoritative and coercive status of power. Economic activity, being crystallized, if only in part, in objects such as property or goods, can be expected to entail no such distance. The object which it produces is for the satisfaction of wants from which it is, in principle, inseparable, though separated from them in actual experience for the simple reason that no object is identical with any one of us. But, as a matter of principle, every object is produced for the sake of each and every one of us—or, at least, of some of us. An economic product is for the sake of consumer utility; political power is not, though its existence does imply the possibility of using it to protect man's existence or to satisfy his ambitions as a consuming and, as such, an economic creature. That is precisely why one must not transfer the structure of economic activity to the political domain. Being in a process of production and having no lodgment in products as property or objects, the political domain must be at some remove from the men who produce it and has to occupy the status of an emanation or projection. Otherwise, it would be entirely identical with its denizens, and there would be no political domain as distinct from the men dwelling in it. Economic activity, however, projects no abstract entities such as power or institutions. As containing products, the economic domain is rightly subject to the demand that they be subservient to man and be accorded neither an independent status nor an independent logic. Because economic property is for utility's sake, one can always measure it by the yardstick of whether it serves human beings or they serve it and, by so doing, pervert their relationship to it. But because the political domain is not entirely for utility's sake, one must preserve its projectivity and refrain from making that aspect merely useful or subservient to utility's demand. This projectivity makes it possible for an individual or a group to claim at all times that the state falls short of its essence and represents expression not of collectivity but just of instrumentality for interests or subservience to them.

Since the economic product must be returned to its point of departure, which is physical man as an existent and consuming being, one can require that the process of economic activity not be allowed to stray too far from its starting point, not be alienated from the human being who is its causal origin. In the political domain, by contrast, there can be no proximity between the political product—namely, power—and its starting point—namely, the men who constitute it.

The relation of the state to territory is not analogous to the relation of an individual to a plot of land upon which he plans to build a house. Not being an object for use, certainly not in terms of its relation to the state, territory represents mainly a groundwork, and not property. In a sense, it becomes an accumulation of property composed, for example, of soil for cultivation or of mining areas, from the point of view of economic activity, which manipulates it according to its own logic and turns it into cumulative or comprehensive property. But in the political domain, it is not property, nor is its status abolished when it is opened up for economic utilization.

The political domain cannot be reduced to another product of history, namely, the division of labor among men—Plato's theory to the contrary notwithstanding, as discussed before. For Plato's correlation of the two presupposes that the existence of the public domain concerns the directedness of some human beings only—to wit, the philosophers—and that all the others direct themselves, at most, only to their own limited field of occupation and those with whom they share it. But the presupposition is untenable on Plato's own premise. According to him, it is not only that a man's occupation is the measure of his nature but also that a man's duty to concern himself with his allegedly predestined occupation is the measure of his moral status. It follows that there exist realms of occupation transcending the particular occupation of a particular individual, realms into which he must not slip—for the man of war it is the realm of craftsmanship, and for the craftsman it is the realm of war. It also follows that Plato recognizes the existence of a common and general public domain, only that, to his mind, it is a negative existence for people other than the philosophers. But if the public domain exists in a negative manner, it exists positively as well. To assume its existence is to assume men's awareness of that, although, unlike the philosophers, they know neither its nature and meaning nor its relationship to the principle of juctice. It squares with Plato's own line of reasoning to conclude that people whose economic occupation constitutes the measure of their political status are not circumscribed within the tight limits of that occupation and barred from entering the common public domain, but are, indeed, in it. Yet the common public domain, if it exists at all and not for philosophers only, cannot be equated exclusively with an arena for diverse economic operations. For it is just that diversity that differentiates human beings in terms of their real occupations, their functions in the economic system, their respective positions as producers and as consumers, or as producers in relation to one particular matter and as consumers in relation to others. The more expansive the economic system becomes, the less do men figure as producers in relation to themselves and the more as consumers of production that transcends them. In the political domain, though, those present in it direct themselves towards the collective; differing from that of the economic, the structure of the political domain is not characterized by a relatedness to a portion and part, that is, to that portion and part with which each one of us is actually occupied as a *relatum* in the economic system. If there is a comprehensive economic system, we are related to it from our own real and partial place. Whereas, in the common political domain, there is at least the demand that we relate ourselves directly to the collective state in general. Therefore, it is necessary, dissenting from Plato, to maintain that the existence of a common public domain and men's directedness towards it constitute positive and independent factors and cannot be conceived as ramifications of, or corollaries to, the relations of interdependence and reciprocal service that obtain among human beings from the point of view of the division of labor and the process of production.

The question whether it is possible to equate the political and economic domains must be distinguished from the question whether, and to what extent, politics and its twofold pupose of contituting power and shaping it are influenced by economic factors. That it is quite possible for economic matters and ambitions to impress their mark upon the shaping of power is attested by the use of power to protect property, develop markets, or distribute the national income in one direction or another. But the instrumental subservience of power to economic matters implies neither that its structure is identical with that of economic activity nor that its *raison d'etre* is merely that of protecting or fostering economic interests. The dovetailing of the political and economic domains in the historical process neither obliterates the difference between them nor abrogates the essential relationship of each to the historical domain. Since the product of political activity is always historical, and the product of economic activity also is, history may be regarded as a meeting ground between the two activities, where they can make reciprocal use of each other. But, as *post factum*, the encounter does not affect their essential interrelationship or cancel the purposes and structures characteristic of each. Yet, owing to the *post factum* nature of their encounter, it is impossible to determine *a priori* which will regulate or control the other. History tells us that men are likely not only to harness political power to economic interests but also to ignore economic ends for the sake of maintaining it. To set the constituting of political power over and above economic purposes or interests is to give the safeguarding of social togetherness priority over socio-centric and anthropocentric aims which benefit individuals as individuals. This is demonstrated in the prevailing trend towards national independence even at the cost of economic advantages, sometimes even elementary ones.

The difference between the orientations of the political and economic domains accounts for the paradox that whereas the status of the individual is safeguarded in economic activity, in political activity it is not. In the economic domain, even when man is a reflection of products and his wants and desires are dictated by the economic process, he himself is the customer; economic activity cannot abolish his status without abolishing itself at the same time. In the last analysis, it is interested in sustaining the individual and even stimulating his appetite, if only for its own sake. So far as it is concerned, then, the more individuals sustained, the better; whereas political activity presupposes a concourse of individuals characterized not by a relation of "give and take," but by an acknowledgement of common togetherness. Being the product to, togetherness and orientated towards sustaining the cohesion of togetherness, the political domain does not secure the status of the individual. Hence, we do not need economic means to sustain the individual in and for the economic domain, but we do need political means to sustain him in and for the political. This will be examined more closely when we discuss the principles of justice, liberty, and equality.

IV

Thus far, the connection between history and politics has been considered in terms of its bearing upon the shaping of the future. Let us survey it form the angle not of shaping but of understanding. By 'understanding,' we mean directedness towards the present in its relation to the past and not in its relation to the future, for the second belongs mainly to shaping, not to understanding. Political activity involves historical understanding and this follows from the occurrence of political events within the empirical limits of a determinate historical situation obtaining in the present but created by the past. As directed towards a historical situation, political activity takes its departure from given factors which it transmutes into conditions of, or opportunities for, the achievement of its purpose of constitutiong and shaping power. Without historical understanding, we would be unable to discern the situations against whose background we propose to act. This is far from implying that historical understanding must take the form of historical research in the disciplinary sense of that term. Nevertheless, recognition of a situation as a historical product is an implicit and essential element of political activity, which takes its departure from the present. The points of departure of politics, foreign or domestic—such as discernment of situations, or gauging of men's attitude towards institutions, of their esteem for of indifference to symbols, or of their readiness or reluctance to defend prestige and interests—are all products of history. Politics takes into account the modes of human response that have been shaped by historical processes and weighs the favorable or unfavorable bearing of these processes upon the courses of political action about to be undertaken.

The relation between historical understanding and political activity precludes unique political activity of unique content. It is possible to understand the real, historical relationship between the present and the past, in more ways than one. One might, for instance, observe that there is a connection between the present political image of Asia and the rule of colonial powers to which Asia was subject in the past, that some features of it have been shaped by Asia's own culture as well as by its exposure to Western influence. But this historical understanding does not of necessity involve a wish to sustain the dual influence or—in keeping with the current tendency to declare independence of the West—to expunge all traces of Western dominion, such as the maintenance of a managerial class or modes of economic development, from the insitutional forms of the East. Courses of political action yield different practical conclusions from any particular historical understanding.

Although historical understanding cannot be identified with political activity, they are closely related: political activity in a sense represents a metamorphosis of historical understanding from its contemplative state to one of real occurrence and intervention in the course of events. Political activity is not historical understanding, but it is—again in a sense—a conclusion drawn from the present towards the future on the basis of an historical understanding directed towards the present as the product of the past. Historical understanding is fostered by a discernment of the double orientation of politics—towards power-constitution and the shaping of power—not only in the political activity of the present but also in the events of the past, that is, those no longer open to our political intervention. The perspective for historical research afforded by the study of political activity permits the view that the relation between political activity and historical understanding is reciprocal.

V

The ultimate ground of the interrelationships between history and political activity is man as a rational or reflective creature. Were it not for his relation of abstraction to the projected product, to power, there would be no political domain. What makes the relation possible is his capacity for reflection, for contemplating reality. Political activity presupposes relatedness to a purpose, which, in turn, would not be possible were it not for man's ability, as a reflective creature, to detach himself from the given moment and look beyond it towards a not-yet-present dimension. Because the political domain is created within history, it cannot but presuppose, as the condition of its possibility, the status of man, as defined not from within the historical process but by a transhistorical structure, not by reference to relationships obtaining within time and its dimensions but by his very relation to time itself, that is, by the relationship of reflection. If history is the product of reflective man, then the political domain is a product within a product.[1]

NOTES

1. See the present author's *Between Past and Present, An Essay on History*, Yale University Press, New Haven 1958. Reprinted by Kennikat Press, Port Washington, N.Y./London 1973. Also his: *Time and Meaning in History*, Reidel, Dordrecht 1987.

CHAPTER SIX

Politics and Morality

I

We shall examine now the question of the relation between politics and morality. To approach the political domain morally is to assume the validity of moral principles on the horizon of politics of state and determine the nature of the principles by which it is, or out to be, governed. Here we will review only the first aspect of the moral question, namely: Is there a connexion between moral conduct and political activity? If we find the moral consideration present on the horizon of the political domain, we may pass from the bounds of the descriptive analysis over the threshold or the normative domain.

One cannot presume that the nature of moral conduct is unequivocal and uncontroversial. In the present analysis, the term will be understood as those modes of human behavior which are controlled by considerations which, as a matter of principle, lend themselves to moral evaluation by reference—be this to rational principles or to emotional motivation. This is a purely structural designation of the moral sphere, but it should suffice— as the first step for our purpose.

II

Let us tackle an architectonic issue: Are there grounds for raising the problem of the moral-political relationship at all, or is the relationship exactly like that, for example, between art and morality or science and morality? Of art and science, it can be claimed that they are subject to the moral consideration only if one is contemplating their results in terms of human behavior. So, Plato grappled with moral or political questions in his survey of artistic works because he approached them from the point of view of their effect upon human beings. It might, however, be argued that, in so far as one deals not with the effects of a particular activity, say, of art or science, but only with its intrinsic nature, there is no warrant for concerning oneself with its relation to moral standards. If art and science are left alone and allowed to develop in conformity to their own inner logic, there appears to be no relation between them and moral conduct. Leaving aside the validity of this particular conception, we shall try to show that there is a relation between politics and morality that it is not external but internal, and that it follows from the nature of political activity.

By definition, politics is an activity directed to the constitution, maintenance, and shaping of power; that is, to a purpose that lies beyond itself. Therefore, it is not a self-contained activity. One can speak of science for science's sake, since the purpose of scientific activity is, in a sense, that activity itself or the quest for truth; one cannot justifiably speak of politics for politics' sake. Politics aims at a purpose that we have ourselves projected, and we can evaluate the purpose from the aspects of its essence and importance, its relation to other purposes, its position in the scale of preferability, and so on. Once the question arises as to the importance and preferability of a particular purpose, there is no evading the moral issue; moral conduct is distinguished, among other things, by an act of our preference for one mode of conduct above another, because we find the first morally superior to the second. The purpose of political activity likewise implies a preference, to engender power rather than not. Like other such instances, the preferred purpose of power is open to question respecting the grounds for preferring it as an order.

III

That there is an internal relation between politics and morality follows not only from the end of political activity but also from its content. Political activity is characterized by a trend towards integration, but integration is unrealizable without the integrating activities of human beings. Considering that this activity is subservient to a purpose which presupposes men's deliberate directedness, it is impossible not to maintain that the ends and the means of political activity are open to moral considerations—in fact and in principle. If one justifies the political purpose of integration on the ground that it emphasizes togetherness, one is inevitably faced with the further question: What justifies togetherness? Likewise, if one considers politics from the point of view of the activities composing it. It is always feasible to ask, for instance, whether men's activities are, indeed, directed towards integration, and whether they reflect the attempt for reconciliation between orientation towards the common public domain and partial interest. Political activity does not lie beyond the horizon of moral evaluation. This is not to aver that it is necessarily moral; no activity is, because the realization of morality is never automatic. What we mean is that politics is open and exposed to moral evaluation if only in the sense of an assessment of political elements unacceptable to moral judgment or violating moral principles. Machiavelli did not claim that the antimoral is moral; he only held it possible to justify antimoral politics, their antimorality notwithstanding.

That political activity is open to moral evaluation follows from a second aspect of its content. Politics is orientated towards the public domain. As channelling our conduct into standardized moulds and as imposing demands upon it, the public domain fulfils a regulative function for our activities; it requires our orientation to integration; implicity, it has the status of a tribunal before which individuals are judged and evaluated. We are judged in terms of whether we contribute to the creation of the public domain and whether we sustain its existence by restraining propensity towards isolation from the collective, or even subversion of it. The contact established between individuals in the public domain can be said to reveal the factually normative position occupied by it as inhibiting extreme egoism or preventing its outward expression. In the public domain, man's conduct is controlled, willy-nilly, by consideration for his fellow and for the public domain itself, which thus plays a double normative role, insisting upon integration and curbing anti-integrative behavior. This implies that the public domain is invested with an initial moral authority entailing one man's consideration for another, a consideration that is a necessary, though not a sufficient, condition of moral conduct. Thus, the public domain is open to morality not only because it is exposed to moral judgment and evaluation, but also because it requires the factual realization of a first moral behest. One might even affirm that—at least at first glance—every bidding to curb egoism is morally justified, for that restrain opens an expanse for the existence of one's fellow. It is only those modes of an individual's conduct which relate to himself and are not egoistic that lend themselves to ethical criticism. It is in these circumstances that the public domain figures as a tribunal before which individuals are judged in terms of whether they curb their egoism.

But that tribunal status is double-edged, and bares the dialectic of the judgment relationship. The judge is always also judged. By passing judgment and evaluating individuals, the tribunal is itself judged and evaluated at the same time. The authority of the public domain to impose demands upon the individual is open to question from two angles. Structurally, the existence of the public domain turns on a marked togetherness and, consequently, on the curbing of the noncollective—that is, the egoistic—behavior.

If it is to be sustained, men must demand of themselves that they uphold the collective, and justify this injunction to themselves or call upon the public domain to do so. Materially, the public domain does not merely require that the individual sustain its existence by contributing to interindividual collectivity, but translates the requirement into specific measures, such as taxation, military service, and judicial verdicts. These measures are open to judgment and evaluation even on the assumption that they are manifestations of the public domain, whose authority, as a matter of principle, is not doubted. At least one criterion for measuring these manifestations is moral: one can always judge them in the light of their stimulus to men to adjust intentions to deeds, of their fostering of justice and equality, or of their sustaining man in his moral, and not in his a-moral, private domain. If we weigh that at least one criterion to measure the political domain is moral, it is because our present purpose is not to establish the parity of moral and political considerations but to expose political considerations to moral scrutiny and show that their sphere does not lie entirely outside moral considerations. That politics is within the reach of morality, and the the circumference of the moral is wider than of the political sphere, follows even from the would-be "political" approach to politics. For the existence of the public domain is held to be no less worthwhile in the context of political considerations, be its worth assessed by the yardstick of the benefit which men derive from its protection and mediation or by that of the good realized by underlining men's togetherness and suppressing their egoism. That a factual relationship obtains between morality and politics is accordingly our premise, and our task is to determine their respective positions.

IV

As soon as the power-factor enters into human reality, men come to be regarded as power-units within the collective power of the state. A minimum of regard is shown for one's fellow—whether as an isolated individual or as a group—when his existence is recognized, and also when he is recognized as a unit of political power of the state. But the ground of truly moral regard is his existence as a fact. If the moral problem arises it is not because one, so to speak, invents one's fellow to provide an object of regard, but because his existence is given *ab initio*. Not every claim of his may be said to occupy a moral status, but his mere existence can, as it is revealed in his claims upon us. Therefore, regard for him as a power-unit represents not only a political or power-conscious consideration but a moral-conscious awareness as well. This duality underlines the importance of toleration in the political domain as a mode of conduct between men, reflecting reciprocity of consideration. Even when I dismiss my fellow's claims—e.g., in the religious or economic spheres, be they on matters of opinion or practice—I dismiss only them and not the claimant. Differentiating thus between his views and contentions and his existence, or his "other-status," I am tolerant towards him, licensing him, in some degree, to express himself because I acknowledge or have regard for him as the other. Toleration is sponsored partly by political and partly by moral consideration: politically, it reflects the need to maintain interindividual concourse, the diversity of men's opinions and beliefs notwithstanding; morally, it reflects the imperative to take my fellow into account and so much respect him as to allow him to entertain beliefs and enter claims, though I cannot myself accept them.

V

The purpose of collective power is to maintain the order that exists among men by freeing its sustained existence from the exclusive dependence upon the goodwill or spontaneity of the constituent individuals. The question with which politics is constantly confronted is, therefore, a moral one: Is political activity subservient solely to the purpose of maintaining power as the projection and guarantee of order, or also to other purposes? Does the creation of the public domain as the first purpose of political activity imply that it is at once the last or supreme purpose? Does the secure sustenance of order exhaust politics and constitute its only justification? Or, to employ again the Aristotelian distinction between the creation of the state for the sake of mere life and its existence for the sake of the good life: Does the creation of power for power's sake imply that the existence of power is for that sake only?

In itself, the constitution of power brings about a change in human reality, by introducing into the circle of existence an element that is nonexistent at the level of order where state-power is lacking. Reliance upon manifest power alters the reliant order and sets limits to spontaneity upon the horizon of existence. The moral question of the relation between spontaneity and nonspontaneous is, accordingly, an intrinsic and inescapable question of politics. That duality is emphasized by the status of the law, as a formulated content, relying upon the possible imposition of sanctions. At times, law is the tool of the maintenance of contents—such as refraining from abuse of one's fellow—towards which spontaneity would do well to direct itself; it does not, however, abandon the content of nonabuse for dependence upon spontaneity but affords it the further, nonmoral, support of sanction qua coercion. As the instrument of a moral principle, law relies upon an incentive which is not strictly moral, that is, not being generated by spontaneity.

Where the moral consideration stands in the political domain can be illuminated from another angle by a second recourse to Aristotle's distinction. It might be argued that a minimum of good life is achieved through the maintenance of mere life: where life is not, good life is impossible. In certain historical situations, protection of life is the primary concern of political power, as in the case of enemy invasion and its inherent danger to men's physical existence or the existence of order. There may well be a clash between the demand to preserve order and to alter it. For instance, when people fight for the political freedom of their ethnic group, they disrupt the established order represented by the foreign dominion whose yoke they seek to cast off. Just as the demand for mere life and for good life may collide, so may the demand for order and for reforming it, or even occasionally for demolishing an established order so as to replace it. So-called revolutionary situations are those in which certain demands—say, the demand for a new order—are given preference over others—say, the demand to sustain the existence of the current one—even when subversion of that order is entailed. In general, there may be a contradiction, as regards political status, between mere life and good life. Take the present-day controversy between those who argue that for the sake of sustaining life in the primary sense, one can endure an undesirable political regime, and those who argue that a life without content is none, and that to submit to a despised regime for the sake of mere life is to destroy life itself. Better red than dead, say some. Better dead than red, say others. Our purpose is not, however, to take sides in the ideological-political debate but to circumscribe its position and point out that it exhibits essentially a moral problem of politics. By its very nature, politics must answer the question whether its primary purpose—the constitution of power—is comprehensive and so preferable to all others, or merely one purpose among many. The conclusion to be drawn from our analysis is that there is partial justification for both viewpoints, that the clash between them is not incidental, and that its resolution—whatever the direction of it—is based on moral preference. It turns out that, far from lying beyond the reach of moral considerations, the political domain is not only open to them but that they even regulate it.

VI

Although power plays its double role of manifesting and sustaining order in the political domain, the significance of the role is not purely political, but, in a sense, also moral. If order implies the demand that each of us conduct himself in conformity to his allotted place, then it also implies an aspect of refraining from the transgression which deviation from that place must imply. By so refraining, we manifest a certain measure of regard for our fellow's existence, and, with it, a minimum of morality. Order implies the sustenance both of interindividual concourse and of individuals in concert within the togetherness. Morality is concerned with order because, within it, individuals exist together as individuals and as "together." That does not make the moral demand and the demand for order identical. Morality might possibly call for the heroic existence of the individual; or the subversion of order by separation from it or by attempting to institute a new one; or the intellectual cultivation of the individual against the background of order, but from above. For all this incommensurability of the two demands, the moral expanse still harbors a demand for order as well; order occupies a moral status, however partial, because within it, individuals live and have their being and cannot help taking each other into consideration. This is where the moral problems of politics come in. The demand for order, regarded in its moral status, might be presented as a comprehensive moral demand or, at any rate as if it had priority over all others; in such a presentation, however, one makes several different moral demands. For the moral expanse encompasses the demands for order, and for changing it, and for self-regulated individual conduct. The incompatibility of the three is to be conceived as a conflict not between moral and nonmoral considerations but between diverse moral demands; and not only in the political domain: there is, for instance, a conflict—or at least a difference—between justice and mercy, between honesty and courtesy, between discipline and licence.

Looked at in its relation to politics, order may be taken as a partial realization of morality or an instrument wielded by morality in pursuing the realization of its more far-reaching demands, including one for recognizable changes in the established order. But there is the reverse side of the correlation of order in its broad, moral sense, and in its narrow, political, sense; namely, the price paid by the moral standpoint for the emergence of politics upon its horizon. By uniting with politics, morality commits itself to the material end of politics as well as to the means by which it is realized; and coercion, too, appears upon its horizon. It may be true that, as regards function and content, in keeping each of us in his allotted place lest he trespass upon the other, politics is the servant of order; nevertheless, even as such, it is subservient not to individual inclination regulated from within by the principle of regard for the other's existence, but to power, manifest in coercive sanction, among other things. Even when that sanction is imposed for the sake of a moral end, say, to protect man's existence as the other, the difference between the means and the end is and cannot obliterated. It is true that, in and through constituting power, man seeks to throw off the burden of personal inclination, announcing thus as it were, that he does not always rely upon the dictates of his heart as guides to decision or action. In the political domain, he sometimes depends upon his product, as power invested with coercive force, more than upon himself. That domain concretely testifies to his double evaluation of himself, as knowing the good, and as liable—in his deeds—to fall short of knowledge. Coercion is one means of healing the breach in this self-evaluation, the power of sanction making up for dispositional weaknesses of character. Even assuming that coercion occupies a compensatory or protective status in relation to conduct, one cannot obscure its factual character, or overlook the elemental discord between conduct springing from inner disposition and controlled by inner principle-preference, and that called forth by constant potential confrontation with the possibility that coercion will be exerted if we deviate from patterns of conduct dictated from without. We may predicate that coercion amounts to the sanction to be laid upon a man who fails to act in conformity to what he demands or expects of himself. Yet this makes the sanction no less external to him and no less incompatible with his self-criticizing morality. Hence, even were we to admit that coercion is an indispensable guarantee of good conduct, we would not consider that status as a sufficient reason for calling it "good." The good is integral to man as a deliberating subject; its purpose is to protect his status as such and permit him to live and act in such a way as to realize and secure it. To oblige him, through coercion, to act as if he were other's keeper, sustaining, as a subject, the other's status as equal one, is to contradict that human characteristic. But coercion is the price which morality must pay for political protection.

Coercion is not the only contradiction in the status of the subject that flows from the confrontation of morality and politics; subordination is another. The mark of political reality is the subordination of men to men, even when they are said to be so subordinated not to men as men but as the representatives of nonpersonal or abstract power. For it is in the hands of men that power as government is concentrated. They are men who have been raised to representation of collective power and order, though they are just individuals among other individuals, living and acting within the periphery of the collective order. Hence, the organized system of the political domain necessitates this subordination and the resultant inequality among men, as visible, say, in the relation between those with initiative and those without it, between those who plan and those whose acts must conform to a system which they have not themselves designed. Corroborative description is found in sociological literature, employing the term relative status, or a relation that obtains when some men have something which others lack. This implies that there would be no government were there no one who did not have this something and, consequently, that if there were no inequality, government would not exist. Political activity may be controlled by acknowledgement of the principle which holds that men are equal, yet inequality in fact is the upshot of the existence of government. Even if we disregard its involving the deprivation of those who do not share in it, and approach it from the standpoint of its status as a partial actualization of collective power, government still breeds inequality. Because government, as actual, is partial, while power as collective is abstract, the hierarchical stratification of men within the ambit of collective power and order is unavoidable, and hence the moral standpoint and political reality collide. From the moral standpoint, every man is a subject and must be treated as one. If all men are subjects, then they subsist on the same level and, in from the perspective of morality, there are no hierarchical differences between them. In the political domain, there are such differences, due to its structure and not to the moral imperative, which, of course, insists that there is no difference whatsoever between one man and another from the angle of morality. From that angle, men are undifferentiated, no matter how diverse their socio-political positions, all being subjects and their status as such being ontological, not social. His social status—whether from the internal angle of the social hierarchy or the external one of intersociety division—has no bearing upon a man's moral-ontological status as subject. The political domain, however, divides mankind not only vertically in a hierarchical stratification but also horizontally into manifold societies distinguished by diverse types of order and power. Thus, the clash between coercion and spontaneity is not the only one implicit in the encounter of morality and politics. An analysis of the concrete consequences of the nature of the two domains shows that whereas in morality, conduct is controlled by acknowledgement of man as subject, in politics it is, in effect, controlled by subordination even when as a matter of principle it is recognized that subordination must not entail infraction of the principle which demands that acknowledgement.

VII

All this has been said to demonstrate the significance of moral considerations to politics, and to invite attention to those constituents of the political domain that contradict the inner logic of the moral. The claim is not that political conduct is moral, but that one can appraise political conduct by moral standards, in full awareness of the limits of applicability of that measuring rod in that context.

The problem of the relation between politics and morality can be approached in another way, namely, by maintaining that the grounds for the state's justification are distinct from the individual's, because the state is a moral substance occupying an autonomous status which dictates its activities. The idea is Hegel's and, in a sense, represents an idealistic crystallization of the notion of *raison d'etat*: the state is characterized by an independent logic which raises it not only to a moral position of its own but even to the ethical status *par excellence*. In the light of the preceding analysis, the idea seems untenable.[1]

The moral status of the state seems to be, in a certain respect, analogous to the individual's. The justification of political power is twofold: in terms of its existence and of its works or agency. The reason and justification for its existence are that it is a manifest expression of togetherness. The reason and justification for its agency are the security which it affords to togetherness, by protecting it or by embedding it in laws regulated, for example, by the principle of equality. Just as power is viewed from the dual perspective of existence and agency, so is the individual: on the one hand, he is approached as an existent fact; on the other, as an agent whose deeds either do or do not conform to the principle of man as a subject. This double standard is behind what might be termed the two faces of the moral situation.[2] The duality of existence and agency in state and individual alike postulates the existence of a corresponding parallelism between their domains.

Political power is measured according to whether it sustains order as imbued with initial moral significance or shapes it in conformity to certain moral contents, such as the principle of justice or of equality. Those moral contents include what is implied by the relation of power to the individual as a constituent of order, as a bearer of integration, and as a moral subject. The political domain involves a relation to concrete human beings, who, morally regarded, are subjects. Hence, there is no avoiding the question whether man's status as subject is or is not sustained in the state, and, if sustained, whether not only as a matter of fact but also as a matter of principle. These questionings are internal criteria for the evaluation of political power, and, from this perspective, it is a moral evaluation. For, since man, towards whom power is directed, occupies a moral position, evaluation of the state's relation to him cannot be regulated by his status, and the state cannot possibly occupy a separate, let alone a superior, position towards the human beings who compose it and relate themselves to it integratively. This link with integration in actuality connects the state with its agents or components from the angle of their ontological and moral status. The assertion of this nexus implies that the state may be measured in terms of whether or not the nexus exists, and, given the validity of the moral claim that it is possible or can obtain, one can assert imperatively that it must obtain.

Just as the public domain is distinguished by a specific character as crystallized togetherness, so the individual has his own distinction; while he lacks collective power, he possesses something wanting in the public domain, namely, consciousness. This character of his is not erased by the collective creation of the public domain; the created public domain is an objectivization of many individuals, but the consciousness of each and every individual is given and is not an objectivization. Therefore, since the existence of the public domain is of a different order from the individual's, there is no justification for maintaining the priority of state-orientated over individual-orientated considerations. To support the subordination of individual to state considerations, this view claims that the existence of the state not only differs from the individual's in term of mode or form of being but is superior to it in terms of the principle of the good. The reasoning seems to be invalid. For to grant the difference between the form or mode of the state's existence and that of the individual by no means warrants the conclusion that the existence of the state is "better" than the individual's by the criterion of the principle of the good. Asserting the possibility of grading the modes of existence of the indivudal and of the body-politic in a scale of preferability is tantamount to asserting that diverse modes of human conduct for example, intellectual and moral, may be so graded. The first assertion, to be sure, refers to modes of existence, the second to modes of conduct; but the two are analogous all the same. There is a tendency in the view that seeks to "stagger" realms and modes, and neither allows them to exist side by side nor will recognize possible contradictions or collisions between them. The mode of the individual's existence does differ from the mode of the state's, and the difference entails differences in status from the aspect of the principle of the good. The individual's status is given, and his moral condition as a subject is planted and entrenched in this situation of his as an individual entity. Considering his given status, he may be said to call for no justification in the first place. The state, however, is not a given product; it is a created one. As the outcome of human creativity, it is of value; but, like every other created product, it is open to such questions as: What reason is there for its existence? What is its inner logic? How is it structured? Of every product, one may ask what its justification is, even if justification is only to be found in the relation of product to producer. It is, therefore, unwarrantable to arrange the existence of the individual and of the state on a graded scale. The individual faces the demand to acknowledge the public domain as a realization of the value implied in transpersonality; the public domain faces the demand to acknowledge the ontological status of the individual whose existence is invested with moral significance. In relation to the individual, the state can claim that its own existence occupies a certain moral status because it is a manifestation of human creativity in general, and its content, as a product of creativity, represents crystallized order. This moral status is not unique, nor is it the highest or most exclusive. For over and against it stand the concrete status of the individual as subject, or of individuals as subjects, and the ideal status of material principles such as justice and truth.

VIII

The opposite view to that of Hegel's contends that, if the public domain does indeed differ from that of the individual, it is precisely because it is unmitigatedly worse, not better, than his. Conduct in the public domain—so the argument runs—is always sponsored by a choice of the lesser evil, never by the pursuit of the realization of the good. Bluntly, every political action is performed with the hangman in the background. In judging the importance of politics by moral standards, this approach dwells upon a single constituent of the political complex which we have analysed, holding that the existence and importance of coercion overshadow all its other factors. It is, of course, necessary to call attention to the evil of coercion, but one should add that the presence of coercion need not obliterate other aspects of the public domain, say, its instrumentality in shaping society or its status as order manifest or its function of setting limits to each and all of us. Nor can this view obscure the fact that the political domain is also a manifestation of human creativity, not the sole one or the highest one, but one nonetheless. The excessively negative evaluation of the political domain mirrors the assumption of a radical antithesis between love and every other mode of relationship between men or between man and the universe. Coercion is not dependent on man's openness to his fellow, his readiness to be attentive to him or to help him, or his wish to awaken him. It is a deliberate effort to put man in a particular place even if he would rather not be there. So it certainly is contradictory to love. But this contradiction ought not to make us forget that love does not exhaust man's relation to the world and to his fellowmen. In the human domain, the confidence relationship is of importance. Without it, man would not be free of the suspicion that the other intends to abuse him arbitrarily. Actually, even coercion presupposes a certain measure of confidence in man; it presumes that he will behave himself in a certain way, if only because he is made to. To have confidence in man is to be confident that he will behave what is described as reasonably, will understand what he must do either because something in him rouses him to a recognition of his duty, or because his duty is forced upon him by external coercion. Hence the existence of coercion cannot crush him, for, in the very act of submission to it, he responds to coercion as a reasonable or rational creature, at least in the pragmatic sense.

That an overly adverse estimation of the political domain lacks warrant is demonstrable from another angle. With power as its center of gravity, the existence of that domain is neither self-sustained nor self-contained. We do not approach it as a created product as we do other created products, such as poetry and painting. Them we approach as observers; the political domain we approach with moral demands and desirous of permeating it with imperatives and principles, because, being perpetually created, it is perpetually exposed to further shaping, and this we do in entire cognizance of its relation to power. As created—although, unlike other creations, such as finished work of art, that bar further creativity related to itself—it stirs men to create, its existence calls for that kind of creativity with prevents the abrogation of the relation between the transsubjective creation and the creator as subject. We have seen that,—by the very nature of its existence,— the political domain does not lend itself to thoroughgoing depersonalization. It is constantly wrestling with the problem of sustaining the link between, on the one hand, semiobjective shaping of relationships, structures, institutions, and moulds, and, on the other, individuals who are subjects and whose subject-status cannot be translated or metamorphosed into the semiobjective forms of the political order.

IX

Most discussions of the relation between morality and politics go on to review the difference between the ends and the means of politics. Dialectically, the moralizing conception of the political domain as totally evil is likely to yield the conclusion that nothing is forbidden there, since only through evil can evil be realized. There is much the same argumentation in the view that, even conceding the moral importance of the purpose of sustaining order, the means to that end are still not moral as a matter of principle, and concurrently that the political domain must be assessed not by its means. We do not assume the existence of intrinsic good in it, but we do hold that the moral distinction between good and evil applies to it. Indeed, coercion is evil, but it does not follow from this to give evil unlimited free rein is to draw the logical conclusion from the evil that is in coercion. On the contrary, where evil exists, its automatic unleashing must be prevented or protested, but it must be recognized as such, and it can be recognized only by reference to what is not evil and if we assume that it does not exhaust the total expanse. The question is not whether coercion exists in fact, but when it is permissible to exert it.

To answer the question we must go back to the conclusions of our preceding analysis. The coercion of political power exists because that power is not a physical entity and its existence and agency lack the strength inherent in individuals in their capacity as limits to other individuals. There is always a possibility of coercion being exerted for the sake of sustaining the existence of an entity that has no existence of its own. This, truly, is the upshot of Machiavelli's contention that, owing to the perpetual possibility of the state disintegrating, special strategies are requisite if that contingency is to be averted. Do we not tend to assume that if the existence of the individual domain is endangered, the use of nonmoral means is warranted by the moral end for whose sake they are employed? Is not this the background for our justifying manslaughter in self-defence or in battle, for our sanctioning theft when the thief is starving? The assumption that if protection of existence is the end, then the use of foul means is fair, applies to the individual domain too, except that, there, the contradiction and duality between end and means must be accompanied by a recognition of the means as equally foul when they subserve a justified end. The idea that the end sanctifies the means is false. The end uses means, knowing well that they are foul and that their use creates no continuity but a contradiction between them and itself. This seems to be true, also, of the political domain, which resorts to foul means such as wars when its survival is threatened from without, or propaganda, persuasion, subterfuge, and concealment when that survival hinges upon its citizens and creators of the domain. Using foul means does not blot out the difference between the fair end of existence and the foul means of securing it; and, besides, the use of foul means is always open to criticism by the users or public opinion, or both. If the political domain is sustained by the integrative intentionality of its occupants, then the more spontaneous the integration, the greater its chances of surviving; the ampler men's acknowledgement of each other in their mutual, order-encompassed encounter, the deeper the roots and the sounder the stability of the state. Yet acknowledgement of the other is a moral content. Thus, dialectically, when it infringes the individual's subject-status, if only for the sake of its own survival, the state, by that same infraction, endangers its own existence, for it is lopping off the branch that it rests upon. Having no physical status of its own, the state cannot afford to be indifferent to men constituting it or to their moral consciousness. So, the more estranged the men who direct themselves towards the state, the stronger the coercion exerted, but the weaker the political order straddling the recalcitrance of the men in it.

In sum, while the coercion of the state makes up for its lack of stability, too much coercion can engender too much distance between state and stateward-self-directing men, undermining its stability and possibly its very existence. Some gap between men and the state is essential to the state's existence and is, therefore, legitimate. But widen it too far and you are likely to drive the state out of existence. Yet, if it cannot afford complete separation, then it is exposed to perpetual evaluation of its ways of power-shaping, the principles controlling its operations, and the extent of its regard or consideration for the human beings who, as moral subjects, are capable of criticizing it. For one revelation of the subject-status is criticism.

X

We may apply the "dialectics of realization" to the politics-morality relationship. Every act directed to realizing an end seeks to translate the given end from a content of the act into an object in the realm of reality. Every act of realization is limited, for no act can fill the expanse of reality. For one thing, the end to be realized is particular and partial; for another, the act places the realized content in a wide context of reality. That context is of a different order from the content, realized not only because it is more extensive but also because it has not been realized by us in the act as has the content. Thus, in the act, we establish an encounter between the content towards which we direct ourselves and the context of reality, which is not the product of realization.

It is through the acts which create the public domain that the realized content of the domain is brought into contact with other contents, with other public domains (other states), with nature, with a territory, with this or that historical period. The act which realizes the content of the political domain does not sustain it in its separation or isolation, but puts it in a context. It is not because the intended content occupies a status of its own that no moral intention can guarantee its morality. One cannot, from its morality as an object of intentionality, infer the morality of an intended content as realized. This is so because, through the act of realization, both the realized content and the context of reality in which it is realized are altered—the content by confrontation with other contents subsisting in this context, and the context by the absorption of the content. That no act of realization guarantees its outcome is obvious in the individual and, also in the public domain. Insofar as it is created, a given public domain is differentiated from others. There is no assurance that different public domains will not collide, and here arises the insistence on refraining from making moral demands of the political domain; facing the constant hazard of disintegration and even annihilation, it must not be tested by the same standards as apply to other sections of reality whose survival is guaranteed. At least *post factum*, it is plain that owing to the dialectics of realization, the less a realized content depends upon the agents of its realization, the more it depends upon the context of reality in which realization has set it. Hence, it is pleaded, when the state is set in reality by men's integrative acts, it must not, nor can it afford to, depend entirely upon them. Over and against that extent of dependence, it is also dependent upon or caught up in the context of, for example, historical, military, and geopolitical existence.

Only up to a point can this reasoning be upheld. Obviously, no one intention monopolizes reality. Every intention aiming to realize an aspiration submits to the judgment of the context of reality into which the content of its ambition will be thrust. But the dialectics of realization operates in the reverse direction as well. Once involved in the context of reality, the realized content becomes even more dependent upon acts of directedness. Where it is endangered by existence, more intensive integrative activity must be conducted by men if the state is to be preserved; consider a time of war when the existence surrounding a particular state is fraught with danger for it, and it cannot meet the danger unless it contrives to inspire loyalty, adherence, and the like. Where the state is concerned, realization never separates the realized content from the agents of its realization. The difference in this respect between the state and the body of scientific findings, or between it and a work of art, has to be mentioned again. Be realization never so dialectical, it could not rely upon enmeshment in the context of reality were it not that the human beings who realize and sustain integration at all times are enmeshed in it. This being so, the state cannot permit itself to be indifferent to men's inclinations or to disregard their evaluation of its existence, agency and ways of shaping and being shaped. Because man has inclinations and an evaluating status, his actuality, which no dialectics of realization can undo, is implicated in the circuit of realization. Indeed, realization stresses the actuality. Not that harmony between men's inclinations and state-conduct is either factual, automatic or even necessary; all that we mean is the encounter of state-conduct with inclination and evaluation is essential and inevitable.

XI

Further light can be shed on our problem by a critical analysis of Max Weber's well-known theory of two types of morality,[3] one of which he holds to be peculiar to politics. His theory may be summarized as follows. There are two types of moral conduct, each with its sphere of applicability and operation. One is the moral conduct of intentions *(Gesinnung)*, the other of responsibility. Of the two, the second is the concern of politics and politicians. Weber describes the man whose actions are controlled by intentions as interested in (or "responsible" for) only one thing, to kindle, tend, and fan the flame of pure intention—for example, the flame of protest against injustice in the social order—lest it be quenched. Judged by their results, says Weber in his characterization of the ethics of this man, his actions are irrational. The moral conduct of responsibility, however, is interested mainly in results, evaluated in terms of the sustenance and management of society; the person who so behaves is concerned to align his deeds not to his intentions but to his given situations, to his attitude towards those situations, and to his assessment of the probable consequences of his conduct. Moral conduct of "intention" may be described as being actuated by the decrees and open to the criticism of a man's own inner tribunal. The moral conduct of responsibility is a revealed conduct concerned with the possibility of influencing events. A man who comports himself morally in this sense holds himself responsible for his acts in the public domain, and assumes their consequences to be open to demands made of him by either himself or his fellow. Underlying the contradistinction is the presupposition that the concern of politics is the shaping of external events and not of man's inner tribunal, which is his own affair. If this is, indeed, the case, then only conduct whose morality does not contradict the revealed and public character of acts is moral conduct compatible with the public domain. But whoever entertains a different conception of the nature of politics must question Weber's distinction.

This differentiation between a moral conduct of intentions and one of responsibility evidently is parallel to a familiar theme in ethical theory, distinguishing the type of moral theory which measures conduct by its motives from that which measures it by its consequences. Conduct in conformity with motives is conceived as absolute moral conduct. And, at times, conduct conforming to consequences is conceived as relative in terms both of its conditions and its results. Ethical theories which measure by motives shift the center of gravity of moral evaluation to the relation between the agent and the principle, assuming that conduct may be regarded as something external: Kant, for example, divides conduct motivated by the moral principle from that which only conforms to the principle. Measured by consequences, the assumption is that only actual conduct instances moral conduct, that only as actual is conduct measurable; actual conduct is revealed in actual consequences. As to the moral value of the agent's intention, inclination and identification with the principle or imperative, one is necessarily left in the dark, since that is a matter of introspection to be settled by man himself. It may be said that, to Weber's mind, moral conduct of inclination is subjective and only subjective morality is absolute. As for revealed moral conduct, namely, actual conduct in the intersubjective domain, relativeness and evaluation by consequences are the *quid pro quo* for its revelation or actuality. What Weber did was to enclose the moral conduct of consequences within the political domain, whereafter he could not help coming to the conclusion that there are two types of moral conduct: he, so to say, translates into sociological terms Hegel's distinction between a principle of conduct in conformity to virtue and the moral principle of conduct of the state.

In discussing the morality of responsibility which is peculiar to politics, Weber does allude to consequences, yet never specifically characterizes politics by reference to them, and one is at a loss to know whether by "consequences" he meant utility or progress. But the crux of the matter is that he speaks not of a morality of consequences, but of one of responsibility, as distinct from a morality of inclination; he characterizes the type of moral conduct which he differentiates from the moral conduct of inclination solely by reference to responsibility, namely, to the standpoint, attitude, or motivation of the agent. The conduct of a man of politics as a man of responsibility is controlled not so much by an assessment of the consequences of his act as by an anticipation of men's response to them, which is likely to take the form of calling him to account for his acts and their upshot. His conduct, if moral, implies an acceptance of responsibility for that upshot and a recognition of the possibility that he will be asked to render a reckoning. Thus, although his characterization of the politically orientated type of morality makes allusion to consequences, Weber cannot get away from the standpoint of the agent. Emphatic as may be his separation between the inner domain of intention-orientated morality and the outer domain of responsibility-orientated morality, he cannot—and does not—omit the personal standpoint of the agent in describing the type of moral conduct compatible with politics. It is not by chance that he characterized the morality of intentions as an irrational mode of behavior; it was his hint that the man of intention is unaccountable. But, wishing to open the inner domain to criticism, he set up the public consequences of it as a critical tribunal, with the proviso that, while the tribunal of criticism judges according to the public consequences of the act, the agent under criticism is not judged. As Leo Strauss has rightly observed, the pointed polarity of Weber's thesis that intention-orientated conduct is irrational and that consequence-orientated conduct is rational can be traced to the distinction between this-worldly and other-worldly ethics.[4]

By confining the morality of intentions to the inner domain of the subject by maintaining that it was not concern of politics, Weber excluded the moral tribunal from the political domain. Still, he was reluctant to present that domain as if ungraced by any moral category, and accordingly introduced a special one to apply to it. But what permits us to assume that the moral significance of conduct is controlled by assessment of consequences and acceptance of responsibility for them? Weber himself suggested no explicit answer. It seems possible, however, to answer our question within the limits of Weber's own teaching. Even on his premises, the two types of moral conduct share two significant features. First, neither is automatic, for both presuppose adoption of an attitude towards the intended conduct, the intention to carry into effect; whether the intention is oriented towards the act or its consequences is a secondary issue. Second, in both types, a man is judged, evaluated, and measured in terms of what he ought to have done, because either he himself, or other people, expected him to do so. At all events, in Weber's system, the moral domain as a whole features a certain formal unity, perhaps more than formal, for both the man of intentions and the man of responsibility are called to account; it appears, then, that he did not succeed in preserving as sharp a distinction between them as he would have liked.

XI

We may attempt now a critical examination of Weber's thesis. One wonders, first, what precisely is meant by the theory that consequences in the political domain may be conceived as a criterion of moral conduct and a nucleus of a special type of morality. For clarification, let us return to the problem of politics, which, in truth, is the problem of its existence. There can be no difference between the consequences of politics and the character of the political domain as concerned with mere existence and as concerned, *pari passu*, with a particular mode of existence. Any segment of existence, as such, is characterized by a particular mode. The existence of nature is characterized by a mode governed by nature's laws and composed of natural elements. The existence of a state is characterized by a mode manifest in its concrete shape, its attitude towards men, its relation to their intentions, it concern for safeguarding the conditions requisite for the perpetual creation of the public domain by men's integrative activities, and so forth. All these aspects must be surveyed in a discussion of political consequences; to see to it that man's existence be sustained, its openness to the poltical domain encouraged, and himself inclined, among other things, towards political integration is the business of the domain of consequence-orientated political activity. Only if Weber had assumed—but he did not—that the "man of intentions" is closed to the political domain would there be warrant for his distinction between types of moral conduct. There is no denying the possibility that consideration for his fellow, acknowledgement of his place in the order, and recognition of power-protected collectivity are—or at least may be—included among a man's intentions. Granting the existence of a type of moral conduct regulated by the responsibility-principle, does not this imply that responsibility, without quotation marks, exists? And does not its existence in the political domain imply the existence there of responsibility towards men's intentions? A man open to the state is the state's concern, and "openness" to the state is also the concern of the man of intentions. Man's rational character as an understanding being who directs himself towards the abstract political domain is bound up with his rational character as inward—inwardly *rational*, not inwardly *irrational*. It is, therefore, impossible to separate the political domain from rational man who, being rational, is characterized by an inward, subjective, and personal mode of moral conduct. The domain of inwardness, as bound up with that rational human character, is at least partly rational. If man can be called to account, it is because he is rational and his rationality is revealed by, among other things, his contribution to the sustenance of the political domain. The implication is not that he man of intentions might be inclined to isolate himself from the public domain, but that it is unnecessary for intention-orientated conduct to take the form of self-isolating conduct. Applying this to the purposes of politics, one can say that of its two primary ends, existence and mode of existence, mere life and the good life, the second can include concern for man's intentions. It is, of course, possible for moral conduct to be apolitical, orientated not towards the shaping of the political domain but to asceticism, or heroism, or pure contemplation. Yet it is impossible for political conduct to neglect to account for men's morally significant intentions. Weber did not come to grips with historical conceptions, such as Plato's or Aristotle's, affirming the interaction or dovetailing of modes of moral conduct and the moral relevance of the political domain itself. Beneath his approach is the historical and philosophical assumption that the links between the realms had been snapped, which is why, for him, the moral domain proper is identified with the inward realm of the individual alone. It cannot be held that the political domain represents realization of moral conduct, but it can be held that it does not lie outside the horizon of a conduct measured by moral standards. And if it lends itself to moral evaluation and criticism, it can claim a moral status for its existence above and beyond the compensatory position secured for it by coercion. This is not to affirm a complete combination of the domains of morality and politics, but to deny the possibility of a full separation of them.

The individual's inward domain, and the political as the domain of interindividual publicity, share yet another material aspect. Between the individual and politics, there is a relationship of mutual responsibility. It is not only for his own existence and self-fulfilling conduct that the individual is responsible; the spectrum of human creation is also his responsibility; he is responsible for those creations in which he has a part not as unique creator but as one agent among others of human creativity. The public domain as a creation is another realization or revelation of the human potentiality, except that, here, the potentiality creates a general concourse of many human beings for itself. Just as the individual is called to acknowledge the importance of a creation which, as an individual, he creates, so is he called to acknowledge the importance of a creation which is not exclusively his but in which he partook, one which occupies the status not of a work of art or intellect but of a public domain. In acknowledging the importance of that creation, he acknowledges the importance of the nonindividual. Transcending the potentiality of the individual is a revelation of human creativity for which the individual, as such, is responsible. To realize himself as an individual, he must rise above his individuality. For an individual, rightly understood, is not a windowless monad but a realization of mankind's general potentiality, which surpasses individuality.

For what, now, is politics responsible? It is responsible for the consequences of political conduct and the conditions of its possibility; for the stability or instability of the state, its belligerence or nonbelligerence, its victory or defeat, and for the favorable or unfavorable conditions of perpetual political creation; and for the orientation or nonorientation of men towards the state as a purpose. Were the existence of the political domain automatic, politics could afford to disregard individuals, their moral reactions, and their value judgments. But the political domain depends upon perpetual creation and is therefore open to morality, assuming that morality is one constituent of human life, an assumption not denied even by advocates of the theory that political conduct is controlled by a logic of its own. The political domain and politically orientated activity conducted within it are responsible not only for the individual's moral status but also for his activity as the *conditio sine qua non* of that status. If activity is absent, there is no political domain. Mutual responsibility does not necessarily imply harmony, but it does imply the impossibility of total severance.

XIII

Had Weber pursued the full implications of the concept of responsibility, he could not have employed it as a nucleus of a distinct and autonomous type of morality. For, correctly taken, the concept precludes the possibility of isolating a mode of moral conduct which can permit itself to dispense with the man of intentions. Man's ability to answer for his conduct implies the concept of responsiblity, and the act for which a man is held responsible is not self-contained but related to and dependent upon the agent, who occupies a position above and beyond it. A man can be held accountable for a deed that he has done, a crime that he has committed, or a decision that he has made, because, as a man, he occupies a position transcending them all. Man is accountable just because he can respond to criticism and the demand that he accounts for his conduct. Responsibility accordingly implies relatedness to the deed and to the doer alike. Man is held responsible for his act because it is conceived as one of his manifestations. The act is a departure for calling to account; but the call is addressed to him as an agent, that is, as a subject. Thus the concept of responsibility, implying relatedness to the doer, forbids us to draw a distinction between the doer's inclinations and the deeds which have transcended them. One manifestation of responsibility is his acceptance of the consequences of what he has done. The call to responsibility is a rational one; to measure a man and his actions by the standard of responsibility is to measure them in terms of whether or not they have conformed to rational criteria. And the rational criterion is whether man as a rational being has been sustained in the deed or been suppressed, crushed, dismissed. It is a measure of conduct in the political and in the moral domain.[5]

NOTES

1. *Hegel's Philosophy of Right*, tr. T. M. Knox, Clarendon Press, Oxford 1942, p. 337.

2. Compare the present author's chapter on "Two Aspects of the Ethical Situation," in *Humanism in the Contemporary Era*, Methuen, Hague 1963, pp. 87 ff.

3. See his *Politik als Beruf*, Duncker & Humblot, München-Leipzig 1926, pp. 57–58.

4. Leo Strauss, *Natural Right and History*, University of Chicago Press, Chicago 1953, pp. 35 ff.

5. Richard McKeon, "The Development and the Significance of the Concept of Responsibility," *Revue Internationale de Philosophie*, XI (1957), pp. 3–32.

PART THREE

Principles

Chapter Seven

Of Justice

I

We leave the limits of our morphological analysis of the political domain to examine the principles and norms of political conduct. Our examination will turn on the question of the factors to which the domain owes its capacity to integrate certain moral norms.

Does the capacity of the political domain to absorb moral norms make them significant for the interhuman relations of the socio-political order and to the relations between the individual and the body-politic? Our starting point is the assumption that the political domain exists as a fact; its existence is founded not only in its crystallizations in the course of the historical process but also in the transempirical grounds of man's essence as a reflecting creature.

The problem of the relatedness of certain moral principles to political facts can be tackled from one of two points of view. Certain facts may be conceived in terms of their origin in moral motivation. For example, helping or protecting one's fellow may be thought of as prompted by moral principles or attitudes. Other modes of concrete conduct, however, cannot be said to originate in a moral source or to owe their factual existence to the working of moral principles. An analysis of such modes, with respect to their relation to the principles of morality, must consider whether they lend themselves to regulation by moral principles, and, if so, how. To take a salient instance: the operation of a man's intellectual powers has no moral source; but the intervention of moral principles can harness them to moral activities such as taking care of man, equipping him for the struggle for survival, and caring for his health. Neither the intellectual powers nor the concrete circumstances of the man who exercises them owe their existence to the moral norm by which they are shaped. Here the moral conduct has recourse to given powers which it channels in the direction indicated by moral norms: in the first case, norms create conduct; in the second, they utilize given powers and shape them in conformity to their content.

The first step towards establishing a connection between the principles of morality and the political domain was taken in preceding chapters. The factual existence of the domain is a manifestation of moral shaping insofar as it constitutes a crystallization of order and the allocation of a sphere of activity to each and every individual within the order. One may not infer that the emergence of the political domain as a fact can be traced to a moral source—say, to the norm of sustaining or protecting man; the sole warranted inference is that the factual functioning of the domain is permeated by a certain element of moral meaning. This permeation, from the point of view of morality, creates more problems than it solves. Being shaped by moral norms, man's character and conduct constrain us to undertake further moral shaping, in the name either of his particular personality or of universal moral demands. Coming within the horizon of morality, an individual can be expected to respond to further—and perhaps higher—moral demands. This is even truer of the political domain. For, implicit in the existence of might is the problem of justifying its exercise or restraint, and from that problem to the problems of morality is but a short step. The moral problems of the political domain are accentuated by historical conditions, such as those prevailing in present-day reality as a result of the rise of the centralized state invested with concentrated power—at times by democratic decision in the name of the persons subordinated to power. Since power connotes the capacity not only for action subservient to ends such as defense or division of labor but also for being shaped by norms, the more power there is at the state's disposal, the greater the demand for moral shaping. Perhaps only the mighty can be righteous. The more functions the state fulfils, the more executive power it commands, the wider the field of power-operations and the greater the opportunity—or at least the call—for regulation by norms.

II

Why, in examining the principles which govern political reality, we begin with that of justice will become evident after our analysis of its nature and function. At the moment, we can only remark that justice is associated with the state in both philosophical discussions and everyday language and thought, an association derived from the relation between state and law, for legal problems are not far removed from the problem of justice. But the roots go much deeper. As defined by classical philosophers, especially Plato, the concept of justice applies to two distinct domains. According to him, justice is equally a virtue of the soul and of the body-politic. In both, it is one of four cardinal virtues—together with courage, moderation, and wisdom—and in both, the relations between that trio are controlled by justice. With Plato's help, we can mark out the place of justice. In his teaching, it is a principle of relationship within a manifold; in the soul's domain, the manifold is composed of psychic faculties or virtues, but one can abstract this formal connotation from Plato's specific context and define justice as a principle of relations within a manifold.

The conclusion drawn by Plato from his definition may be worded as follows. The purpose of the principle of justice is to confine each particular faculty of the soul and each particular human occupation within its proper limits. A given virtue or occupation is said to be ordered in conformity to justice, and hence is just, if it stays within those bounds. Politically, this signifies that a justly ordered state is one whose members—differing from each other—apply themselves to their proper occupations and abide within their proper limits and refrain from overstepping them. As the ordering principle both of the psychic manifold and the political, justice entails curbing of faculties or virtues in the one case, and of occupations or activities in the other. Once the proper nature of each virtue and activity, each in its due place, is secured, a harmonious whole of virtues and occupations is sustained. Plato does remind us of one material aspect of the meaning of justice. But did he recognize its central aspect? He seems to have overlooked the positive connotation of the principle, which is the positive, outgoing, concern of man for his fellow. From Plato's premises it follows that, provided each man does his duty and stays in his place, just order will be sustained. That is why Plato is faced with the problem of discord, why the prevention or restraint of discord is doubly guaranteed; for man has his proper place demarcated for him in fact, and the principle of justice expects or commands him to stay in it. Yet, on his own premises, Plato's description of justice seems to be lacking, for more regulation than he allows is presupposed even by justice understood as a curb. It is not enough that I recognize my proper occupation, its place and status. To confine myself within its limits, I must also recognize the place and status of my fellow's occupation, and not only in a negative recognition that he is forbidden to transgress his limits but also in a positive sense of recognizing his right to act within them. I am expected not only to refrain from exceeding the limits of my allotted place but also to act within them, to recognize that the position of my occupation is mine and the position of his is his.

The regulative character of the principle of justice is more evident in the political domain than in the domain of the individual soul. As the ordering principle of the manifold of the soul, justice may be deemed not a principle but a trait, a character, or a crystallization of personality. In the political domain, it is impossible to rely merely upon the well-ordered psychic faculties of the individuals living and acting in it. We need regulative shaping by a principle which, in this respect, may be regarded as abstract, as a principle proper. Where a norm is not realized in the soul as a given reality; there is no option but to introduce regulative principles and invest the intervention of the normative element with authoritative importance.

III

Thus, even the negative connotation of justice as a formal principle of placement bespeaks an element of positive content, in the twofold sense of recognition of the other's place and of the regulative authority of norms. Content-wise, the principle of justice carries two further connotations: the one positive, in the sense implied by the concept of positive law; the other moral, in the strict sense of the term. The positive one belongs to the political domain, to law-abiding conduct, to control by legal rules and regulations, to what in German is called *Recht*. In everyday usage, to say that a certain act is "just" means that it is a law-abiding one. The moral connotation is analogous to that of natural, not positive, law. An act that conforms to positive law can conform to natural law at the same time, as when a law is binding upon all persons without discrimination. But the status of non-discrimination, as formulated in positive law, seems to be far more fundamental than the status, say, of traffic along the right-hand side of the highway, which may likewise be formulated in positive laws, rules, or regulations.

In the fifth book of the *Nicomachean Ethics*, Aristotle maintains that the primary connotation of justice is the fair apportionment to each man of his share; a formulation of the same notion appears in Ulpianus. Taking it as an apt point of departure in analyzing the positive connotation of justice, we need do no more than expose the tacit premises upon which it is based to show why justice is justifiable. In a sense, it is the intellectual revolution of modern times that makes it possible to bring those premises to light. Perhaps the modern world affords real opportunities for a revival of the idea of justice. Behind the idea of fair apportionment of his lawful share to each is the more fundamental one of man's lawful right to get his share. The principle of justice is inset in the idea that the demands of man possess a legitimate status; his right to be taken into consideration is its major premise; because he deserves consideration, his demands occupy a position which bids consideration in general and specific courses of considerate conduct in particular. To take a simple illustration: it is held just or right to rectify a wrong that a man has suffered, or to make good a loss that he has incurred. Our judgment that this is bidden by the principle of justice, and our conduct in conformity thereto, are based on the ground that here is a man wronged or deprived and meriting concrete consideration in redress of the wrong or in restitution of the loss; considerate conduct takes the form of concrete retribution or reparation. But conduct in conformity to the principle of consideration implies more than, and is not exhausted in, the behavioral aspect of the act of retribution or reparation; it manifests action motivated by norm, by our acknowledgement that it is right or just to take man into consideration in principle and in practice.

IV

The principle of justice may, accordingly, be said to play a double role: it justifies the demand of every man to be taken into consideration, and clothes that idea of consideration for man with its own authority. More important, it embodies it on the plane of concrete conduct as a command to take man into concrete consideration, that is, concretely interpreted, to give every man what he deserves. It asserts that to do so is to respond to his demands, as a matter of principle and also through particular acts of allotment.

A relation of dialectical interdependence may be said to exist between the principle of justice and the consideration for man. The principle of consideration is the conceptual premise of the principle of justice; if we did not acknowledge the principle of consideration, we should not arrive at the concept of justice. On the other hand, justice enjoins upon us to regard consideration as just and to recognize that our response to man's demands is called not only by his ability to impose them but also by the principle that to respond is right or that to take him into consideration is just. The demand formulated by the principle of consideration is consequently enforced by the principle of justice insofar as it induces us to meet or respond to that demand. The principle of justice may be said to perform the further function of weighing and balancing demand and response, to be the measure of the rightness or wrongness of a particular demand for allotment and of the corresponding response. In itself, the demand for consideration is always right or just; but the specific demands for allotment which articulate it concretely are open to discussion and deliberation in the light of the principle of justice; to give or not to give is a question which must be decided upon by reference to that principle.

As to weighing and balancing concrete demand and response, the principle may dictate a negative response to a particular demand. Here, too, justice plays a double role, determining which demands deserve a positive response and which demands do not. To take an extreme example: according to the principle, man's demand to participate in the elective procedures operative in the political domain deserves to be taken into consideration. But it is by no means necessary to conclude that because that demand is just, a minor's insistence on voting also is; conceivable, if measured by the principle of justice, the minor's demand will turn out to be unjust and a just response to it would, therefore, be negative.

The idea of consideration can mean conduct not merely towards our fellow man as an individual but towards the body-politic as a whole as well. According to the principle of justice, the projected nature of the state is conceived as deserving of consideration. The demand made by the state of its individual members that they conduct themselves in such a way as to manifest consideration for it is justified by the principle of consideration. In discriminating between demands for consideration, whether imposed by individuals or by the body-politic, in terms of the positive or negative response which justice prescribes, we are guided by the principle of justice in its capacity to weigh and balance demand and response. Thus the principle applies to three distinct modes of relationship: between a particular individual or the manifold of individuals and the state; between an individual and his fellow man; and between man and the state as an entity subject to the demand that it take him into consideration.

In the political domain, the principle has two parts to fill. It upholds the legitimacy of the demand of man to be taken into consideration by the state in such a way as to be afforded the opportunity to engage in its affairs and partake of whatever it has to offer. And it upholds the legitimacy of the state's demand to be taken into consideration by its individual members in such a way as to be allotted its due portion of directedness towards its perpetual constitution, the prevention of its disintegration, and the rendering of political practice open to regulation by principles. Man takes the state into consideration because he conceives it as his creation, achievement, or possession. According to Kant, the principle of justice establishes the right of every man to his legitimate share of property; in our present context, it may be said that it establishes his right to his share of—and in—the state. Here, the principle entails concrete conduct conforming to its prescriptions and facilitating the factual realization of this legitimate demand of his; it calls for the creation of such real conditions as will make possible his sharing in the diverse kinds of property in general, and in the state in particular.

V

Plato and Hegel sought to establish the grounds of justice by correlating its essence or content with the content of a harmonious whole. For both, the specific nature of this correlation is dictated by the general presuppositions of their systematic outlook. In Plato's eyes, the cosmos at large seemed to feature an ordered harmony; in Hegel's, history as a whole seemed to be moving towards a harmonious unity. According to Plato, approximation to the cosmic order is the norm of human conduct; according to Hegel, progression towards a unified order of history is the norm. The principle of cosmic relationships, or of historical, becomes the principle of political life. There seem to be two reasons for criticizing that hypothesis.

1. For one thing, it is far from certain that a cosmic order exists of which the human order is an image, or that a universal order of history exists into which all streams of human action flow. Suppose a universal order of history does exist. Then, it can exist only as the progressively emergent product of a process nourished or sustained by human beings who direct themselves towards constituting it by their own concrete acts. But granting, for argument's sake, that there is a comprehensive order and that it is destined to serve as a norm of human conduct, then, if such an order is to fulfil its normative function, its essence and normative status must be perceived in theory and acted upon in practice by the human beings. Yet the grasp of the men who understand the cosmic or historical norm is not comprehensive even when they conceive that the norm is; they neither take in its full meaning nor grasp the relation of the comprehensive norm to the particular actions occurring here and now. Hence, even were we to assume that the principle of justice is one of comprehensive order, we would still be none the wiser as to how we ought to behave towards human beings conceived as denizens of the order.

2. The needlessness of linking the principle of justice to a comprehensive order is also suggested by its human import. We are expected to take man into consideration and to express our concern for him in practice, whether we conceive him as a dweller in the cosmos, abiding by cosmic law, or as a unique creature attuned to his own rhythm of being and action. We encounter him in the realms of social, political, and historical reality, which are, at least partially, man-made products or creations, superimposed by man upon the given order of the cosmos. It is within their limits that we present the problem of justice. The tangible starting point of our conduct is marked by our confrontation with man and not by the cosmic order. Our problem is to shape the order of man and not to synchronize the rhythm of human reality with the harmony of the cosmic spheres.

VI

To fathom the meaning of justice, one must do more than correlate it with the idea of order as a comprehensive reticulation of interhuman relationships. If our approach to man is guided by an order-orientated principle of justice, and if we contemplate him according to his mutual relations, we are likely to lose sight of him as man and begin to see him only as a *locus* of relationships, as entangled in a relational structure of roles, occupations, and classes. If you look upon it as an ordered relational structure, consideration for man signifies circumscription of realms within the order; and the principle of justice, as tied to the idea of consideration, signifies enforcement of that circumscription. But man is different from the order in which he subsists. He is in the *order*; but *he* is in the order. The structure around him does not exhaust his whole essence. To take man into consideration is to have regard not only for his status or place in the structure, but also for his essence as implicated in the diffused existence of relations and roles. It is not that the concrete role, rank, and activities of man do not call for consideration, but that his total essence calls for it too. For that matter, conformity to the principle of justice involves transcendence of the socio-political perspective. Consideration for man in terms of his role and rank in the social order need not necessarily conform to the principle. Confined to a socio-political perspective, consideration is likely to be dictated not by norms but by expediency. For example, conduct designed to foster the development of men's powers and talents may be calculated to guarantee efficient performance of their social or political functions; the decision to sustain men within the order may be prompted by awareness that, lacking maintenance of its human components, the order itself would perish. To discern the nature of authentic consideration as the ground for, or the justification of, justice, one must turn from his empirical mesh of roles and relations to man's transempirical essence, which is never fully revealed and still calls for consideration. Not being a unit of power, it must be taken into authentic consideration, for no reason of expediency, economy, order-enforcement, or the like needs allow for it. The principle of justice, in that conception, is no longer relative to any particular social or political theory; its elucidation now presupposes a theory of human nature based upon the fundamental assumption that man is a being occupying a status of his own, whose essence and, therefore, status are not fully identical with his place in the socio-political reality.

But in that case, justice is not a matter of custom, position, personality, temperament, or will, and the principle of it could not operate without a concomitant understanding of man's essence, of the fact that every individual partakes of that essence, which finds diffuse realization in the manifold of human beings. Adequate consideration of man is the necessary consequence of the rational perception that he is the object of consideration and that the subjects demanding consideration are men, individual and diffuse partakers of his essence.

A rational perception of man's transhistorical and transpolitical essence enables justice to operate, but the purpose of the principle is to realize consideration of and for man on the historico-political plane of human reality: its justification is metaphysical, its normative grounds are moral, its realm of realization is historical. Yet, because it is subservient to the realization, in historical reality, of authentic consideration for man, consideration called for and vindicated by his outological essence, the principle can never find complete and final realization; the mutability, flux, and fragmentation which characterize historical reality are bound to imply its realization only piecemeal. On the stage of history, the demand for consideration may be for education, preservation of life, equality, or human rights—the particular form being contingent upon the setting or circumstances of realization. Moreover, complete and final realization is precluded by the nature not only of history but also of man's essence, which we may define in this context as a superabundance of creative potentiality over actual creations, or of transempirical essence over any empirical part played or place held, so that it necessarily makes impossible a complete realization in history. Our neverending confrontation with the problem of justice attests the existence of a basic breach between man's total essence—which is not only historical—and its historical manifestations, between that essence and the relational environment in which its historical realizations set it. The principle of justice bridges the gap by moulding historical reality in the image of man's total essence or affording that transempirical essence the empirical consideration expressed in institutional patterns and procedures. It formulates or expresses the recognition that to treat a man justly is to treat him as an embodiment of man's essence and consider him as such. As justified by that consideration, it in turn justifies the realization of the consideration by deliberate directedness and deeds.

Consideration for man is consideration for one's fellow and, therefore, entails a circumscription of realms of conduct in general and of the individual's private domain in particular; for example, to take our fellow into consideration is, among other things, to respect his privacy both in principle and in practice. Earlier we said that he commands our acknowledgement by virtue of his existence as a fact. Now, it turns out that this acknowledgement is demanded not only by his presence but also by the principle of justice, which upholds the right of man to be taken into consideration. Man, as commanding consideration, is encountered within the order, and the principle of justice demands that we arrange that in such a way as to permit consideration for him to be realized. The foundation of the political domain is the factual order; the regulative authority of this fact is founded upon, or upheld by, the principle of justice.

VII

Our regressive analysis has led us from the idea of justice to the idea of consideration for man, and from that to the ultimate ground for justice, that is to say the conception of men as partaking of the human essence; practical consideration for man presupposes theoretical recognition that it is he who is the existent encountered. The idea of human essence and the theoretical understanding of it are thus the theoretical premises of practical consideration for man in attitude and in action. To conceive that he partakes of, or embodies, the human essence is to recognize that he is an understanding creature; if each of us were not one, men would not consider one another: men's mutual consideration presupposes their mutual recognition or understanding. Our considerate, and thus understanding, attitude towards our fellow man is governed by the assumption that its object is a subject characterized by understanding; because understanding is his attribute, we take him into consideration and for the same reason expect him to consider us. But understanding is not only an attribute of man's universal essence but also an ultimate fact realized solely by concrete and particular men.

It is assumed that justice requires equitable consideration for all, and, at the same time, that particular circumstances deserve special consideration. For example, justice demands housing for all, but first of all for the homeless. Just conduct in conformity to the principle of consideration implies more than recognition of the universal human essence; it extends to perception of man's particular circumstances. Not that there is any reason to think that the two faces of action that conform to justice will square automatically, any more than there is to assume that any mode of action will automatically conform to a principle. Not to acknowledge men's right to be taken into consideration is unjust in principle. Yet no empirical translation of the demand for consideration is guaranteed *ab initio*, and it is far from self-evident that one can be found at all. In itself, the demand is always just, with a justness that is never contingent upon particular circumstances. Yet it can only be realized in particular circumstances, seeing that the men who make it live in particular circumstances. So a man, rightly or wrongly, may feel that the response to his demand for justice is unjust. This structure, turned towards man's transempirical essence one way, and towards the empirical situation of particular men in particular circumstances the other, results in a conduct conforming to the principle of justice, being problematic; there is no certainty that the two visages will tally, or even touch.

In this respect, the principle of justice may be regarded as the point of encounter of two distinct planes: the transempirical of man's essence and the empirical of men's existence. The transempirical dictates the demand that man and his status be recognized and considered; the empirical insists upon specific allotments, an insistence based upon, inherent in, and concretely translating the demand implied by consideration for man's transempirical essence. Underlying demands for rights, possessions, property, development of abilities, and so forth, made on the empirical plane is our consideration for man as deserving of his due. One can always evaluate men's empirical demands, and the responses to them, in terms of whether they are regulated by consideration for man's transempirical essence or sustain it. We have seen that man's total essence can never be realized on the plane of historical or empirical reality; we may add that no empirical requital of his empirical demands represents a full realization of that essence. All the same, concrete expression of our consideration for it is demanded by the principle of justice, which bids us not to leave man's essence in the transempirical isolation, and forbids us to suppose that, so long as man is master in his inward kingdom, justice is unimpaired even if he is a slave in the empirical domain. Justice is, at once, incompatible with a dualistic view of this sort and demands, in fact, that we endeavor to close the distance between our transempirical essence and our empirical existence. As a principle of conduct, justice aims to guide us towards concrete expressions of our transempirical essence by shaping our empirical existence in its image. The political implications of justice in that sense will be considered presently.

VIII

Justice, in its double orientation, demands that we understand man as partaking of a universal and transempirical human essence and as living and acting in particular empirical circumstances; the principle presupposes the objectivity of that understanding, that is, of seeing things as they are. Therefore, it is correct to maintain that the norm of justice is objectivity, though objectivity is primarily a norm not of conduct but of understanding. Guided by the principle of justice, we endeavor to translate objective understanding into conduct, that is, into conduct controlled by our taking into account on the transempirical plane the actual state of affairs of the universal human essence and on the empirical plane that of particular individuals and their special circumstances. A theoretical assessment of man can sponsor practical consideration for him by way of empirical procedures and empirical allotments designed to satisfy his concrete demands.

To deny the possibility of understanding man's essence—even partially—or recognizing his special circumstances—again, even partially—is to deny that there can be concrete conduct conforming to the principle of justice. Implanted in understanding, the principle of justice rests not only upon the principle of consideration for man but also upon the principle of principles, the principle of truth—recognizing the things as they are.

IX

What, then, are the concrete conclusions of this analysis? On the plane of empirical reality, we find a tendency to interpret the underlying demand for consideration as one to share in the goods which the world has to offer, or to regard that sharing as the empirical correlate of the transempirical demand for consideration. Owing to this tendency, in part prompted by a greater awareness of the principle of justice, modern man is inclined to approach the world, and especially those areas of it created by men in the course of the historical process, as potentially his possession. He tends, in the name of justice, to claim the right and the concrete opportunity to acquire the goods produced by human history; he is not given to adopt an ascetic attitude towards the opportunities opened by the march of civilization. The result is man's constantly deeper submergence in the empirical kingdom of goods. In the empirical domain, however, requital of his demands—in conformity to the principle of justice—often makes him a possession-seeker at the expense of his transempirical essence, whereas conforming to that essence would make him a truth-seeker; on the transempirical plane of essence, he is an understanding creature with a contemplative, not an acquisitive, attitude towards the world.

Empirically interpreted, the principle of justice warrants man's demand that history or civilization showers its goods upon him. In the long run, his quest for worldly goods may transform him into an image of the goods granted him in the name of justice. The irony is that this quest removes him farther and farther from his essence, from the starting point of his pursuit of possessions. Submergence in history, pursuit of civilized goods, the possession-orientated idea of culture, and the acquisitive attitude towards the world may very well make man a being determined not by his essence but by goods. Together, they can effect the levelling of reality in the basic sense of reducing human existence to a single, empirical plane, and, by restricting him to it, cut man off or maroon him from his essence—at least as regards his self-understanding. Man cannot, without contradicting himself, drown himself in theory as in practice in the sea of worldly or empirical goods. Even abandonment to the pursuit and enjoyment of the wealth which empirical reality has to offer presupposes understanding, improper, to be sure, but understanding nonetheless. Even self-alienation presupposes conscious deflection of understanding from its proper end and activity, which is contemplation, to the pursuit of possessions and the process of their production. The way of understanding is not predetermined, and it may be the path of infidelity to contemplation or the path to its subversion. From the standpoint of the principle of justice, the modern world is marked by a paradoxical development in the direction of what one might call the self-overthrow of the basis of justice.

As an end in itself, there is no justification for his pursuit of possessions. Besides, as a possession-seeker, man demands justice in the sense not of consideration for his essence but of requital of his wants. So he comes to be looked upon not as a contemplative and creative but mainly as a consuming and pleasure-seeking creature. The paradoxes generated by the process of translating justice from a principle of consideration for man into concordant practical conduct provide a vivid illustration of the dialectics of realization, of which we examined one aspect in connection with the relation between politics and morality. Justice can and must be realized in different ways and in radically diverse circumstances in a developed, possessions-saturated, and affluent civilization, one undergoing an unobstructed process of possession-production, and no less in an underdeveloped, poverty-stricken, and privation-haunted civilization. In an affluent one, to demand justice may mean—at least sometimes—to demand renunciation of possessions, abstinence from the pursuit of worldly goods, in the name, or for the sake, of sustaining the orientation of man's existence towards its essence, of preserving his detachment from, or transcendence of, the plane of empirical reality. In a poverty-stricken, privation-haunted civilization, the demand may mean the requital of men's wants or, at least, banning or discouraging an identification of poverty with normative asceticism or its justification for asceticism's sake. Civilization is men's collective creation, and every man has a right to be part of it and share in the goods that it has to offer. But a man can choose to draw a line between his transempirical essence and civilization as a particular realization of the creative powers possessed by the universal human essence. Then he can go on to decide to approach civilized goods as possessions to be sought in so far as they sustain his essence and renounced if their pursuit makes for alienation from it. Inside a civilization, those who have acquired goods can be bidden, in the name of justice, to restrain their acquisitive appetite, and justice may bid that those who have not partaken of civilization's goods be granted their due share.

Renunciation of pursuit, or ascetic detachment from it, may also appear as a refusal to regard human creations as potential possessions and nothing more. This stems from the recognition that certain creations—works of art or the body of scientific knowledge—owe their existence to human activities controlled by their own proper and intrinsic principles and are motivated by dedication to them and not by the pursuit of possessions. If man were to uphold the intrinsic worth of such modes of human creativity and creation—and this applies particularly to knowledge—sustaining them without regard to market value, he would fortify that contemplative position which can find sustenance in no quest for possessions, however "successful." In contemporary circumstances, realization of justice may indeed call for the abandonment of the aimless pursuit of acquisitions and of the satisfaction of wants, for the sake of sustaining or preserving the duality of transempirical essence and empirical existence. Not that the empirical must contradict the essential, but its tendency to realize the essential in such a manner as to demolish the dual structure of human reality must be checked.

A specific example may help at this point. Until not very long ago, the culture of Asia assigned a prominent place to contemplation for its own sake. Today, that high ranking is threatened by a tendency, which emerged in the West centuries ago, to harness intellectual energies to the pursuit of instrumentally valuable possessions. Thus today, the call to asceticism in the sense of a refusal to own admit the fact that possessions constitute an authentic mirror of man, and can be sounded to the four corners of the earth. But the call to some form of asceticism in the sense of, at least, a need for abstinence from possessions in the literal-material purport is addressed primarily to the developed-affluent areas of the twentieth century.

X

Another aspect of justice comes to the fore when we consider the ambivalence of the term 'just' in the usage of everyday life. When we say "Your action or standpoint is just," or simply "You are right," we may mean that you have judged or acted conformably to the principle of consideration for man, or that your opinion or conduct corresponds to the state of affairs as it is. In the second case, we are using the term 'just' or 'right' loosely, and what we really mean is that the opinion, judgment, or demand in question is valid. In asserting the validity of a particular viewpoint, one has evidently measured it by reference not to the principle of giving each man his due but to the criteria of validity. Certain viewpoints, however, may be described as just or right in both senses, for the realms of right or considerate allocation and of right or valid judgment are liable to converge, as when I adopt a particular standpoint and maintain that its adoption is warranted by particular circumstances. For example, in certain circumstances I am obliged to pursue a certain course of military action, adopt a given political line, or undertake a specific educational project. To say that such standpoints are right is to make two distinct assertions. One avers a factual correspondence between my diagnosis of the circumstances and the conclusions to which it points. Using my (intellectual) judgment, I have diagnosed the situation, and my diagnosis will, therefore, be measured by criteria of validity: that is to say, my belief that the enemy is about to invade my country, or that, in the social conditions prevailing, social improvement can only be realized through education, is based upon an analysis and should be assessed in terms of whether it is right or wrong, valid or invalid. The other assertion avers the conformance of my action to the principle of justice: I maintain, as well, that my adopted course of action is warranted or justified by the principle of consideration for man or men. This is the meeting place of the realm of theory and its criteria of validity, and the realm of practice and its principle of justice. Here, the diagnosis must not only correspond to the circumstances but also prescribe practical courses of action open to evaluation by reference to the principle of justice.

Are all standpoints subject to this double standard of right and wrong? Or are there cases where the question of whether the standpoint to be evaluated conforms to the principle of consideration for man has no bearing on whether it is right or wrong? If a man were to suggest a new scientific theory and it met with opposition, he would surely not suppose to defend it by appealing to the principle of justice, by asking his opponents to take both himself and the novelty of his suggestion into consideration. But what of his opponents? Supposing that, measured by the criteria of validity, the theory turned out to be valid, could the prosecution claim that, nevertheless, it shows no consideration for earlier theories which it explodes or for the feelings of the men who believed them to be true, and that, being inconsiderate, it must be suppressed? Surely not. In this and like instances, one and the same standpoint might seem both right and wrong, measured by the double standard. If, however, a judgment based upon the criteria of validity or truth clashes with one based upon the principle of consideration, one must follow the directives not of that principle but of the principle of validity or truth. This testifies that the problem of justice as consideration for man or men may arise even in connection with standpoints whose adoption is irrelevant to questions of consideration; even a scientific theory can be approached, if only tentatively, from the perspective of the conflict of principles or of realms.

At times, the conflict of principles can and must be resolved by a rejection of the claims put forward by the one—say, the principle of consideration—and an acceptance of the other—say, the principle of truth. There are occasions, however, when it is impossible to cut the Gordian knot. Here are some examples. Upon diagnosing the situation of a particular man and finding that he has abused society or one of its members by violent action, I conclude that he must be subjected to the coercive force of state-institutions. Or, finding that another man, by neglecting his health, has failed to safeguard his existence and that this neglect endangers also the health of other members of society, I deem it necessary to adopt coercive measures to oblige him to take care of himself. In the second case, the use of coercion may be regarded as a mere technicality, seeing that it is prescribed by the principle of justice as the principle of allotting to each man his due deserts; justice demands that the man be granted his health and afforded the living conditions conducive to fostering it. It may be regarded as a technical use of coercion, since it is orientated not to the coercive machinery of the state but to the principle of justice which, in the name of consideration for man, demands that he gets his due; coercion is necessitated by that principle of consideration, despite the contradiction implicit in its use to realize the principle.

But when a man is penalized in the name of justice, the problem is far more acute. Justice demands that, if A suffers a loss as the result of B's action, coercion must be applied to force B to make it good; the principle of justice or of consideration is taken to imply consideration for the injured party and that, in turn, to imply punishment of the injuring one. Punishment is regarded as a means of obliging B to take A into consideration, and B redresses the wrong done by his failure to conform to the principle of consideration by submitting himself to coercion and accepting the penalty which it inflicts. Here, too, the demands of justice are said to conform to the principle of consideration, except that the applicability of the principle is restricted to the injured party, who is identified with man and is accordingly regarded as the one who deserves consideration. In taking A into consideration, we believe we are acting in conformity with the principle of consideration, though, by restricting its applicability to A, we inflict injury upon B, whose earlier action breaches the principle; for coercion, when it penalizes, is injurious even when it is allegedly consequential on the demands of justice. This applies *a fortiori* to the extreme case of the death penalty, where consideration for a man whose life has been taken by another is said to entail the taking of that other's life. The contradiction involved in annihilating B's existence out of consideration for his victim A is patent, yet the act comes according to that interpretation under the heading of conduct conforming to the principle of justice.

Here we revert to the ambiguity of the term 'just' or 'right,' as denoting both a true or valid diagnosis of a state of affairs governed by the principle of truth, and just or considerate practical conclusions drawn from the diagnosis conformably to the principle of consideration. In the case cited, the two meanings figure. By the criterion of truth, the verdict that B is guilty of taking A's life may be right as asserting a state of affairs. But the diagnosis upon which it rests gives no guidance as to the concrete course of action which we have to follow if the principle of justice, as the principle of consideration for man, is to be realized. Only the principle of justice can help us, for the principle of truth tells us nothing about what we are to do to B and cannot suggest how much importance we are to attach to his extreme transgression of the principle of consideration. And it cannot counsel us as to the conclusions to be drawn concerning the application of the principle of consideration to a man who has so radically abused it. Here, the regulative value of the principle of justice emerges.

The matter merits emphasis for the light that it sheds upon our conception of justice as the principle of allocation in the realm of empirical existence, regulated by consideration for man's transempirical essence. Here, allocation or giving in the realm of empirical existence out of consideration for A is giving him what has been taken from him by B by taking it back from B, so to speak—even if this means taking B's life. Thus justice in that realm would seem to warrant annihilation of B's empirical existence. The question, however, is this: How can one realize justice if empirical existence itself is not sustained? And, conversely, if it is sustained, what must one do if the demands of man's transempirical essence and of sustaining his empirical existence conflict? One possible answer is asceticism. Just as, in the name of sustaining and safeguarding man's transempirical essence, one can call for an ascetic attitude towards possessions in the realm of empirical existence; so, in the name of sustaining that existence, one can call for asceticism towards man's transempirical essence lest overconscientious consideration for it leads to the annihilation of the existence in which such consideration must be made concretely manifest. For only through the agency and in the domain of real men who endeavor to shape their empirical interrelationships in the image of their transempirical essence can the principle of justice be realized. As justice can undermine itself by myopic concentration upon requital of acquisitive demands on the empirical plane of human existence, so it can also by the same kind of concentration upon conformance to the demands of man's transempirical essence. Nothing in excess, not even justice. The two faces of justice must check and balance each other, for not even justice is so infallible a principle as to require no control or restraint by complementary principles. As a matter of fact, such control or restraint is required by the very nature of justice as here understood. Consideration for men being the essence of justice, their existence is the intrinsic limit of justice. Annihilate a man's existence and you annihilate justice's foundations in consideration for man. Concern for his existence is consideration at its minimum. His existence stands over and against any other demand that the idea of justice might put forward. Justice which demands the extermination of the man to whom its principle applies is, to say the least, one-sided or one-dimensional. To abuse man's existence is always unjust, no matter how persuasively it be argued that in certain circumstances—say, on the field of battle—sacrifice of human life is unavoidable. But a battlefield is one thing, a court of law another. And standards of right and wrong which may be valid in combat cannot conceivably regulate the judgment which society passes upon one of its members in court.

Here is another illustration of the problematics of bifacial justice. It is not easy to draw a line of demarcation between a man's life and his opinions. Yet this is precisely what is attempted by those who argue that if a man's opinions can be crushed without crushing his existence, then to attack them does not violate the principle of justice as based upon that of consideration. But we must ask whether the very assumption that we can draw a sharp distinction between a man's life and his opinions does not often transgress the principle of consideration for man. To understand a man's life—and understanding, as has been shown, is the *sine qua non* of consideration—must we not understand the opinions or beliefs which render his life meaningful to him? Say, for example, that because we cannot accept the religious belief of a particular man, we try to persuade him to abandon it, we try, in effect, to crush it. Can this attempt be said to conform to the principle of consideration for man, or, in our case, for the believer? There can be no pat answer to this and like questions. One can only offer a sort of guidance in these terms: Has our approach come near to the principle of justice at least to the extent of maintaining a balance between consideration for man's essence and for his existence? Is it "just" or "considerate" to try to crush a belief or an opinion that we ourselves cannot accept? The guidance which we suggest would seem at least to indicate that to take our fellow's opinions into consideration does not mean silencing our own, since the principle of consideration demands not only that I respect his opinions but also that he respects mine, and that I respect mine as well. Not abstaining from repression, represents the limit of respect for a man's opinions, beliefs or customs. In this context, consideration verges upon toleration or implies it. Here, once again, we encounter the convergence or dovetailing of principles by which the texture of men's life and activity in concert is marked. We note here that no principle can be treated in complete isolation from the others with which it is interwoven in the fabric of inter-human relationships.

XI

Is there an internal connection between the principle of justice and the socio-political domain, and, if so, what is its nature and what does it rest upon? Such a connection is attested by the factual structure of men's life in concert. That their life is corporate necessitates demarcation of the respective domains of all individuals who live and act in concert. Where the demarcation is not merely factual but also well-founded, where it is demanded not merely by the brute fact of our fellow's physical presence but also by our acknowledgement of him, the principle of consideration for him is operative in actuality. The principle of justice maintains that our consideration for our fellow is just. As the order of men's life in concert, the political domain, by its very nature, is related to the principle of consideration. Conversely, by its very nature, the principle of consideration is related to men's life in concert regarded as a given fact. Simply because our life in concert demands reciprocal consideration, corporate life is a manifestation of the social significance of the principle of justice.

Is there also a relation between the principle of justice and the political order as distinguished from the social, that is, as an institutionalized order? There is—and its nature is as complex or multifaceted as the nature of the political domain itself. From one angle, it can be traced to the instrumental facet or function of the political domain. There is a sense in which political power may be considered instrumental in realizing the principle of justice; when it is so, the state and the power at its disposal may be regarded as a means of realizing and enforcing consideration for man, at least in certain spheres. The relation of the principle of justice to the political domain differs from its relation to the social. On the social plane, the principle requires consideration for my fellow-man, as empirically encountered in the concrete course of life in concert. In the political domain, it requires consideration for man in his generality as distinguished from the particular individual whom I encounter. This shift in orientation, from man as my concrete fellow to man as such, is due to the existence of the political domain as an abstract or projective entity. The state is neither related to particular persons nor is it a particular person, and it cannot occupy the status of a fellow; it is related to all its denizens. As a means of realizing the principle of justice, it is subservient to the realization of consideration for all men within its bounds.

In its instrumental capacity, the political domain is related to that principle inasmuch as it manifests consideration for man and enforces its realization concretely. Law is one of its major means of enforcement. For example, the principle of consideration can find legal expression and sanction as a prohibition of abuse or injury of men by men or by the body-politic. Law either prescribes preventive rules protecting man from harm or, these rules failing, sets right the wrong that a man has suffered either by literal retribution, by granting the injured party monetary reparation or by penalizing the offending one. Or it can implement the principle of consideration by guarding the individual's private domain, his possessions, his property, or by forbidding slander, and so on. All these are patent exemplifications of the relation between the political domain and the principle of justice, against the background of the subservience of power-invested state machinery to the realization and enforcement of the principle of consideration.

But the state can be a means of realizing consideration for man in the positive sense of cultivating his powers or helping him to bring out his latent abilities. Political machinery can be geared to educational projects conducing to fulfilment of man's capacity for knowledge or to establishment of employment opportunities promoting the fulfilment of his capacity for work. In these and like consideration-orientated undertakings, the state is related to man not as the other but as man, and is guided by some conception of the nature of human abilities. Were there no conception of that kind, there could be no consideration for man. Such a guiding conception can not be formulated *a priori*. The conception of human capacities controlling the state's anthropocentric activities is necessarily relative to changing historical circumstances. Justice demands that, with due allowance for those circumstances, the state translate consideration for man into the creation of concrete conditions conducing to the fulfilment of his powers or, at least, that it acknowledge its potential instrumentality for promoting that fulfilment. Here, too, one observes the character of justice as orientated towards man both as an embodiment of the universal and transempirical human essence, and as a concrete individual living and acting in particular empirical circumstances. In aligning itself to the principle of justice, say, by undertaking to realize universal education or universal employment, the state must have regard for both aspects of demands of man. Justice enjoins that the state turns towards him in theory and in practice, and be the medium for translating—if only in particular and piecemeal terms—his transempirical essence into the specific empirical circumstances of men's historical existence.

As realized and enforced by the state and its power-machinery, the principle of consideration can also be expressed as a demand that man be permitted to partake of the goods which the progress of civilization provides. Justice requires that, if civilization has furnished tools or commodities, men must have them put at their disposal by the state. If civilization has achieved advance in the economic and technological spheres, then it demands that the state give men a chance to benefit from the advance. Here, the state is servitor of the principle of consideration being a means not only of securing the development of man's capacity for knowledge and work but also of bringing civilization to men and making it their possession.

XII

Now, we shall examine this relation between the principle of justice and the political domain from the standpoint of the state. The principle emerges in the context of the demand that every man be given a chance to share in and partake of the state and join forces with other men in the joint and perpetual endeavor to crystallize and constitute its collectivity. In this regard, the state itself is, as it were, a possession in which man deserves a part according to the principle of justice. If—as occupying a position of partial distance from man—the state takes him into consideration, then, by opening itself to the shaping exertions of its occupants, it gives men the opportunity to realize their status as shareholders in the collective political domain through their own efforts. Here, the relation is reversed and the principle of consideration realized not by the state's efforts to shape man out of consideration for his, as yet, unfulfilled powers, but by men's efforts—as submitted to, and encouraged by, the state—to shape the state out of consideration for their status as shareholders in it. In that sense, a "just" state is one which promotes and guarantees men's active part in the shaping of its own form and features. Since the state is a power-invested projection, and power is liable to be translated into coercion let alone over-coercion, that consideration presupposes the curbing of coercion: the greater the consideration for him, the less does man have to submit to coercion; the more power is controlled by the principle of consideration, the less hastily or arbitrarily is it used to coerce.

Thus understood, the principle of justice may be said to play two roles in the political domain: it justifies men's demand to share in the state and to contribute towards its constitution; and it regulates the relation of reciprocal consideration between the state and its denizens, authorizing both (a) the state's demand that men acknowledge and respect its status and essential features and (b) men's demand the state acknowledge and respect their inviolable status and proper essence, lest these be extinguished in the act of constituting the political order. In that capacity, the principle may be conceived as one of adjustment, with the function of striking a fair or equitable balance between the respective, and possibly opposing, demands of the state and its denizens to be taken into consideration. The origin of the word "adjustment" itself, by the way, would seem to speak for an internal relation between the content of the principle of justice as one of equitable authorization and requital of demands and the very idea of adjustment.

XIII

The sphere of applicability of the principle in that meaning extends beyond the realm circumscribed by the reciprocal demands for consideration put forward by the state and its members. In corporate life, consideration and adjustment go hand in hand. All through men's life in concert, this principle, as that of mutual consideration for each by each and for all by all, takes the form of a principle of channelling and balancing men's diverse demands for consideration. This is not to imply that justice by definition or by nature entails adjustment; its essence is not adjustment but consideration, but, on the empirical plane of men's concrete interrelationships, an element of adjustment enters into the principle of justice in men's concrete expressions of mutual regard.

The state plays a significant part in the realization of justice as a principle of balancing rights and duties. The state can protect the rights of all and guarantee that all be taken into consideration by all and each by itself. Being the emanation not of any particular person or group, but of all in a certain area, it is equipped to act as an institution of adjustment. For only an institution related to none in particular, and thus obliged to respect no special (and as such unjust) demand for consideration, is qualified to fill the role of 'adjuster'. To be sure, the impersonality of the state pertains only to its essence as an abstract projection of togetherness and not to its concrete embodiment in government. The instrumental machinery of the state does, of course, fall into the hands of certain parts of the body-politic (such as classes and parties and individuals). Yet it is precisely the contradiction between the state subservient to all and the political machine as controlled by particular parts of the body-politic that warrants the demand (not the reality) for equal consideration raised by the under-privileged parts. Those parts which have no control over the state in its instrumental capacity have the right to demand—in the name of justice—that the state be loyal to its essence and origin as the amanuensis of justice, to its agency of the principle of adjustment or equalization of men's respective demands for reciprocal consideration. Of the operation of the principle of justice as one of adjustment of rights there are any number of historical illustrations. It often happens, in the course of the historical process, that certain parts of a body-social or body-politic appeal to the abstract principles upon which the socio-political structure is founded, demanding that the state be true to its underlying principles and manifest equitable or non-discriminatory regard for all parts of the body to which it owes its projective existence. Thus, throughout the period of their emancipation, the Jews fought for their rights in the name of justice or equality as the principle of the state. And all under-privileged groups likewise make their protest against discrimination in the name of the principle of justice or of the law-abiding state as the principle's concrete embodiment. Justice demands accommodation of diverse claims and the satisfaction of those for unprejudiced consideration which have yet to win recognition and response.

Still another aspect of the nature of the political domain figures in its relation to the principle of justice. As an abstract entity, that domain is qualified, and can be expected, to orientate itself to another abstract entity, to the universal human essence. Since every empirical human being is a partial embodiment of that essence, consideration for it means consideration for each and all of its partial embodiments as well as recognition of their right to demand it, and consideration for them out of consideration for the essence which they share cannot be equitable. As an expression of collectivity, the state is to show consideration for partial empirical embodiments of the universal human essence in such a way as to allot each no more than its due; as consideration for man's essence, justice disallows the assignment of excess worth to any empirical manifestation of it. And to recognize that, from the perspective of the universal human essence, the status of all its embodiments as equal is to recognize that, from the point of view of its essential worth, no embodiment deserves a surplus of consideration. Justice demands that the state sustain a constant, impartial orientation to the human essence on the plane of men's empirical existence or translate its acknowledgement of that essence into an acknowledgement of the inviolable status of each and every individual man or group.

In saying that, by its very nature as an abstract entity, the state is qualified to orientate itself to the transempirical human essence as another such entity, we did not intend to blur the basic distinction between the two kinds of abstract entity, or to imply that consideration for the state—as consideration for an abstract creation of all men and for no empirical man or group of men in particular—is analogous to consideration for the transempirical human essence as the pool of man's creative potentiality. Each and all of us are embodiments of that essence; none of us are embodiments of the state nor is the state a condition of our creative activities. On the contrary, those activities are its condition, for, as we have argued, if we did not acknowledge it, and direct ourselves towards the constitution, the state would not exist. Accordingly, to take the state into consideration is to acknowledge its status as an abstract entity which owes its partly self-sustaining power to our very acknowledgement. Its abstract status might appear to be in danger of demolition by the sheer physical mass of concrete entities, concrete persons and their concrete aims and ambitions, or of another state composed of concrete persons and their aims and ambitions. If consideration for the transempirical human essence is to be sustained, the state, too, must be sustained as an abstract entity, which is tantamount to sustaining its status as isolated from concrete human beings and their concrete particular and partial aspirations. Here the principle of justice, in its manifestation as adjustment, must step in and prevent short-sighted consideration for the state from bringing about its radical separation from concrete men and their ends. No less, it must prevent such short-sighted consideration for them as would reduce the state to a rubber stamp of their concrete intents or a guardian of the particular and partial interests of a given group of them. It would be instructive to watch the workings of this polarity in the historical process and see when, and why, emphasis is laid upon the state's consideration for men, and when, and why, upon their consideration for the state.

The part played by the principle of justice through the instrumentality of the state in striking a balance between diverse, and at times conflicting, claims represents one concrete manifestation of the principle of consideration on the plane of men's empirical existence. Realization of consideration for man often requires coordination or adjustment of men's reciprocal demands. As an emanation or expression of the entire body-social, the state must act in conformity to the principle of justice in that sense. As the projection of all, the state is qualified to represent and uphold a synoptic view of each and all as candidates for equitable consideration. A similar view can be adopted by the individual members of society: each man can conceive of all his fellows as candidates. Thus the idea of man can be related to men's empirical existence in either or both of the following modes: if the state represents and upholds the idea, then its individual members can shape their concrete interrelationships in conformity to it; if the state has not yet adopted the idea, then its individual members can endeavor to shape the political order in its image. Insofar as the state subserves the idea of man and the principle of consideration for him, it will seek to adjust and requite men's concrete and reciprocal claims. It can respond to the demand of a particular man for redress of the loss which he has suffered at the hands of another, either by obliging that other to make monetary amends or by giving the injured party a share of the funds which it has collected through taxation. In either case, it is acting in conformity to the principle of justice as adjustment, at least on the plane of men's empirical interrelationships.

XIV

In traditional discussions of the concept of justice, it is customary to distinguish between commutative and distributive justice (*justitia commutativa, justitia distributiva*). Commutative justice regulates interindividual relations by enforcing contracts and pledges, redressing wrongs, and so on—and the state is one instrument for fulfilling that function. Distributive justice primarily regulates the relationships not between individual members of society but between them and the body-politic. In the modern world, more and more areas have been, and are being, brought under the control of distributive justice as a result of the state's growing intervention in the economic sphere, as manifest, for example, in the economic opportunities afforded men by the state by way of employment and insurance. The difference between the commutative and distributive aspects may now be formulated in terms of the different modes of "consideration-realization" which they may be taken to represent. As with commutative justice, the principle of consideration carries with it restoration of a material loss that a man has incurred or redress of a wrong that he has suffered. And, as with distributive justice, it calls for the endeavor to accord man his due deserts, regardless of whether his deprivation reflects the loss of something that he had before or a lack yet to be supplied. For example, distributive justice can demand that man be afforded the opportunity of developing his talents and a real chance to partake of the various benefits of the civilized world. Commutative justice is a manifestation of consideration for man under the aspect of situations as they are, distributive of consideration for him under the aspect of situations as they ought to be. Both aspects uphold his right to his due deserts: the commutative, his right to be compensated for any loss incurred; the distributive, his right to be given a genuine opportunity to display his qualities and satisfy his wants and potentialities.

Both aspects are operative in a particular process of realizing consideration for man. Take the act of emancipating slaves. This might be viewed as a realization of commutative justice, in the sense that through it, man regains liberty lost, justice having demanded that liberty be restored to him that has been dispossessed of it; it is assumed that the lack of liberty is due to a loss incurred if not on the empirical then on the transempirical plane. For on the transempirical, liberty is held to be man's birthright even if he has never possessed it on the empirical. From another angle, however, the act of emancipation may be said to realize distributive justice, in which case the assumption is that man ought to be given what some, but not all, men have, namely, liberty. Through the act, a possession hitherto existent on the empirical plane, but partaken of only by some, is made the possession of all. Whether the act is justified commutatively or distributively, it affords an illustration of the principle of justice working within the realm of concrete reality in such a way as to shape it in the image of man's transempirical essence (liberty, in our example), or, conversely, in such a way as to assign to man's transempirical essence a regulative role in the shaping of men's empirical existence. But the fact that the principle of consideration can be realized in more than one way does not absolve us from deciding which way is preferable in the given circumstances; rather does it oblige us to decide. In itself, as upholding the right of every man to such consideration as would give him his due deserts, the principle does not prescribe which of its aspects shall be applied, or how. The mode of its realization is not predetermined, so its translation into concrete courses of conduct is, in this respect, uncertain. To be sure, the conditions of applicability of commutative justice are more readily determined than those of distributive. For instance, if a man's home has been damaged or destroyed, commutative justice would seem to demand that we restore his loss either by repairing the damage or by giving him another apartment. But what of members of society who live in slums? Does the principle of consideration not require that we apply the distributive aspect of justice to them? Must we not measure their actual housing conditions by the higher standard of what they ought to be if men are to get their due? And if, so measured, their actual conditions are found wanting, does not the principle of justice demand that we give the slum-dwellers what they deserve to have but lack? As a matter of fact what constitutes decent housing is not a question for which there is a ready-made answer. A question of commutative justice provides its own answer, for the loss that a man has incurred is the measure of the compensation which he merits. No such answer, however, is available for questions to do with the realization of distributive justice, which, by definition, rejects the measure of what a man has as a standard of what he ought to have. What does, and what does not, constitute a situation calling for shaping in conformity to the distributive justice is a question which must be asked anew and grappled with anew always. Attention must be directed towards determining how men's empirical existence ought to be, for never before has the state had so much power to alter it. But where to alter it, and how, are open questions. When it comes to acting in conformity to distributive justice, all we can do is study the circumstances as they arise and decide how that justice demands that we then act. Our insistence that the circumstances be heeded in determining what aspect of the principle of justice should guide our shaping of the situation is far from implying that the bearing of the principle itself upon the situation is relative to the circumstances. On the contrary, it is because the applicability of justice to the situation is taken for granted that the question as to which of its aspects is the more applicable arises at all.

Our examination of the aspects of justice would appear to permit the general observation that the principle of consideration can be realized in two ways. One is to protect man's existence, as it is, from injury or loss and to restore losses incurred; the other is to shape it, as it is, in conformity to an idea of what it ought to be. The first conserves man's given situtation, the second alters or reforms it; both represent possible interpretations of the meaning of justice. The problems set by the multiple meanings of justice, and by the relatedness of the mode of its realization to an intricate network of circumstances, cannot be treated in all their complexity until we have considered the principle of equality and its relation to the principle of justice. But one can say this: Granting that consideration for man is necessarily consideration for him in a particular situation, strict conformance to the principle of equal consideration for all may very well be unjust if it means ignoring those aspects of men's concrete situations by virtue whereof they are not equal. Here we must chart a course between the Scylla of equal consideration for empirically unequal parties and the Charybdis of unequal consideration for equal parties. Equal consideration—e.g., for invalids and noninvalids—is as unjust as to deny a musically gifted child the opportunity to cultivate his talent because we do not offer an opportunity to children not so gifted. But when the empirical differences between individuals must be taken into account by our interpretation of the principle of consideration, and when they can and must be ignored—this is a moot point. Does consideration for man, for instance, oblige us to take men's particular religious beliefs into account or, in our endeavors to shape society and state in conformity to its demands, to proceed as if there were no religious differences between men? Even a superficial glance at the history of men's searching for an answer to this and like problems would seem to show that a final, infallible interpretation of the principle of justice, and of the anchoring principle of consideration for man, is beyond our ken.

XV

We can now examine the relation between justice as a principle and the political domain as a concrete order of men's life in concert. The ultimate grounds for that relation are not in the political domain but in the universal principle of consideration for man, as such, by men. In this sense, the principle of justice transcends the limits of the political domain. Since the essence of justice is consideration for man, the principle applies directly to man as such and indirectly to him as a social being. If it is also the regulative principle of society and state, it is because the man for whom it claims consideration exists tactically within a socio-political framework. Accordingly, the principle of justice cannot be identified with the principle of the good. In terms of its essence, the principle occupies an independent position and at the same time represents one particular manifestation or implication of the principle of the good. That principle upholds man's existence as a subject; the principle of justice demands concrete endeavors to shape men in their circumstances in the image of man as a subject. Were one to formulate the supreme principle of the moral domain as an imperative of acting in such a way as always to sustain man's existence as subject and endeavor to create conditions conducive thereto, then the corresponding formulation of justice as the regulative principle of the empirical domain would be to shape men's existence in such a way as to guarantee them the conditions necessary to be "subjects." The principle of justice may thus be said to occupy an intermediate position between the principle of the good and the empirical domain; it may be defined as the principle of empirical conduct in conformity to the principle of good.[1]

NOTE

1. Consult Ch. Perelman, *De la Justice*, Bruxelles 1945. Perelman relates the idea of justice to the idea of equality and not to the notion of concern for man. On the relation between justice and equality, see Chapter Nine below. Also H. L. A. Hart, *The Concept of Law*, Oxford 1961, pp. 15 ff.

John Rawls's: *A Theory of Justice*, The Belknap Press of Harvard University Press, Cambridge 1971, is concerned with justice as distribution. It would be out of place to deal here with that theory and its impact at length, though it seems to be possible to enlarge Rawls's coordinates and deal with the issue of human essence. Rawls himself refers to elements of Kant's philosophy in his Dewey Lectures: Kantian constructivism and moral theory-Rational and full antonomy, *Journal of Philosophy*, 77, No. 9, September 1980. Observations on the approach formulated by Rawls are presented by the author in his paper: Public Culture of a Democratic Society: Comments on Professor Rawls' Dewey Lectures, *Journal of Value Inquiry*, 17, 1983, pp. 143 ff.

On the whole issue consult Paul Weiss: *Toward A Perfected State*, State University of New York Press, 1986, mainly pp. 317 ff. Also, Michael Walzer: *Spheres of Justice, A Defense of Pluralism and Equality*, Basic Books, New York 1983.

CHAPTER EIGHT

Of Freedom

I

Our task now is to analyse the modes in which the principle of freedom does or can contribute to the shaping of the political domain. The underlying premise is the freedom's authority as a regulative principle of politics springs from man's status as subject. It is by virtue of its essence as a prepolitical or transpolitical attribute of man as subject that freedom also occupies the regulative position in question. Hence, our analysis is based upon the assumption that freedom is the primary manifestation and the active realization of man's existence as subject.

In that sense, freedom may be described as a factual attribute of man's given status. As a fact, it has the authority to function as a principle of politics; to demand that man's status as subject be acknowledged and taken into consideration by the political domain. An analysis of the political domain, its structure, activities, and norms does not permit of a systematic demonstration of the status of freedom as an attribute or manifestation of man's place in the universe, since that pertains to metaphysical rather than to political theory.[1] Still, to fashion a scheme for our analysis, from the aspect of freedom's role in the political domain, it might be advisable to explore what the concept signifies. For its multivalent meanings are mirrored in its numerous concrete manifestations as a principle of political reality.

II

Freedom connotes—first—and reflects a fact more basic than, though correlative to, itself, namely, the 'distance' between man himself and the circumstances in which he exists; man as a concrete subject is active in relation to his circumambient situation. As a subject, man is detached from those circumstances by virtue of his consciousness-sustained relationship to them. Even when he is acted upon by his surroundings, as a subject, he is conscious of that impact; insofar as he is even conscious of his passivity in relation to them, he is at the same time active.

It is not as though, in being conscious of his objective surroundings, his consciousness or understanding is not determined by the object of which it is conscious; indeed, to the extent that his attention is focussed upon that object and upon no other, his understanding may be said to be determined by it. When my attention is turned to my desk, and not to my bookcase, the desk determines my understanding because it, and not the bookcase, occupies my mind. Yet the relationship of determination between the understanding and its object is not analogous to that between cause and its effect. By occupying my mind, the desk is translated from an opaque object or thing into a content. My understanding of it as content cannot be conceived as the effect of the piece of furniture before me. The relationship between consciousness and the object-as-content which determines it is not definable in terms of efficient causality; rather, the act of understanding, as focussing upon content, frees us from the determination of causality by subjecting us to the determination of a significant content. The context of our acts of going beyond the causal determination through shift of focus to a significant content is a context of efficient causality in which we are also determined by our circumstances. But the act of understanding itself cannot be identified with its context or background.

Furthermore, the relationship of meaningful determination between the understanding and its object does not involve the understanding's total determination by its object, and, indeed, a gap between the *relata* is the precondition of their encounter. If there could be total determination, the object could exist without understanding, but no object can become a meaningful content without it. The transmutation of object into content presupposes a reciprocal relationship between the object and the understanding, and that, in turn, presupposes a gap between the *relata*. If a complete merger or identification of the understanding and its object were possible, all understanding of objects would be impossible. An understood object is one that we can name or label. When we name the object before us a "desk" or a "book," we assign a label to it that is not identifiable with it. A name denotes a reservoir of meaning into which the object can be integrated only if we understand it. Were the name in which the understanding is crystallized be attached exclusively to the object and identified with it, understanding would remain void of content, for there would be no way of transforming the object into a content. Hence, a certain remove between the understanding and the content upon which it dwells is the *conditio sine qua non* of understanding. Thus it may be said that a twofold distance is presupposed by man's relationship of understanding to his circumstances: that between the understanding and the object holding its attention, and that, within understanding itself, between the acts *through* which it is realized and the contents *in* which it is crystallized. It is this twofold distance which constitutes the point of departure of the present analysis. Freedom is founded on the fact that understanding resists exhaustive translation into either contents or objects.

III

The basic relationship between man and the world is one of understanding or, at least, one sustained by it. The distance presupposed by this relationship cannot be annulled by any human act. Every human act may be described as an endeavor, undertaken from a standpoint of detachment from the world, to intervene in the world. The structure of all modes of men's activity is a dialectical one of approach through detachment.

In its primary sense freedom is the corollary of the distance between the understanding and its objects, and, as such, may be described as nondetermination by circumstances. If we were asked why we framed our description negatively as nondetermination rather than positively as spontaneity, we would reply that the analysis, thus far, does not afford the necessary groundwork for a consideration of spontaneity, although it does for a consideration of nondetermination. Our definition is of freedom as detachment from the circumstances not only of the cosmos but also of history. As created by human activity, the historical process is all the more subject to the dialectical rhythm of human activity, that is, of approach through distance or detachment. In the course of its creation, history is crystallized in a nexus of circumstances, which, like all circumstances, are approached by man from a standpoint of detachment. The understanding's detachment from, and its incommensurability with, the circumstances understood not only cannot be cancelled by the historical process but is even a necessary condition of the process and of the activity which sustains it.

The idea of freedom here expounded is opposed to the idea that it consists not in detachment from the circumstances but in identification with them, an idea that Hegel had in mind when he spoke of being with yourself when being with the other.[2] As formulated by him, the identification-theory of freedom likewise stresses the difference between a man's own standpoint and his standpoint as seen by the other, but considers it an obstacle that must and can be overcome. In Hegel's view, the distance between man and his circumstances constitutes an antithetical point of departure which must be transcended if freedom in the sense of comprehensive or total sovereignty is to be achieved. That is possible only when the factor which we have called "circumstances" and Hegel calls "other" is no longer differentiated from and alien to me, only when the other and I are one. Behind this identification-theory is the notion that nothing less than total potency, absorbing its circumstances into itself, can constitute freedom; the theory would not be satisfied with freedom within limits, as detachment from, as opposition to, and as intervention—from the position of detachment—in, the circumstances. It is concerned not with man's position but with his ultimate achievement. Only through achievement is identification possible; only through it is the notion controlling my endeavors, that is, my purpose, identified with the product of my endeavors in such a way as to become one with myself. If achieved identity is the measure of freedom, it is only plausible that freedom will not be found either at the beginning of the historical process or even during the concrete course of its development, for, at either stage, man is not identical with his circumstances but detached from them. Men's historical activity, their very striving towards unattained ends, bear witness to their own partial existence of their failure to absorb the other into themselves. Process, as such, implies that the activity sustaining it is not total but partial, incomplete, short of consummating the identification at which it aims. Hence, not until the process of history comes to an end will there be complete identify between man and his cirsumstances, and the two factors be synthesized into a total status of identity.

This interpretation of freedom is untenable for several reasons. No real process can overcome the basic distance between man and his circumstances, because that distance is an attribute of his place in reality. But let us assume, for argument's sake, that an identificaiton of man and the man-made circumstances of historical reality is possible and that, in history, I might find myself "in the other" and "the other with me." Still, identification would not constitute the final achievement. As a product of the historical process, identification is vulnerable to the turns which that process might take in the future. Achievement of identificaiton is no guarantee that it has been achieved once and for all. Supposing man had achieved identification with his historical circumstances at the start of this century; does that make him identical today with the then unforeseen historical circumstances of conquering the cosmos? Surely, the endeavor to conquer outer space has opened new horizons, formed new gulfs to be bridged, revealed new circumstances still to be absorbed into the circle of identification. Or, to take a more shattering illustration, say, the historical process wreaks unforeseen horrors on masses of mankind. Is the historical phenomenon of mass annihilation a circumstance that the identification-hypothesis can cope with? History itself creates new distances and calls forth new human standpoints in relation to the new circumstances which it perpetually brings into being. Never will we be able to say that the end of history has come and that the process of man's approach to the world which he himself has made is complete.

An additional objection to the identification-theory concerns its very premises. One cannot help asking if an identification of man with his circumstances can be conceived as a matter of principle. Is there any possibility that I might find myself "with the other as being myself"? It seems that the answer is no. Even were I so to find myself, I should still have to understand, as mine, the situation in which I found myself. A distance between my *understanding* of my identity with the other and that *identity* itself is presupposed by identification itself. Without that distance, the identification would be opaque and I myself transformed into a virtual other or even object. The theory assumes that nothing less than total achievement, as total absorption of the other into an all-encompassing circle, can constitute freedom as absolute sovereignty. Freedom, however, does not consist in absolute sovereignty. It is a condition, or an attribute of the human condition, not an achievement; it represents man's power to act detachedly upon his circumstances, not his completed actions. As an achievement, freedom—like all realized actions—is partial. The reservoir of potentiality or potency, being a comprehensive whole, is prior to any of its partial realizations. As a comprehensive reservoir of potentiality, freedom is not an unlimited potency, its limits being set by the circumstances upon which it must act and which it can never completely absorb into a synthesis of total identity; limitation is the price of freedom as an active manifestation of man's detachment from his circumstances. Conversely, loss of distinguishing detachment would be its price as his total identification with his circumstances. On the premises both of the identification-theory and of the detachment-theory, man must pay for his freedom. According to the first, he must forfeit his distinguishing mark, according to the second, he must renounce his aspiration to total sovereignty over his circumstances and face the bounds circumscribing every act of freedom, every act whose structure is a dialectical approach through detachment. One might put the detachment-theory another way by extending Aristotle's definition of the free man as a man who lives for himself,[3] that is, who does not live solely "with the other," because he can never reach total idenfication with the other or his circumstances. To be free is to be detached from the circumstances constitutive of surrounding reality.

IV

As an active revelation of the distance between man and the circumstances constituting reality, freedom may be likened to a barrier fencing off man's position from the realm of objects and preventing his transformation into an object. Because freedom in that sense is a fact, man may be confident that no objective complex of circumstances and no crystallization of his own creative powers can evict him from his subject-position vis-a-vis the world of objects in which he lives. No human creation whatsoever may be conceived as a full realization of freedom, for its essence is not to be realized in any creations but to be real in the status of man as subject. Yet the empirical reality of freedom is not given automatically. On the contrary, how to find empirical expressions for the standing of freedom as an active revelation of detachment, or guarantee it the status as principle of empirical conduct in general and of political in particular, is one of the gravest problems presented by the given fact of freedom. It is already evident that freedom can be neither granted nor made by the political domain. The most that the political domain can do is to acknowledge it through active endeavors to find concrete translations, whereby to shape its own empirical features and activities in the image of that acknowledgement. Consequently, in contrast to our analysis of the concrete modes in which the principle of justice is reflected in the political domain, we shall dissect the modes in which freedom finds, or should find, political expression against the background or our analysis of man's position as a subject. For, whereas the relationship between the principle of justice and the political domain is founded on the principle or idea of consideration for man as a subject, that between freedom and the political domain expresses the fact of his subject-status and the facticity of freedom as an active revelation of it.

V

The foregoing argument may now give place to a positive review of the meanings of the concept of freedom. One way of defining freedom is to differentiate it from two kinds of necessity, one imposed by law-abiding objective processes and the other by compulsion. As distinguished from objective necessity, freedom means that mode of conduct which is not exposed to total determination by any objective and law-abiding process whatsoever—physical, genetic, or historical. As distinguished from compulsion, it means that mode of conduct which is not subject to an exclusive determination by coercive use of force, that is, a use entailed by the laws neither of nature nor of history, but by human decision and action. Coercion is, of course, involved in objective, law-abiding, processes also; but, while objective coercion is inexorable and unavoidable, that of compulsion is not. Compulsion is, by definition, the use of force where that is not necessary by the nature of the state of affairs. Were men to act in a certain way out of physical, genetic, or historical necessity, no compulsion would be needed to make him to act so. Nature "coerces" him to breathe. But only men compel other men not to "breathe" a word of protest against the circumstances in which they live and breathe. Men are subjected to coercion by nature and to compulsion by man. The basic difference between the relation of freedom to necessity and to compulsion, respectively, may be formulated as follows: The distinction between freedom and necessity does not carry the negation of necessity in freedom's name, but the distinction between freedom and compulsion does carry such a negation of compulsion. Freedom does not entail the negation of objective necessity any more than the standpoint of the understanding subject—where freedom rests—entails the negation of the object understood. But it entails the negation of excessive coercion, just as the standpoint of understanding does the negation of excessive determination of the understanding by its object. Freedom negates not the inexorable determination of men as subjects by the necessity of their circumstances as objects, but their excessive determination as subjects by their fellows as men. From an objective point of view, the breaking of one man by his fellow through torture is obviously possible, but, from the point of view of the principle of freedom, for man to take advantage of that possibility is wrong and forbidden.

Another way of defining freedom is to describe it as the absence of hindrance. Thus defined, it does not mean total overcoming of the hindrance presented by the circumstances of man's existence. Limitation by circumstances is the price that freedom must pay for its status as the active manifestation of man's posture. Were there no circumstances to oppose, there would be no freedom. Thus freedom does not demand the total negation of the said hindrances. What it demands is the negation of avoidable hindrances, that is, of compulsive ones not inherent in the circumstances. It is true that as regards the man-made circumstances of human reality, whether economic or social or historical, the distinction between hindrances in the sense of inescapable circumstances and in the sense of avoidable inhibitions is far from clear. As to what constitutes objective necessity and what arbitrary compulsion, in this respect, there are indeed differences of opinion.

Nevertheless, one can say that men do not tend to regard circumstances of their own making as analogous—in terms of the hindrances which they present—to those over which they have no control, say, those produced by physical or genetic processes. Should we consider for example, the difference between tall and short men as identical with the difference between rich and poor men, at least not in terms of the possible remediability or irremediability of the feature involved in the difference? One can also say that the boundaries between necessary or inexorable circumstances and compulsory or remediable hindrances are subject to shifts as a result of man's intervention in natural processes. So while freedom is opposed to compulsive hindrances as a matter of principle, the precise nature of compulsive, as distinguished from necessary, hindrances does not lend itself to an indisputable definition as a matter of fact.

VI

The possibility of choice is yet another meaning of the concept of freedom, being a corollary of the more general meaning of absence of total determination by objective circumstances. If man were completely determined by his circumstances, he would have no possibility of choice. A certain distance between the agent and the context of circumstances in which he acts is, therefore, the necessary condition of action in conformity to choice or promoted by it. As contingent upon relative indetermination by circumstances, possibility of choice can mean a chance either of choosing one among several courses of action afforded by the circumstances confronting you, or of choosing to act upon those circumstances in such a way as to alter or fashion them. Man makes a free choice in the first sense when he chooses to live under the conditions of Australia rather than of Britain, and in the second, when he chooses to act upon the wilderness in such a way as to transform it into a place of habitation. In both cases, his choice is relative to the circumstances, and its range of possibilities is determined by them. Man is free to choose to transform the wilderness so, because, as a matter of principle, it lends itself to that transformation; he is not free to choose to transform Mars in that way because, so far as we know now, Mars lacks the conditions or circumstances which make human life possible. But, as Mars is beyond the compass of possible human existence, its reality cannot be conceived as a limitation of human freedom in the sense of freedom of choice. Freedom means not unbounded possibility of choice but its possibility within the limits of human capacity. Hence man's freedom may be said to be infringed by such circumstances only as they lend themselves to transformation by his own efforts. Just as, in the sense of indetermination by circumstances, freedom is constricted only by the avoidable determination of compusion, so, in the sense of possibility of choice, it is constricted only by avoidable or remediable circumstances. Thus the impossiblitiy of living on the moon or on Mars cannot be taken as a curtailment of freedom of choice, whereas the impossibility, for example, of moving to the West rather than live in Eastern Europe may.

We have thus advanced from the negative definition of freedom as absence of total determination by objective circumstances to a positive definition of it as a possibility of acting within, or even upon, objective circumstances on the basis of choice. This possibility is, indeed, partly afforded by the circumstances themselves, but it is linked to a further aspect of freedom, namely, the capacity of self-originating or spontaneous action. The interdependence of freedom as absence of total determination, as possibility of choice, and as spontaneity may be put in this way: If man's actions are not subject to complete determination by objective circumstances, then they cannot be totally accounted for as the effects of an objective nexus of determining factors and causes; and if his action upon his circumstances is not merely a reaction to stimuli originating in them, there is ground to assume the existence of a self-originating source of human action. The existence of some measure of indetermination by circumstances and of some possibility of choice warrants the conclusion that freedom is possible in the sense of a spontaneous source of relatedness to, and action upon, the circumstances. Just as the relationship of the understanding to its object is established not by the object but by the understanding's intentionality, so some phases of human action, at least, are not called forth by the circumstances acted upon but originate in the agent's spontaneous directedness towards them.

VII

Freedom figures in the threefold sense of indetermination, possibility of choice, and the power of self-originating action. A fourth sense is offered by the philosophical tradition, in which freedom has frequently been defined as rational conduct. Freedom as indetermination, and also as choice, pertains to the conditions of possibility of action; and as the power of self-origination, to the source of action; but as rationality, it pertains to the *content* or direction of free action. The first three senses refer to freedom *from* excessive hindrances, the fourth refers to the freedom *to* act in conformity to rational deliberation or norms. In what sense, then, does an action determined by a specific rational content and proceeding in a defined direction fall under the heading of free actions? One way of answering would be to consider the implications of the idea of spontaneity as the power of self-originating action. For spontaneous action is action characterized by a structure. The self-originating activity of understanding is characterized by a two fold structure or rhythm of synthesis of impressions into objects and translation of objects into concepts or contents. Understanding, therefore, is an activity in which spontaneity and structure are not mutually exclusive but are actually correlative factors. Spontaneous action is a structured action moving along a well-defined course, and, insofar as an action's direction is of that character, the action may be said to feature a trend towards rationality.

The relation between rationality and freedom can be explained by demonstrating that only in a reality controlled by reason can freedom find concrete realization. The existence of freedom, as explained before, presupposes a certain distance between the agent and his circumstances; and if there were no circumstances, there would also be no freedom. A further precondition of freedom is the rational organization of reality, or at least of social reality in terms of patterns of behavior, namely, legal systems that conform to such patterns as will permit concrete expression of freedom.

VIII

From this exploration of the divergent meanings of freedom we may move to an analysis of the different possible manifestations of those meanings in the domain of politics. The basic assumption will be that this domain is not a mere image or reflection of the transempirical but a realm in its own right, with its own distinguishing marks. Although analytically distinct, the empirical and transempirical realms of human reality are not independent of each other. Just as the political domain is open to shaping by principles, so the transempirical is open to the empirical and, to a certain extent, dependent upon it. The transempirical existence of freedom is guaranteed by man's position of understanding. Of itself, political life is no warrant that man's capacity for understanding will be developed, let alone expressed. There is no guarantee that his transempirical status of understanding and its active expression in freedom will find reflection in political life and activity. Nevertheless, the very fact that his empirical status as a political creature inheres in his transempirical status as an understanding one, makes the political domain the target of legitimate evaluation and criticism guided by the norm of his transempirical status. Concurrently, it warrants moral judgments as to whether political inhibition of human freedom is right or wrong. Because man possesses a twofold status, transempirical and empirical, the transempirical has the authority to function as a measure and a regulative principle of the empirical. If political reality is appraised by this standard and found wanting, it can be required to adjust itself to the norm of man's subject-status and guarantee its sustenance. Man is the creator of political reality, and, in creating it, reveals his status of detachment or distance from the world. As man's creation, the political domain presupposes—as its precondition—the rational or understanding-endowed nature of its creator.

Because the existence of the political domain is not static but dynamic, because the domain is created and re-created, the primordial conditions of its creation are at the same time the present conditions of its continuous creation and re-creation. There is, accordingly, no justification for assuming that once upon a time there was a free or understanding creature who created a political domain and, having finished the work, lost or gave up his creative powers of freedom and understanding. If this assumption is a fiction, it is because it has invented a temporal sequence which has no correlate in reality. The political domain is of the same character as another fundamental human creation—language. Man's creative powers of comprehending and manipulating symbols are the conditions of the creation and the continuous re-creation of language. With language as with political reality, primordial origins and present capacities of self-originating re-creation are aspects of one and the same status. Political integration is sustained as an historical-empirical fact by the very status and power of freedom through understanding which is the transempirical condition of its existence.

But, although the criterion of man's transempirical status is not entirely extrinsic to the political domain, it may not be conceived as an intrinsic criterion of it either. That status of his is not entirely intrinsic because it reflects his prepolitical and transpolitical essence, and, equally, not entirely extrinsic, because man occupying it lives his empirical life and conducts his empirical activities within a socio-political framework. From the angle of its relation to the political domain, freedom through understanding may be conceived of the threefold sense of a fact, an end, and a regulative content, norm or value. It is a political fact if its existence is acknowledged by, and manifested in, the political domain; it is an end if men's aspirations are directed towards its realization there. And its projection as an end originates not in an arbitrary whim but in an essential content, which—as a principle of preference regulating conduct—is a value.

IX

If the nature of the political domain as a field and a product of human activity renders it liable to evaluation and regulation by the principle of freedom as the condition of that activity, the problem arises of how freedom in its various senses can be preserved under the concrete conditions of political life and activity. To be a political creature is to overstep individuality and contribute one's share to the collective endeavor of political togetherness. But freedom in the original sense belongs to man not as an agent of integration but as an individual subject who, as such, aims at understanding the world and not at joining forces with his fellows in an effort to create and sustain an integrated collectivity; political integration presupposes collective activity, while understanding is promoted in the activity of individual subjects. The crux of the problem of political freedom is the difference between the *conditio sine qua non* of understanding—namely, individuality of consciousness—and of that political existence—namely, transcending individuality towards collective integrating endeavor.

Another reason which renders the realization of freedom in the political domain problematic is this: political reality is fraught with coercive elements and upheld by created and concentrated power. Freedom, by definition, is opposed to, and infringed by, a measure of coercion exceeding that inescapably immanent in the objective circumstances of man's existence. Yet the circumstances of political reality include, as an essential component, just that coercive power which, as man-made or constituted, represents not the circumstantial necessity compatible with freedom but the compulsion opposed to it. If an element of compulsion is part and parcel of the circumstances or conditions of political reality, how can that activity possibly sustain freedom when its primary aim is to constitute its antithesis, namely, potentially compulsive power?

Further impediments to the realization of freedom in the political domain are introduced by the character of that domain as a partial integration of particular human beings in particular geographical-historical or spatial-temporal circumstances. The domain does not effect an encounter between man and the entire cosmic expanse but brings him into contact only with a limited range of possiblities circumscribed within definite spatial-temporal bounds. As a nexus of circumstances, the domain is itself a hindrance, not, indeed, in the sense that physical circumstances represent hindrances, but in the sense of limiting partialness. Man, as an understanding subject, stands against the total range of physical and cosmic circumstances. He occupies his position of detachment or freedom from those circumstances as an individual, and not as a member of any particular body-social or body-politic. Since all men, as such, occupy that position, in freedom all are equal, but political reality creates differences between them, dividing some, uniting others. Given this partialness, how can freedom, as an attribute of man's universal essence, be realized within defined political bounds? Or, if the demands of his universal essence and his particular political circumstances clash, how much importance are we to attach to the demand of those circumstances? Thus, by virtue of the integration which constitutes it, the power which supports it, and the spatial-temporal or geographical-historical bounds which circumscribe it, the political domain superimposes its own hindrances upon those immanent in the nature of things, which inhibit the realization of freedom.

Another factor contributing to the problematics of the encounter between the transempirical and empirical planes of human reality is a tendency to regard the empirical crystallizations of man's creative capacities as possessing a value equal to, if not greater than, that of creative potency or potentiality in itself. It leads to the view that human creations in general, and the political domain in particular, are concrete revelations of what is best in man. The tendency is exemplified by suggestions in literary criticism that evaluation of a literary work of art, rich and complex as it may be, need not, or even must not, take account of the rich and complex character of the creator and the creative process. Further evidence of that tendency is the idea that the artist as a man is likely to be far less admirable than his work of art. Even if we conceded the tenability of this respecting artistic or even scientific creations, we should not follow an attempt to consider the political domain, as a creation, analogously. The mode of being of a work of art or a scientific text is not the same as that of the political domain: once created, a work of art or a scientific text no longer depends on its creators for its existence, but the political domain always does. Evaluation of the political domain cannot isolate it from its creators, because it is an ordered construct or form, whose "matter" or content is the life and activities of its creators.

To raise the political domain to the status of *realized* freedom is to assume that freedom is realized not in its source, which is man as a creative subject, but in the context of circumstances to which, by definition, the status of the creative subject is opposed. The political domain, as a creation, is still a revelation of human freedom, but, also as a creation, it is incommensurable with the status of freedom occupied by, and only by, its creator; beyond the creative subject, freedom does not exist. Because freedom cannot be projected into political moulds, because the tension between the status of men as free subjects or creators and of the political order as their creation can never be overcome, the problem of political freedom affects the very heart of political life. Poles apart from its creators in its ontological status as a creation, opposed to the freedom of its creators as a complex of circumstances and hindrances overlaid upon the circumstances and hindrances of nature that exist of necessity, and liable to transgress the freedom if its creators with the coercive machinery at its disposal—how can the political domain possibly make room for expressions of man's status?

Grim as the prospect may seem, there are grounds for assuming that, at least in certain areas, there is capacity and call for freedom within the said orbit, and for demanding that the empirical domain acknowledge the trans-empirical status of freedom in its threefold capacity as fact, end, and norm, and submit to its regulative authority. But why wrestle with the problem of political freedom at all? Why not avoid the intricate labyrinth of the encounter of so ambiguous a transempirical factor as freedom with so multifaceted an empirical factor as the political domain? The issue itself leads us to face it. The assumption of our analysis of the relation between the planes of political reality and of principles is that political practice is not, or ought not to be, void of conception, of conscious conformity to transempirical principles in general and the principle of freedom in particular. There is nothing utopian in this assumption; it does not claim that a kingdom of freedom can be established on a politically organized earth, nor does it propose to abandon the political earth for a heavenly kingdom of freedom. But, for the very reason that it recognizes that the political domain is here to stay, our exploration intends to demonstrate that, ontologically, it is not cut off from the realm of freedom.

To show that empirical expression of man's status within the political domain is possible and necessary, though by no means automatic, we must scour areas of empirical reality where freedom can strike root. The major aspects of the problem of political freedom are these:

1. Given the factual existence of that domain, is it possible to sustain such modes of activity as are free or exempt from political concerns? Granting that men's life and activity in concert are ordered in relational structures conforming to the logic of the political domain, to the logic of integration, placement, and power, is it, nevertheless, possible for men to engage in activities controlled by an inner logic of their own being unchecked by the logic of that domain?

2. Given the factual organization of the domain in political moulds and patterns, are there, all the same, certain areas in it that can be shaped in conformity to nonpolitical patterns and ends?

3. Given the patent tension beteen the coercion-fraught political order and the status of freedom, is it still possible to sustain free activities not only within but even for the sake of the comprehensive body-politic?

The first two aspects concern the possibility of being *in* the political domain without being *of* it; the third concerns the possibility of being in the domain and for it, rather than against it, by free directedness towards it. All three are reducible to the ultimate problem how, within the domain, man's status of detachment or distance from his circumstances can be upheld, not only with the permission but even with the aid of politics.

X

If the problem can be stated in terms of the first and second aspects, it is because the political domain and the activity sustaining it are only one field and mode of human activity among the many wherein the comprehensive essence of man is revealed; it is also revealed in other, apolitical, fields and modes of activity, such as scientific inquiry, philosophic speculation, and artistic creation. If these are legitimate manifestations of it, it would be improper to try to subordinate their structure and aims to the logic of political activity. That there is no case for ascribing to the logic of political activity a comprehensive jurisdiction over all modes of human activity follows from an analysis of the nature of intellectual activity, whose essence is a perpetual endeavor to decipher the riddle of reality by translating opaque data into meaningful relational structures. As a legitimate revelation of human essence, it cannot and need not submit to the guidance of the logic of political activity. Controlled by a different end, the logic of intellectual activity necessarily differs from the logic of political activity. Directed not towards interindividual integration but towards the universe at large, intellectual activity is itself universal and inheres in man's status as an understanding subject. Political activity is partial, for it is directed towards the integration of particular individuals who live and act in particular circumstances. It is true that intellectual activity fosters human cooperation, since deciphering of the riddles of reality is the common end of all who by intellectual inquiry seek to transform facts into meanings. But intellectual and political cooperation are not the same thing: intellectual activity creates interindividual communication, political activity creates interindividual integration.

Intellectual activity, directed towards an interpretation of the world as it is, is subordinated to the principle of objectivity as the principle of fidelity to things, or to states of affairs, as they are, whereas subordination in the political domain is to power. It would be a blunder to try to compare the two kinds of subordination, if only because power commands the submission of political activity not as a state of affairs to which it conforms but as a product which it creates; again depersonalization, which is essential to intellectual activity, is impossible in politics. Intellectual activity involves depersonalization; political activity, directed towards projectivity cannot be completely depersonalized. Differing from political in purpose, structure, and inner logic, intellectual activity is a clear example of manifestation of man's comprehensive essence, which presupposes freedom from politics so as to function in conformity to its own regulative principle. The same would apply to other—let us say, artistic or literary—apolitical activities, where the principle of freedom can be realized only on the condition that the differences between their respective domains and the political are acknowledged, respected, and upheld. To sustain freedom as freedom from politics, the political domain must eschew assumption of authority to regulate other legitimate modes of human activity. Here, freedom from politics means freedom to act in conformity to apolitical principles.

That, so understood, it is or can be of political moment follows from a consideration of the place, in the political domain, of free intellectual analysis of that domain itself. Such an analysis, governed by the principle of objectivity, discloses that the activities by which the domain is sustained are controlld not by objectivity but by projectivity. Any theory of politics flows from the inner logic of a theoretical approach and not from the logic of political activity. The norm of objectivity to which political theory must conform is not to be found in the realm of political practice; politics or political practice cannot be objective or depersonalized, but political theory can and should be. One can and should require of political theory that it conform to the principle of objectivity, even though its object—the political domain—cannot be expected to. To guarantee freedom of apolitical activity, it is not necessary to have recourse to positive political legislation; all that is required is acknowledgement, by the political domain and policy, of the legitimate status of activities regulated by their own and not by political logic. Freedom from politics will then be safeguarded if politics and political activity recognize the limits of their own sphere of jurisdiction and do not transgress them.

Recognition of activities which the logic of politics does not fetter would also give latitude for freedom of choice. For where there is room for more than one legitimate mode of human activity, man's choice of occupation is unshackled by any need to worry whether the one chosen is or is not compatible with the logic of political activity, and it will not be dictated from without but spring from his own spontaneous preference. Freedom of choice, as being also freedom from politics, implies—among other things—that, whether, for example, a particular metaphysical or physical theory holds or does not hold good, the reigning political ideology has no bearing on a man's option of the theory that he will adhere to; choice is free if its object is not the business of the political domain. Such freedom can find active expression in the demand that the political domain mind its own business and resign physical and metaphysical theories to those activities which are qualified and authorized to deal with them. If latitude is left for activities which politics does not shackle, some measure of freedom as rational conduct is secured, for there is then place for free discussion, debate, methodical airing of doubts, and so forth.

XI

The limited authority of political activity does not, however, imply the unlimited applicability of the logic of apolitical activity. One must take issue here with the theory that the inner logic of intellectual activity can be imposed upon the political domain. This assumes that subordination to power can and ought to be identified with subordination to objectivity in such a way as, sooner or later, to reduce political coercion to mere rational subordination. Refutation of such a theory is essential not only to an analysis of the structural differences between the realms of intellectual and political activity but also to an exposure of the fallacy at the heart of the political ideology which uses the theory as a rubber stamp of totalitarianism.

One cannot overemphasize the importance of the fact that, whereas intellectual activity is characterized by subordination to the principle of objectivity and consequently by depersonalization, the political domain is characterized by subordination to projected power and order, and consequently by the impossibility of a thoroughgoing depersonalization. The possiblity of complete depersonalization is contingent upon subordination to objectivity as conformance to a rational norm or demand which, by its very nature, is universal and, as such, impersonal. The paradox is that depersonalizing subordination to objectivity may be conceived as a mode of self-fulfilment, since through subordination to objectivity a man expresses his transempirical essence as a rational creature. But in no conceivable sense can subordination to projectivity constitute a mode of self-realization through rational recognition of objectivity. Power and order are, by definition and nature, projected away from ourselves. Because we deliberately project them beyond and against ourselves, subordination to them does not amount to recognizing a continuation of ourselves in them. Creatures endowed with understanding as they are, men are always conscious of the distance and difference between their position and the domain of power and order.

At least one aspect of freedom, namely, freedom of choice, can only be realized on the basis of personal or individual preference, decision, aspiration, and the like. True, not all theories of freedom define it as freedom of choice. And it is not by chance that theories which overlook or deny this aspect of the concept (the systems of Hegel and Marx, for example) point to the reduction of political relationships to an intellectual pattern. The assumption is this: As freedom in general is rational identification with the objective and rational order of things, so political freedom is rational identification with the rational and objective order in society or state. Since their premise is that to be free is to be subordinate to objectivity in all spheres, they do not consider that imposing the ideal of objectivity upon the political sphere threatens human freedom; on the contrary, that ideal, as realized in the political order, would, for them, be its apotheosis.

But just to say that freedom equals identification with objectivity does not validate this equation. Any objective order that men have made, men can unmake. Hence the quasi-objective political order, though it be the realized crystallization of human desire, does not command the same kind of rational identification as does the objective order of things. That is why rational criticism of the objective order of nature is misplaced or at least futile, and why rational criticism of the projective order of society and state makes sense and sometimes bears fruit.

The only way of realizing the ideal of freedom or the intellectual ideal of depersonalized objectivity in the political domain would be, if one may say so, to force men to be free. Since man as a political creature is a concrete person, and since persons are not spontaneously impersonal, they cannot be depersonalized except by the use of coercive force. According to this line of thought, as translated from theory into practice by the Bolshevist regime, if a man is unable to identify himself with the truth of the regime as with the truth of the proposition that two plus two equals four, then the regime must spare no coercive effort to help him to achieve that degree of identification. Of course, perverted intellectual zeal is not the only reason for the use of coercive force by Bolshevism. One of the socio-historical practical reasons for it is the urgency of industrialization, and exploiting political machinery for the conscription of manpower is considered to be an efficient means of industrial advancement. It would, however, be the reverse of perspicacity to take economic, social, and historical factors as adequately explaining the connection between excessive use of coercive force and Bolshevist politics.

Coercion is integral to the ideology of Bolshevism and follows from its conviction that a regime is the objective incarnation of objective historical processes based upon rational unravelling of the riddle of history, rather than a projective crystallization of a particular network of interindividual relationships. Grant a regime a pseudo-objective status, and you authorize it to demand no less acknowledgement than does the principle of truth. Do so, and you shatter that principle even while professing to worship it. Why? To elevate the empirical and projective reality of a regime to the rank of a transempirical and objective ideal, to present a pseudo-objective empirical structure as a scientific decipherment of the writing on the wall of history, as of no less status than the conceptual structures which embody scientific unravellings of the riddle of nature—this is to pervert objective reality while rendering lip-service to its worship. Besides, to use coercion so as to force men to join the regime in worshipping truth is sheer blasphemy, for the proper adherence to truth is free intellectual activity.

XII

What is more important is that the principle of truth commands unwavering acknowledgement only because it is ideal. The price of realization in empirical reality is relativity, not only of the projective realization of human integration in an empirical order but also of the principles which shape it. The political order is not an incarnation of the universal and absolute meaning of history; it is a particular translation of the particular interpretation attached to their own integration by particular persons who live and act under particular geographical, historical, economic, and social conditions. Political integration can be interpreted in more ways than one, depending upon historical circumstances. The same ambiguity and flexibility characterize the interpretations to which ideal principles lend themselves when it comes to applying them in political practice to concrete empirical situations.

The problems of the statesman are not analogous to those of the scientist, nor are the methods of solution comparable. The validity of physical theory is a problem of a different order from that of handling an empirical situation in the political domain even in conformity to the demands of the principle of justice. To solve theoretical problems, man must interpret empirical data objectively and translate them into abstract conceptual constructs; to solve political problems, he must interpret the implications of an abstract principle for his own empirical situation and translate it into concrete courses of action. In the realm of theory, truth, as a criterion of validity, functions as a regulative principle by virtue of its ideal status, which is independent of the thinker's empirical situation. In the realm of political practice, justice, as a criterion of right and wrong, can function as a regulative principle of concrete conduct only if it be not completely detached from the agent and from the situation which he must shape through his action, because the foundation of justice is consideration for man as a concrete person. The essence of truth, moreover, is not relative to the infinite variety of circumstances—geographical, historical, meteorological, and the rest—which are the stage of men's action in concert; the concrete meaning of justice does vary with the circumstances to which it is applied and with the mental make-up of the men who interpret it.

Once you admit that a regime may serve the cause of truth with the machinery of compulsion, you must admit that no truth will be deprived of that service, not even the truth of the regime itself. Of that truth there can be no question, since the regime embodies the objective truth of the historical process. The flaw in this argument is its failure to realize that to suppress all questioning is to choke the fountainhead of that intellectual activity which alone can discover the historical truth allegedly embodied in the regime. Without free intellectual inquiry, no truth can be unveiled, not even political truth, assuming that it exists. And unless intellectual and political activity are separated, there can be neither free thought nor free politics. Thus historical experience upholds the conclusions indicated by a theoretical analysis of the conditions of political freedom as freedom from politics, and makes it quite clear that the existence of realms exempt from the problematics of political integration and beyond the reach of the coercive arm of the body-politic is the *conditio sine qua non* of freedom in that sense.

The more diversified the modes of legitimate activity conducted within, but not regulated by, the political domain, the more latitude there is for freedom from politics. A diversified political reality is likely to be beset by tensions, at times even clashes, between different modes. Believing that each activity is sovereign within its own bounds, people may conclude that any attempt to relax the tensions and end the clashes by subordinating the logic of one activity to the logic of another is illicit and unjustifiable breach of freedom. When the upshot is total negation of all subordination and the denial that, within definite political limits, subordination is indispensable, this reasoning has gone beyond the demand for apolitical islands of activity within the political domain to a jettisoning of politics even within its proper sphere. Radical conclusions of this kind are usually drawn by some creative persons (artists, writers, thinkers), who are so immersed in the depths of intellectual or artistic creation that they overlook the existence of the sociopolitical domain and—in extreme cases—deny it. This attitude is as inadmissible as any attempt to apply the logic of one particular, and hence partial, mode of activity which reveals the comprehensive essence of man to other such modes. To cross diversifying boundaries between patently different and equally sovereign modes and realms of activity, no matter in what direction, cannot be justified. No human activity is *carte blanche*. That a man is, let us say, a creative writer does not give him the prerogative of ignoring the existence of other men, nor is such a prerogative implicit in the concept of freedom from politics. No man could ignore the socio-political domain even if he wanted to. Being a man as well as a gifted artist, he is no less dependent upon interhuman relationships and their sphere to satisfy his daily wants than are less talented men. To take advantage of the public domain and of the men who sustain it is not to rule out or ignore its existence, but to deny that taking implies or demands giving, that rights entail obligations.

In fairness to the antipolitical attitude, it must be observed that it does not always originate in the arrogation to oneself of privileges that one denies to others. A man can honestly believe that dedication to his creative calling requires unreserved negation of the political domain and unreserved allegiance to the realm of creativity. One cannot call a man's sense of consecration amoral, and, if, nevertheless, it constitutes a threat in the political domain, that hardly warrants the hasty suppression of such antipolitical attitudes with the aid of the coercive machine of politics; thoughtless use of force beyond the legitimate limits of the political domain can no more be vindicated than extreme attitudes which flout the authority of politics even within its own limits.

Here enters the problem of more moderate manifestations of the antipolitical standpoint, which oppose not the existence of the political domain but certain policies, forms, and usages found within its recognized limits. Since such a standpoint—for example, that of a conscientious objector—does not reject the realm of interhuman relationships or claim for itself privileges denied to others, it would be hard to object to it on moral grounds and to use the moral argument as justification for its coercive suppression. It might, of course, be contended that conscientious objection to military service involves indirect exploitation of others, since the conscientious objector lets them fight the battles. This contention, however, overlooks the grounds of conscientious objection, the twofold ideal of peace and brotherhood. Here, the antipolitical stance cannot be compared to that of the artist, for example, who in turning his back on the political domain turns it on his fellow-men as well. If we have digressed, it was not to decide for or against conscientious objection or any other mode of antipolitical thought and expression, but to illustrate the complexity of the problem of political freedom as freedom from politics.

XIII

The second aspect of the problem is freedom within politics, or—in traditional terms—political rights. By this we mean the right to conduct certain activities within the political domain without conforming to the integrated poltical pattern, and the authority to expect that they will carry political weight and set their mark on politics. Here, again, the problematics of freedom follow from the nature of the political domain. In our analysis of that domain, we noted that it is but one among many institutionalized forms of togetherness, such as the family, the club, the school, the church, and so on. When these forms command the loyalty of their members, it is impossible to isolate their functions from those of the state. Hence, unlike intellectual or artistic activities, the freedom which follows from, and depends upon, their separation from political life and from educational or religious activities will necessarily come in contact, and at times even in conflict, with political activities. Intellectual activity need not have political aftereffects, because its end is not loyalty-commanding integration but the translation of nontranslucent data into significant contents; the same is true of artistic activity, whose end is not interindividual integration but individual creation. But political repercussions are bound to ensue from religious activity aiming at religious organization. So there can be no simple solution to our problem. The principle of freedom demands that, notwithstanding the conflict of loyalties, the right of partially institutionalized forms, such as religious organizations, to sustain their own patterns of integration be recognized by the more comprehensive order which is the political. On the other hand, the right of religious organization does not empower such organizations to expect political organization or integration to follow their own partial patterns. The demand for freedom of religious organization is subject to the same qualifications as that for freedom of intellectual activity—and for the same reason. Both are authorized by the fact that man's essence is not, and cannot be, exhaustively expressed in any empirical activity or form. Hence the authority of each partial activity within its own limited domain; hence, also, the illegitimacy of any attempt by an activity to venture beyond its own limits into the domain of an activity as sovereign as itself. Just as freedom forbids the infliction not only of political logic on the intellectual domain but also of intellectual logic on the political, so freedom demands not only that the state recognizes the church as a legitimate, though partial, mode of human organization, but also that the church recognizes the state as a legitimate mode of human organization and not adopt an aggressive policy towards it. Just as failure to recognize the limits of freedom from politics can inspire antipolitical attitudes in creative persons, so failure to recognize the limits of freedom within politics might inspire not only attitudes of that kind but even antipolitical action in religious organizations ranging from passive resistance to, or separation from what is understood as the secular order of society and state.

Once more freedom proves to be not incompatible with unresolved strains and conflicts. In fact, owing to the ambiguity of freedom and the multifaceted nature of empirical political reality, the encounter between the two is bound to be ambiguous and tension-torn. These strains and conflicts between the demands of freedom within politics and of political integration permit us to broach the problem of freedom in this sense. To try to solve that problem would be unavailing, but as least one can say that the political domain has the right to defend itself against aggressive expressions of the demand for freedom within politics, though not the authority to present its own claims as if only they were legitimate. Conversely, religious organizations have a right to defend their ways of life and worship against political encroachment, but not by attacking the political domain. The positive implications of political freedom cannot, then, be determined *a priori*, but the negative can. From the principle of political freedom, as inseparable from the partial sovereignty of all manifestations of human essence and the comprehensive sovereignty of none, there stems fundamental negation of aggressive trespass upon the sovereign boundaries of any manifestation.

The problem is how to sustain such institutional forms and functions as are in the political domain, but not of it, within a political ambit. Freedom within politics demands that the political order acknowledges organized activities which have political repercussions but not attributes, which aim at integration and inspire group loyalties but are not sustained by power and law. It does not entail active political acknowledgement in the form of legal recognition of the right of religious or educational institutions to enjoy it, and the state confines itself within certain bounds so as to allow for their unhindered activity. To sustain such institutional forms and functions *in* the political domain, but not *of* it, is to realize a certain measure of freedom as absence of hindrance. It is also to make room for freedom of choice, since men are thereby afforded a possibility of choosing, for example, the kind of school which they would like to attend or the kind of congregation that they would like to join. Freedom, as spontaneity, can also find expression in political recognition of apolitical institutional forms to the extent that they are the products of spontaneous directedness and endeavor. So that, for all the obstacles which it sets in the path of realizing freedom, the political domain can and does lodge diverse empirical expressions of this basic freedom.

XIV

The most overt political manifestation of freedom within the domain is freedom for politics' sake. By way of preamble to a consideration of it, we may survey a mode of political freedom which can be classified under the heading neither of freedom from politics, nor of freedom within politics, nor of freedom for politics' sake, but is a borderline phenomenon verging on all three: freedom of speech. The ultimate justification of the demand for this freedom is transpolitical, for it flows from the nature not of politics but of man as an understanding subject who expresses his understanding in verbal forms; freedom of speech presupposes and reflects freedom of thought. So it might come under the heading of freedom from politics, especially when it mirrors free thought concerning such apolitical or transpolitical contents as physical or metaphysical theories and aesthetic values.

When it mirrors free thought about religious contents, or, rather, free belief in them, free speech is a manifestation of freedom within politics, expecially if it is formulated in articles of faith commanding the loyalty of organized religious groups and thus has indirect, if not direct, political bearing. When it mirrors free thought about specifically political contents, particularly thought about future policy, it is a manifestation of freedom for politics' sake, by which we mean projection of political ends and adoption of political means for their realization. Freedom for politics' sake and political initiative are two sides of the same coin. Political initiative is the ability to intervene in given situations or given courses of events so as to regulate them, as well as the ability to plan future courses of action and get the plans carried out; as such, it is an indispensable condition of the existence of political activity.

Initiative is predicated not only by the power-constituting and integrative activities but also by the activity which shapes constituted power by filling it with content or subordinating it to regulative principles. For the content which power is to absorb, or the principles by which it is to be shaped, must be interpreted; interpretation presupposes intellectual initiative, as does that mode of criticism which contributes its share to the shaping of power, if only by censuring its flaws.

But in its most primary sense, freedom for politics' sake is generation of human integration, acknowledgement of the existence of integration, and participation in the activities which keep integration in existence. It is this freedom that is implied by the concept of franchise, as universal suffrage, which makes for the political crystallization of social integration and, at the same time, is one manifestation of the dynamics of integration or of integration in action.

Political initiative, or freedom for politics' sake, presupposes freedom as the possibility of choice. If men were not somewhat detached from their integrative togetherness, they could not choose to project it into political forms or to participate in its political dynamics. The dependence of freedom for politics' sake upon freedom is also reflected in such multifarious manifestations of initiative as critical evaluation of political data, projection of political ends (both being also revelations of freedom as rational action), legislation, forming of public opinion, formulating political ideologies, planning politics and projects, and so on. Yet, no particular manifestation of initiative exhausts the reservoir of spontaneity implicit in the status of men who manifest it by political action. It is never completely expended in such political revelations as criticism, voting, deciding upon particular plans and policies, or electing a particular party to office. The realm of its possible manifestion is always wider than that of its actual ones. That is why the fund or reservoir of potential initiative makes it possible to object to such particular crystallizations as this particular law or that defined policy. This surplus of potential rests in, and reflects, freedom as distance between man's position as subject and external circumstances. Again we see that the political domain can, even must, accept freedom as a position of detachment from all circumstances, political included. What is more, it can fortify that position by discharging the twofold sanction of power and law for the sake of guaranteeing to man the possibility to express his spontaneity by, for example, creating apolitical institutional forms, or taking part in elections by secret ballot, that is, by free choice, or through legislation.

XV

Realized initiative, like all realizations, is subject to the dialectics of realization. In and through the process of their realizations, the contents aimed at by aspiration are objectivized and thus projected from the realm of aspiring agent into that of forms. The dynamics of initiative are a movement between the pole of the initiating subject and the pole of such forms as institutions or laws which, as objectivizations, occupy a position of semi-independence from the subjects to whom they owe their existence. But objectivization of the contents of initiative does not imply objectivization of the initiative itself. There can be no metamorphosis of initiative into institutionalized forms, or of the subject-status of freedom into the objectivization-status of semi-independence. The gulf between initiative and its own crystallizations is similar to that between man's freedom and the circumstances which he approaches through detachment or distance. Freedom, as initiative, is to its crystallization as potentiality is to its actualizations. Both imply a surplus of unrealized possibilities. If, then, freedom, as a reservoir of potentiality and as detachment even from its own crystallization, is to be sustained, initiative must be permitted to express itself through a critical "taking exception to" its objectivized contents and thereby enable continuous quest for as yet unrealized forms of initiative-expression. It may, therefore, be said that reform and novelty are the objective correlatives of the reservoir of possibilities implicit in freedom as initiative. To express initiative is, accordingly, to seek new laws, new directions, new patterns and meanings of integration, and also to question and criticize old laws, old directions, and old patterns and meanings of integration. As both critical detachment from the entrenched crystallizations of its own contents and constructive quest for new forms of content-projection and self-crystallization, political initiative, or freedom for politics' sake, may be described as freedom of intellectual detachment from the objectivized political domain and freedom of practical participation in the constitution and shaping of that domain.

These two countenances of political initiative are mirrored in two broad categories of objectivized content and contemplation: one includes all the forms and functions in which practical initiative is made manifest, the other all those in which theoretical or critical initiative is. An historical manifestation of practical political initiative, or freedom for politics' sake, would be the constitution of an independent socio-political context possessing power, as created, for example, by the efforts of anticolonial national movements. Other, more partial, manifestations range through elections, legislation, and polls, so influencing public opinion as to achieve significant political results; an illustration is the stages of the victory of universal suffrage thanks to the pressure of public opinion.

The manifestations of theoretical or critical political initiative are less palpable because they are rarely crystallized in fixed institutional forms or in political activities furthering well-defined political ends. The primary crystallization of theoretical political initiative is the critical standpoint itself, one of evaluation, deliberation and questioning. That standpoint may produce political results, especially when its manifestation in free speech influences public opinion. But its primary purpose and function are not to shape public opinion but to reveal man's status as an understanding being detached from political circumstances and hence capable, also, of criticizing them. Not all free thought and its expression in free speech are reducible to a mode of freedom for politics' sake, that is, of political initiative. Scientific inquiry and religious thought and expression are, respectively, modes of freedom from politics and of freedom *in* but not *of* politics. The justificaton of free political thought and its expression inheres in the nature of the political domain itself as one which owes its existence, as well as its shaping by contents and principles, to the initiative of men. They do not only create it through their practical endeavors but also shape it continuously, if only negatively, through their theoretical criticism of contents already crystallized and their theoretical quest for new ones.

XVI

Freedom for politics' sake, as theoretical initiative, means freedom to adopt a critical viewpoint towards such specific political matters as the principles regulating political activity, or the laws ordering political life, or the power by which the political domain is sustained and safeguarded. As criticism of power, theoretical initiative may take a fundamental-philosophical or a topical-historical form. Philosophical criticism of power is manifest both in radically antipower viewpoints such as the anarchist negation of it, and in more moderate opinions which, although they do not deny that power, as coercion, is evil, realize that a modicum of coercion is a necessary evil. Such opinions are based on the assumption that the necessary existence of the evil of coercion follows from men's choice of it as preferable to a social reality void of patterns of conduct sanctioned by coercive power, a reality, that is, in which they would have themselves to shoulder the burden of full responsibility for every decision and action. Moderate philosophical criticism thus dismisses the possibility of doing away with power and directs its critical shafts only against those excessive uses of coercion which overpass the limits of necessity. Criticism that aims not at annihilating power but confining it within precise and inviolable bounds is illustrated by the earlier mapping of human activities that are beyond the legitimate reach of political power and logic.

Topical-historical criticism is the negative evaluation of particular ends to which concentrated power is yoked. How relevant this mode of freedom for politics' sake is in modern political reality is attested by the negative example of attempts to suppress it. A particular state uses coercive force to outlaw and suppress subversive activities and movements. The task of the critic would be to bare the breach of fredom, as freedom of practical political initiative, which the act of suppression implies; he has no right to criticize the act, if only because it is a *fait accompli*. The flaw in this argumentation is plain in the light of the foregoing analysis. The critical standpoint hinges on man's position of detachment from his factual circumstances; if they are inevitable or objectively necessary, freedom does not demand their negation; but, if they are avoidable superimpositions of compulsion upon the natural necessity, it does demand their negation, if not in deed then at least in thought or attitude. It is precisely as an accomplished fact that the coercive suppression of practical political initiative calls for theoretical political initiative as criticism of the fact.

XVII

The strongest advocacy of criticism even of such political facts as are crystallizations of human initiative is provided by the example of dictatorships established by plebiscites. Such dictatorships claimed that their origins in the political initiative of the men who voted them into power gave them license to suppress all further manifestations of initiative. The Nazi regime did not hesitate to justify its annihilation of men of initiative on the ground that it was authorized to do so by the plebiscite which established it. Even supposing that the plebiscite initiative was authentic, and reflected free deliberation, we should still have to deny the authority of any crystallization of initiative to suppress further initiative. The reasons for this position are these: Human initiative being a well of potentiality, no particular manifestation of it may arrogate to itself the authority of an ultimate manifestation; political initiative is a bipolar manifestation of freedom, consisting in theoretical or critical assessment of political reality as well as of its practical constitution and shaping; and the fact that practical initiative produces Nazism does not imply that theoretical initiative will. Accordingly, any regime which rests its authority upon the practical initiative whence it sprang cannot stamp out other revelations of that initiative or its theoretical counterpart. Novelty and reform being the practical correlates of the ongoing reservoir of initiative, to thwart impulses in new directions is to deny the authority of the initiative which is said to authorize that denial. You cannot have your initiative and suppress it. Exposure to criticism and reform is the price that any regime must pay for the authority which men bestow on projections of their freedom for politics' sake.

In the last analysis, practical initiative presupposes the critical one, which alone can manumit men from bondage to political forms invested with the authority and prestige of time and tradition. The higher the prestige of traditional patterns, the more likely is critical freedom for politics' sake to assume "iconoclastic" forms. Before practical initiative can make a move towards to future, the critical must make a move against and away from the past. Thus, one political task of criticism is to clear the ground for practical initiative and defend its right; a more urgent task of critical initiative is to defend itself by resisting attempts to stifle man's critical faculty or, failing that, to present it as a cardinal sin.

There is no graver threat to critical initiative than the efforts expended to equate man's critical faculty with the arch-tempter to political wrongdoing, and to force those tempted to atone for their alleged derelictions by public confession. The methods of "persuading" men to resist temptation—ranging from brainwashing to physical torture—must be uncompromisingly denounced. But, obnoxious as they are, they are a lesser evil and threat to humanity than the end by which they are "justified," namely, the end of converting or perverting man's cardinal virtue—critical judgment—into a cardinal crime or identifying it with humanity. To destroy that vicious equation, to undo the coupling of intellectual liberty with political licentiousness or depravity, is perhaps the first and major duty of criticism for politics' sake.

XVIII

Like freedom within politics, freedom for politics' sake must be safeguarded by the political domain itself with the means at its disposal. Legal recognition and sanction of men's right to create apolitical instititional forms, religious congregations, for example, and to share in the constitution and shaping of power through practical and critical initiative alike represent one mode of this safeguarding. Legal circumscription of the legitimate limits of coercion, physical or psychological, coupled with legal prohibition of any transgression of them by the state represents another mode. Freedom within politics and freedom for politics' sake, as well, presuppose active political support of that character, because both produce political consequences.

One consequence is produced by the conflict of loyalties which each entails within the political domain. If the conflict cannot be resolved, then the problem arises of striking a balance. Man's freedom within politics requires him to coordinate and counterpoise the demands of his church, for example, with the demands of his state; his freedom for politics' sake requires reconciliation of the demands of his practical initiative with the demands of his critical initiative, which call for some measure of detachment or separation from the products of practical initiative. Coordination or counterpoising of loyalties in conflict is a problem which must be tackled if cohesion is to be preserved. One way of squaring them is to inspire loyalty to certain collective symbols invested with prestige and acknowledged by all. Thus, it is said that the body-politic and the body-social equally owe their cohesion to collective participation in symbols that are not subject to criticism. Within the circumference of unifying symbols, critical initiative has its place, provided that it is aimed not at them but at particular political forms and functions subsisting within a universally acknowledged collectivity.

The need to reconcile conflicting loyalties does not arise except within the political domain, and there only in respect of activities which generate direct or indirect political repercussions because of their inspiring loyalty to nonpolitical ends. The tensions within the domain of activities that are free from politics call not for resolution by coordination but for solution by judgment in conformity to objective criteria of validity. For example, if two incompatible physical theories collide, the problem is one not of striking a balance between them but of determining which provides a more adequate account of data; the issue of loyalty is obviously irrelevant. But, where loyalties are divided within the political domain, there can be no question of which is the "valid" one; both are inspired by equally legitimate and equally partial manifestations or revelations of man's universal essence. In view of the authority of the two claims, the decision must turn on preference or choice, which presupposes a minimum of personal initiative and must not be forced upon a man by the use of the coercive machinery available to one institutional form that claims his loyalty, namely, the state. If, to take a concrete example, a Jewish citizen of the Soviet Union is torn between his loyalty to his people, its past and present, and his awareness that his government disapproves of any links between its citizens and realms beyond its own frontiers, the government must not "help" him to resolve his dilemma by forcing him to settle for one of its horns. Equilibration of loyalties on the basis of a minimum of personal initiative is the precondition of expressing freedom as choice and inititiative in political practice on the part of the individuals.

It could, of course, be argued that the coexistence of conflicting activities is a limitation of freedom and that the need forced upon man by a reality that is racked by tensions to coordinate conflicting claims upon his loyalty curbs rather than fosters his freedom. What is wrong with this argument is that it does not take into account that the objective necessity and compulsion are different things. To say it again, inexorable necessity does not constitute a breach of freedom, avoidable compulsion does. In terms of the present problem, the distinction implies that, whereas the clash of loyalties due to the multiplicity of legitimate revelations of man's essence cannot be conceived as an impediment, compulsory "resolution" of the clash through the aid of the state's coercive machinery must be conceived as one. A political reality purporting to be both comprehensive and exclusive, claiming undivided loyalty, and twarting any impulse towards separation from itself by physical emigration or intellectual reservation—such a reality is riddled with compulsion, through and through.

Every universalization of political reality is an interpretation. In itself, an interpretation of the meaning of political integration does not violate but reveals freedom, for it is a mode of theoretical initiative in whose absence political reality could neither exist nor be shaped. But a universalizing interpretation of that reality which portrays the political order as if it were the comprehensive and unique manifestation of man's essence, one which presents the demands of political integration as if their claim upon men's loyalty were the sole legitimate claim, infringes freedom of initiative in both the practical sense, in the direction of participation, and the critical sense, in the direction of detachment. By arrogating to itself the status of a comprehensive manifestation of man and the authority of commanding his unreserved loyalty, the political domain opens itself to fair criticism in the name of the principle of freedom, which can itself only be realized by multivalence in diversity and conflict.

At this juncture, we can enlarge upon the dialectical relationship between freedom as an active expression of man's distance from his circumstances and the necessary confrontation with them. Anything that stands over and against freedom as detachment or distance is a circumstance. In terms of my freedom, the existence of my fellow man is a must one as are the components of natural, social, and political reality, except that he is of a different order from any natural, social, or political circumstace. In confronting him, my freedom is circumscribed not by natural necessity or by political compulsion, but by human freedom itself. Occupying the same ontological subject-status as I do, he has as much right as I have to demand that his status and correlative freedom of detachment be recognized and taken into consideration. His authority to impose this demand upon me, like mine to impose it upon him, is derived from the principle of freedom as disallowance of complete identification of man's subject-status with any objective or objectivized realm of circumstances. Every man is, accordingly, entitled to demand that he be afforded a possibility of taking exception to his circumstances, including those created by political ideology and activity. To claim the right of free faith is to claim it not only for myself but for my fellowman as well. Similarly, to claim the right of loyalty to more than one institutional form is to assume that he too deserves to be granted it. Consequently, from the angle of the principle of freedom, any attempt by a particular expression of man's comprehensive essence to monopolize loyalty is illegitimate. Counterpoise of coexisting standpoints of freedom and adjustment of their conflicting claims are the price that freedom pays, as it were, for itself, and that it must be paid is implicit in the dialectics of realization.

XIX

In certain cases a particular nexus of circumstances, in themselves alien to the essence of freedom, may nevertheless contribute to its realization; for instance, the wielding of political power to enforce universal education. Compulsory education involves a visible element of coercion, especially for parents who would rather not send their children to school if it were not that failure to do so was an offense subject to penalty. But, here, coercion is, so to speak, technical: the direct end of compulsory education is not political integration—although it may contribute to it by cultivating the theoretical and practical initiative which nourishes integrative activities—but the guaranteeing of man's right to self-fulfillment. Its underlying assumption is that the potentialities of human nature can be brought to actualization by an education process. Founded on such an assumption, the use of force for education's sake may even be described as anticoercive; indeed, to cultivate man's power of understanding is to cultivate his power to confront his circumstances open-eyed and detachedly. With compulsory education, the problem of reconciling the claims of politics and education does not arise, since political means are there subordinated to apolitical ends. With coercion for political purposes, say, to safeguard order, a balance must be struck between the standpoints of freedom, which opposes coercion, and of the political domain, which claims the authority to use force when its existence is at stake. Unlike freedom from politics, freedom for politics' sake cannot simply ignore the fact of coercion, or, on the other hand, deny the right of the political domain to resort to force in self-defense. As free for politics' sake, a man cannot disown all allegiance to power. But, he can demand the possibility of coping with the conflict of loyalties between power and freedom on is own initiative, and that the state not cut the Gordian knot by equating loyalty to initiative with temptation to sin or madness. Just as the rights of the state imply man's duty to abstain from anti-integrative conduct, so his rights imply the state's duty to abstain from dehumanizing conduct, from making men mere cogs in the political machine.

To submit that the conflict and counterbalancing of loyalties, the claims of freedom and power are again the price that freedom must pay for its realization in the political domain is far from exhausting the problematics of freedom in the domain where coercion rules. Coordination or counterpoise is a mean between radical negation of coercive power and its total acceptance. In saying that feedom for politics' sake must reconcile its claims with those of power to gain admission to political reality, we do not renounce the right to criticize power. Rather, because coercive power is an inevitable element of political life, the right to detect and resist any trespass of the limits of unavoidable coercion must be upheld. But criticism cannot annul reality; the most that it can do is point the way towards a different order of reality which is possible and desirable but not actual.

Power regularizes the rhythm of political life and makes it possible to foresee the results of action within the political domain; thereby, it excludes the element of surprise and caprice from the round of human relationships established within its sphere. Regularity and predictability are secured by the prohibition of violence, a prohibition which cannot be defied with impunity. Since violent abuse of one's fellow, or of society, is a possiblity open to human initiative, the ban on violence, enforced by coercion, is a curtailment or limitation of freedom as initiative. Here, however, freedom faces coercion not as brute force but as an agent of rational regularity and absense of whim. In that capacity, coercive power channels individual intiative into fixed patterns. Men submit to this not only because they have no choice, but also because the may realize that unlimited latitude for initiative is not desirable, and that a limitation of their freedom which prevents them from violently abusing their fellows, or society, is justified. Conceived as a barrier between man and the destructive course of action in which his initiative might possibly explode, coercion is acknowledge not only as an insurmountable obstacle but also as a legitimate bound to freedom.

Not concord but tension is the distinguishing mark of a political reality in which man's freedom has found partial empirical realization. The interaction of freedom and coercive political power does not cancel out the fundamental polarity implicit in the opposition of the two factors. The problem of political freedom is one not of overcoming the tension between the poles but of adjusting and balancing their antithetical claims. It follows that there can be no final solution to the problematics of political freedom; freedom can never be fully or totally realized in the political domain. Yet the same polarity implies the untenability of such theories as conceive of the political domain as so thoroughly steeped in coercion and compulsion that even partial realization of freedom within its bounds is out of the question. Seeing how complex both poles are, and how complex, therefore and even more, their interaction is, the harmonizing and the anarchist hypothesis alike must be rejected as one-sided simplifications of the problem.

XX

The link between the problem of political freedom and the status of the individual in the political domain is evidenced by the questions of toleration and private property. Freedom and toleration are conjoined, for the justification of man's demand to be treated tolerantly is the principle of freedom; to demand toleration is to claim recognition of his right of free thought and conduct within certain limits. The right is recognized because it is conceded that, up to a point, a man is free to act in conformity to his own interpretation of his own freedom. That is why one who feels himself authorized by his freedom to think or act in an unconventional manner may do so within bounds, but, like other modes of political freedom, toleration must pay the price of tension—or counterbalance—for its realization in the political domain. A man cannot claim toleration for his own right to think and act freely without tolerating the right of other men, who neither think nor act as he does, to think and act freely. The duty to take others into consideration is the counterpart of the right to be taken into consideration by them. For the same principle of freedom authorizes the claim for toleration and the positive response to it. Just as the counterbalancing of freedom by freedom is entailed by the political realization of the principle of freedom, so is the counterbalancing of toleration by toleration entailed by the political realization of the principle of toleration.

Just as the realization in the political domain generates tensions and conflicts which must be assimilated but cannot be resolved, so does the realization of toleration. It can be argued, for example, that the claim of toleration collides with the claims of political integration and social cohesion; one objection to tolerating, for instance, religious freedom is that it is likely to dissolve the cohesion of society and state, and that the claims of that cohesion take precedence of the claims of the principle of toleration.

Yet one can say that the tension itself is preferable to resolving it in a way that suppresses one of its poles. Here, as elsewhere, not an exclusive recognition of single claim but ambidextrous and inclusive counterbalancing of conflicting claims would be the only possible procedure safeguarding the principle of freedom; counterbalancing implies, in this case, that the claim for free interpretation and expression of individual freedom be offset by acknowledgement of the limits set to freedom by the demands of socio-political cohesion. Conversely, the right of society and state to defend the cohesion of their collective framework must be checked and balanced by the right of individuals to be treated tolerantly. And if it be argued that to accommodate the claims of toleration can result in the disintegration of socio-political bonds, then one must answer that failure to do so may end in the same way, by alienating men to whom freedom matters from the state's domain and thus enhancing the chasm between actual human beings and the pojected might of the state.

The call for checks and balances is all the more urgent considering that nonrecognition of the claim for toleration and coercive suppression of free speech and action often go hand in hand. One check to arbitrary coercion is the criticism and opposition which it is itself bound to evoke; criticism controlled by the principle of freedom would demand that coercion be used only in situations that cannot be handled otherwise and also caution us against misrepresenting conflicts that might be settled without the use of coercion as if they were susceptible to that means of settlement alone. Our formulation, here, cannot but be in indefinite terms; it is for human beings to determine in what circumstances the use of coercive force is unavoidable and in what it can be avoided. The principle of toleration is broken whether coercive force is wielded to suppress opinions and actions which might have been accommodated or to guarantee recognition of a particular claim for toleration. Coercive toleration is a contradiction in terms. For example, no religious organization can, without self-contradiction, claim that its right to toleration be recognized by political enforcement of its own modes of thought and way of life; a religion tolerated by the state is not a religion supported by it through the twofold sanction of power and law. Furthermore, toleration of a part of the body-politic by the body-politic as a whole by no means involves harnessing the collective power of the whole body-politic to the purpose of meeting the demands or executing the policy of that, or any, part. There is, too, something self-defeating about the religious sector's campaign to make up for its lack of persuasive power (the power of conviction, debate, proof, education) by trying to mobilize coercive power for the dissemination of its truth. So much for what toleration does not imply. Let us now see what it does.

Inherent in the principle of freedom, toleration can be either an intellectual or a moral imperative. It demands recognition of opinions other than one's own, a demand based upon an awareness of the inexhaustibility of man's essence, and of the partialness of any embodiment of that essence, oneself included. To respect my fellow's opinion is to admit the fallibility and partialness of my own; to acknowledge his right to worship in conformity to the articles of his own faith, even though they do not square with mine, is to be conscious that no religious type exhausts the possibilities of religious thought and expression immanent in man's universal essence. As a particular embodiment of those possibilities, any religion has as much right to toleration as my own. The imperative of intellecutal toleration applies to philosophy and science as well. A man respects a speculative or scientific system other than the one to which he adheres, because he realizes that the totality of potential structures of thought is not exhausted in any of its particular embodiments, and he recognizes the right of all embodiments to be "taken into consideration." Recognition of the other's right to choose his own mode of thought or belief is prompted by a measure of uncertainty as to the infallibility or absolute and exclusive validity of one's own.

But the moral imperative of toleration does not reflect only a man's recognition that his fellow's viewpoint may be as valid as his own, each in its partial way, when both are measured against the gamut of possible viewpoints. It implies sometimes acknowledgement not of a viewpoint but of the man who adopts it, which is why the imperative is in this case moral rather than intellectual. Here, toleration is demanded not by the total range of possibly valid viewpoints but by a particular moral principle—whether it be the principle of justice as inhering in the principle of consideration for man as such, or of freedom as upholding his right to choose his own mode of thought, belief, and conduct on his own initiative, as least within certain limits. A man might tolerate a belief which he rejects on intellectual grounds as a superstitition, or a political view which he rejects on those grounds as inadequate or impracticable, because he recognizes not the justification of the view but the right of the man who adopts a belief or entertains a political ideology to be taken into consideration as a man.

Is there, then, a limit to toleration in the intellectual and the moral sense? Does any and every viewpoint have a right to claim our acknowledgement on the gound either of its partial validity or of the principles of freedom, justice, and consideration for man? Judging from recent historical experience, one may maintain that there is a limit to toleration by the principle of consideration for man as such, which demands that we do not tolerate viewpoints that deny membership in the human species to particular members of it. The most blatant example of an intolerable viewpoint of that kind is the racial theory of Nazism, which refused the Jewish people and it descendants a place in the circle of humanity and degraded its members to the level of crude matter which entitles the regime and its supporters to handle them accordingly. There is neither intellectual nor moral justification for a viewpoint which holds that certain human beings are not human beings; there can be no countenancing people who, in the name of a viewpoint, treat certain men and women as if they were potter's clay or just an organic compound. As a matter of principle, Nazism and Nazis are disqualified by their own viewpoint and actions as possible candidates for toleration. A variant of human thought or belief can claim toleration as such. A man can claim toleration for his viewpoint as an expression of his own status as an embodiment of the human essence. But toleration, as consideration, cannot extend beyond the minium limit of consideration for man as such. Make it your decision not to take other human beings into consideration, dedicate yourself to the exclusion of members of man's species from its circle, deny the outcast the right to be taken into consideration as human beings and you demolish the pillars of toleration and rob society of its authority to grant you the toleration which you demand. Society has no authority to tolerate men who deny the humanity of other men. "Tolerate no view or policy which would banish particular human beings from the human circle" is a rule or imperative that ought to regulate political consideration of the problem where the limit to toleration must be drawn. But what, we may be asked, of less extreme viewpoints, such as those that grade human beings according to degrees of humanity in a ladder of superior and inferior types? We should answer that, though these views have not transgressed the ultimate limits of possible toleration, push them a bit, and they will.

XXI

Let us now consider the connection between the political freedom and private property. In its primary sense, freedom is the active expression of the distance between man and his circumstances; that distance is the scene of operation as well as the castle of the individual as individual, so that the grounds of freedom are also those of individuality. Now it is customery to represent private property as the concrete correlate or manifestation of the independent position occupied by man as an individual; it is said to pertain to the essence of individuality. The connection among individuality, freedom, and property has also been conceptual consideration: property has been defined as one of the rights of man, and Hegel defines it as the external sphere of freedom. Its correlation with freedom cannot be accepted without reservation or qualification.

To start with, the concept of property is ambiguous. The term denotes those things which a man has the right to use; its primary meaning is the authority not of ownership but of utilization, even though, strictly speaking, "private property" obviously signifies the right to use that stems from ownership: property-owners are empowered to utilize materials, machinery, financial means, and various processes of production. But that does not always imply authority of ownership. The development of modern economics has led to the emergence of a managerial class invested with the authority to utilize the means of production, to plan how to utilize them, and to carry the plans into effect. This kind of authority is not founded in, or contingent on, that of ownership in the strict, formal-legal, sense, which usually belongs to shareholders devoid of an active part in activating the means of production. At the same time, it is the legal owners who invest management with its authority to use property, and it is they who profit from the use. There is, therefore, justification for employing the term 'private property' in the sense of authority of utilization directly or indirectly dependent upon the authority of ownership: the dependence is indirect when those invested with the authority of utilization are subject to the control of those possessing the authority of ownership; it is direct when both modes of authority are vested in the same persons, that is, when the users are the owners.

May we, then, or may we not, conceive of property—either as ownership or as management—as pertaining to the essence of freedom? Let us first limit the scope of the question by observing that it arises only with reference to such modes of property as have direct influence on the structure of interindividual relationships in the public domain. The problem of the relation between freedom and property affects only such types of property as contribute to areas of the public domain, or perhaps of the public domain as a whole; for example, ownership of the industrial means of production or of banks. In that domain, whether by property one means ownership-authority or managerial-authority is to some extent immaterial. In either case, it implies the control of the means of production by representatives not of the body-social as a whole but of certain individuals or groups whose interests are vested in the activation of those means. In this context, the problem of property is one of the relationship between two modes of freedom: freedom of initiative manifested by those who have the authority to activate and utilize property, and freedom of those who depend upon its activation and utilization.

It has been shown that a counterbalancing of freedom against freedom is essential to the realization of freedom in the political domain. This means that, from the point of view of the principle of freedom, factual authority neither of ownership nor of utilization invests with authority one man's status of initiative, as distinguished from other man's status of dependence. A status of freedom can be justified only by the principle of freedom; only a status that does not violate the freedom of other men, that does not put them in a position of dependence, can claim the authority of a status conforming to that principle. That those who own the means of production, or who have the authority to utilize them, manifest initiative or freedom is clear, but it is no less clear that the dependence of other men is the counterpart of it. Since such a one-sided initiative fails to meet the demands of the principle of freedom as regards the counterbalancing of initiative against intitiative, it is not a legitimate realization of freedom. For that reason, factual ownership of property and factual authority to utilize it, insofar as they contribute to the shaping of interindividual relationships in the public domain, come under criticism. The criticism is grounded in the principle of freedom which is also the principle justifying ownership.

Criticism of property is controlled both by the principles of freedom and of equality understood as a demand for equal freedom or equal initiative for all. It is a question not of analyzing the abstract concepts of intitiative and freedom, but of coming to grips with a concrete situation in the sphere of interhuman relationships and endeavoring, within that sphere, to uphold the right of every man to a certain measure of independence and initiative.

It is argued that the utilization and activation of private property raise the standard of living by adding to the amount of possessions. Yet whether private property conduces to efficient economic development has no bearing on the fundamental issue of whether it is justified in terms of freedom. It might, of course, be objected that man is willing to pay the price of renouncing his relatively independent position within economic and human relationships for the benefit of a higher standard of living. Yet even this argument must allow at least as much freedom as is required by the preference that men would give to the higher standard; only if the choice is not forced upon them is the argument in any sense valid.

But let us suppose that, on their own free initiative, men elect to raise their standard of living and pay a toll for that initiative. Would we not still have to ask whether freedom can find significant social expression where economic initiative is concentrated in a few hands and economic dependence is the lot of the many? Can men be expeced to manifest initiative in other spheres when, in the economic, they are deprived of initiative of their own? If the answer is no, that is, if social initiative is incompatible with far reaching econimic dependence of some and economic initiative of others, than we face the basic problem of how widespread initiative can be housed as a matter of principles in the economic sphere.

The economic sphere lends itself to the same kind of consideration as is given to any other sphere of human activity which supplies the necessities of men's existence. In one major respect, the status of the economic sphere is comparable to the educational. Education is a service offered by the body-social as a whole to all its members, because it is assumed that only through education can men's latent abilities be developed and that citizenship—as interindividual cooperation and as interest and participation in the life of society—can be taught. The same would apply to the economic process, which supplies the diversity of material wants—for example, food, housing, and clothing—requisite to human existence and is sustained by men's concerted economic activities. Only in the economic sphere, and only through the instrumentality of economic activities can the basic physical needs of man be met; and, as society is responsible for satisfying those needs, it is to society as a whole—and not to private ownership and management—that the economic domain belongs; and it is to public service, not to private profit, that the economic process is, or ought to be, subservient.

What is the difference between a service-economy controlled by society and a profit-economy controlled by ownership and/or management? In the first, the economic process is regulated by the represenatives of society at large for the benefit of all the members; in the second, it is regulated by those invested with ownership-authority for the benefit of those invested with use-authority. Service-economy is designed to satisfy the wants of men, profit-economy to staisfy the wants of owners by way of satisfying the wants of men. In modern society, more and more notice is being taken of the idea of public service, but its relevance to the economic domain has yet to gain widespread acknowledgement, although the need to realize it there is among the most urgent needs of our social reality. Society is presently involved in a contradiction between the objective-teleological status of the economic sphere and the ownership-orientated economic ideology which is at odds with the idea of servive. This contradiction will last until a way is found of counterpoising the service-status of the economic sphere and men's legitimate demand for an opportunity to manifest their initiative there as well. Freedom will not be compatible with the economic structure as long as ownership and/or management are the sole channels of initiative in it.

The connection between political freedom and property can be considered from the angle of contemporary historical reality as well. In the Western world, it has become customary to associate the idea of individual privacy with the idea of property in such a way as to present property as though it were an indispensable condition of privacy. Here, again, the problem pertains only to such kinds of property as contribute to the features of interindividual relationships and not to strictly personal property, such as articles of clothing or furniture. Today, owing to the homogeneity of culture, and the appeal of mass media of communication, the private domain of the individual is being confined within ever narrower limits. The greater that encroachment, the more he inclines to regard property as the last refuge of privacy. In actual fact, however, man's ownership of property does not seclude him in his private domain, but attaches him to the public and implicates him in the complex of interhuman relationships. The correlation of property and privacy is, therefore, doubtful. It is obvious that in Asia and Africa a process of economic development capable of accommodating private or individual initiative cannot get under way until the ideas of property and privacy are dissociated; if the abolition of private ownership of the means of production is not accompanied by a rejection of the property-privacy ideology, it is quite possible that privacy itself—as a major manifestation of individual freedom—will find no warrant. Hence the importance of unlinking the two ideas, especially where economic development cannot conceivably be sustained by private initiative but must be fostered by that of the state.

By "privacy" we mean not only the self-enclosure of the individual's personal life and experience but also his distance from, or relative nondetermination by, processes even when he is economically dependent upon them and upon the policies which regulate them. The historical problem involved in the tension between privacy as partial independence of political activity and economic dependence on political planning, policy and processes may be put this way: Can freedom, as a principle of concrete human reality, be so expressed as to guarantee dissociation of the idea of privacy from the idea or ideology of private property?

XXII

To be precise, political freedom means individual freedom from excessive determination either by other individals or by the political power of the state, the liberty to act on one's own inititiative at least within certain limits. The term is, however, sometimes employed to denote the freedom of the body-politic or of the state, and it is that meaning which will now be examined. The state's freedom of initiative is reflected in its legislative authority and in its sovereignty or power to enforce the laws which it makes. Thus regarded, it may be conceived as analogous to the initiative of the individual as reflected in his capacity to make his own decisions and act upon them. But, unlike the status of the individual as a free agent, that of the state is not a given fact: the state's existence is neither inedpendent of, nor completely sundered from, the directedness and endeavors of human beings towards its sustenance. Considering, then, this status of the state, does it make sense to attribute to its free agency in general and legislative initiative in particular? Surely one cannot ignore its lack of a self-sustaining status, when one employs the term 'political freedom' in the sense of the sovereignty of a state.

The paradox of that attribution of freedom to the state is justified by the very fact that it does not occupy a completely objective status. Were it to occupy such a status and be entirely detached from the perpetual process of integration and from the concrete human agents who sustain that process, were its status as a human creation analogous to that of man's artistic or literary creations, it would be as senseless to speak of its freedom as it is to speak of the freedom of a painting or a book. The statement "A creative artist is free" makes sense, but "An artistic creation is free" does not, because a finished work of art is a self-contained object which can, at most, inspire creation in a subject; it can be studied, or handled, or cared for. But to say "A state is free" makes sense because, although a human creation, the state is never transformed into an object or thing; it is an emanation of men's togetherness invested also with their capacity of free agency. Its freedom may accordingly be defined as a freedom of concerted human activity directed towards integration. If its individual creators were not free, it would not be free either. The freedom of the state consists in the power of decision and action made manifest in and through such state activities as legislation, decrees, signing of treaties, and establishment of international relations. In this one respect, it is analogous to the freedom of the individual, which, as we noted, it likewise a reservoir of potentiality. But the analogy must not be labored, for, unlike the potentiality of individual freedom, which always holds an unrealized surplus of possibilities, the potentiality of state-freedom is equal to its actuality, that is, to the sum total of acts in which the state makes its sovereignty manifest. If the state did not act, it would not exist; if it did not make decisions, it would not be free. A state can make decisions only through the agency of its institutions and, ultimately, the agency and initiative of its individual members. A free state is, accordingly, one sustained in freedom by those members, who grant it the authority of free agency within the sphere of their togetherness.

XXIII

The points of similarity and difference between the modes of expression of the freedom of the state and of the individual must be brought under comparative analysis, controlled by the distinctions which we drew between freedom from politics, freedom within politics, and freedom for politics' sake. That the distinctions apply to the political domain, regarded from the individual's point of view, has been shown. Whether or not they can be applied to the political domain from the state's point of view is now for consideration. With regard to the state, freedom from politics means acknowledgement of the limits of the political domain by the body-politic; the principle of freedom, in that sense, demands acknowledgement by the body-politic of the right possessed by the individuals to whom it owes its existence to maintain apolitical spheres and modes of activity subordinate to apolitical types of logic and not subordinate to the logic of the political domain. This does not mean that apolitical activities must be acknowledged by the body-politic within the limits of its own public domain, for the plain reason that being a projection of the togetherness of men the body-politic does not and cannot conduct intellectual activities, for example. One cannot, therefore, expect the political crystallization of the social domain to allow latitude for unbridled apolitical activity within the political. If the right to sustain a multicolored diversity of activities is to be respected, men must stand up for it by preserving their own diversity and demanding recognition of it by the body-politic. Even from the angle of the state, freedom from politics is the freedom given to individuals to uphold their diversity in the political domain of interpretations of integration; in interstate relationships, freedom within politics demands that no state seek to impose upon another the logic and structure of its own mode of togetherness.

Freedom for politics' sake, too, can be applied to the state. As concerns the individual, it means the theoretical and practical political initiative which individuals manifest in activities ranging from the integrative activity which makes the political domain to the moulding of public opinion. As concerns the state, it is manifest, for example, in acts of decision, adoption of policy, and legislation; legislation, then, is to the body-politic what voting is to individuals, and it may be said that, in the sense of political initiative, freedom of the state and of the individual dovetail. Freedom for politics' sake, or political initiative, is, we observed, the precondition not only of the constitution but also of the shaping of the political order. More than that, it stands in a symmetrical relationship between the state—as regulator of its activities on its own initiative—and its individual members, who, likewise on their own initiative, shape the form and regulate the functions of the political order.

The reciprocity and interaction of the individual and the collective shaping-initiative always render it possible that the two will collide. There is no guarantee that the initiative shown by individuals within the ambit of collective cohesion will sustain that cohesion in actual fact, not even when individual men of initiative are under the impression that their spontaneous actions are orientated to its sustenance. Individual economic initiative is a case in point: the activities sponsored by it may very well create inter-individual division and, consequently, result in the slackening of collective ties. At the same time, the said individuals may imagine that they contribute to collective cohesion because they foster and accelerate the economic development of the body-politic, amplify its store of possessions, and so forth. The conception of the political domain as the sphere of actual collectivity may, in that case, conceivably clash with the conception of it as the field of economic development. This does not necessarily imply that freedom is here manifested only by one party—say, the men of economic initiative—whereas the other—the proponents of collective cohesion—thwarts it. What it does imply is that we are confronted with a collision between two interpretations of freedom, and with the consequent need to counterbalance their respective claims.

That the symmetrical relation between the political initiative of the state and of its individual members is a possible source of tension and conflict is demonstrable from another aspect: a decision by the state to sustain collective cohesion could well conflict with the decision of its individual members to uphold their right to manifest critical detachment from it or loyalty to a particular church. Also, it would be erroneous to identify the state's decision to sustain the freedom of the body-politic with the decision of the individuals constituting it. Because of its projective status as men's creation, the state is partly, though not entirely, divorced from its creators, and its decisions cannot be regarded as a faithful reflection of theirs. The initiative of the body-politic cannot be identified with that of its individual members because no so-called decision of the body-politic is made *by* the body-politic; every one of its decisions is made *in its name*; every act of decision said to reflect the initiative of the body-politic actually reflects that of the particular individuals who represent it. Only an individual can act directly, namely, without representation, for only individuals are concrete beings who come into direct contact with the actual world. The distance between the freedoms of individuals and of the body-politic cannot be bridged even by a referendum, since decision by it divides individual human beings—at least in practice—into groups with diverse viewpoints and deciding in diverse directions. Thus, although it can create majority representation of the body-politic, a referendum cannot cancel representation of the whole by one of its parts. The existence of institutionalized moulds such as legislative assemblies and of institutionalized arrangements such as referendums bears witness to the gap between the ways of state and individual initiative.

Here is further evidence that the function of freedom in the political domain is to uphold diversification and multiplication of both isolated individual standpoints and partial forms of togetherness, as distinguished from the comprehensive form of the state within the domain itself. Multiplicity, diversity, conflict of viewpoints within a single sphere, structural and teleological differences among different spheres, are features of a political reality. The complexity of the problematics of political freedom is due not only to the multiple modes of freedom-realization possible on a single plane of human reality but also to the multiple planes of relationship—for example, the planes of interindividual relations, individual—state relations, and interstate relations—on which the many facets of freedom find concrete expression. This diversification does not make for complete collective cohesion, but neither does it make for complete atomic disolution. Riddled with tensions, conflicts, and counterbalancing of demands, a reality of this kind presents a relational structure that lends itself to an analysis, a structure conforming to the logic of the principle of freedom.[4]

One mode of counterbalancing the political initiatives of the body-politic and of its individual members is illustrated by the fact of political majority and by the principle of majority decision upon which it is based. Only where latitude is left for individual political initiative do we find a political majority; a totalitarian state cannot assimilate the principle of partial agreement among the greater number of its individual members, because, having arrogated to itself a comprehensive status, it professes to be based upon unanimous agreement and strains every coercive channel to create unanimity by suppression. Policies adopted by majority decision come to have the status of policies adopted by decision of the body-politic as a whole, which means that, as expressing the collective cohesion of the body-politic, a majority can shape the body-politic in the image of the policies which it has agreed upon by following requisite courses of action. But, just as there is an intrinsic limit to toleration, so there is to majority action, one set by the acts of initiative from which the majority sprang; which means that every majority action must be accompanied by recognition of its source, that is, by acknowledgement of individual initiative orientated towards interindividual togetherness. The majority can be expected, or required, to abide by the political-moral imperative always to act in such a way as to allow latitude for the creation of a majority in the next stage of the political process, namely, to acknowledge, in practice as in principle, the right of individuals to manifest their political initiative by transcending the majority of the present stage as a step towards the majority of the coming one. No majority is authorized to suppress the initiative which gave rise to it or may arrest the perpetual process whereby new majorities may, and perhaps ought to, be brought into being; freedom of initiative in an unpredictable and indeterminable direction is the limit of majority action. Majority action is bounded by the open horizon of majorities yet unborn.

In another way, its limits can be shown to be fixed by the merely representative status of the majority vis-a-vis the body-politic as a whole.

It must be accompanied by the consciousness that no particular majority is a full expression of that total togetherness of which, by definition, it falls short. To say this, to say that a majority takes note of its position as an empirical product of agreement among particular individuals who have chosen to interpret their togetherness in a particular way and seek to shape the body-politic conformably, is to say that it has recognized the limits of its representative status. And if a majority does that, it necessarily allows latitude for interpretations of togetherness other then its own and, consequently, for other meetings grounds, still to be prepared, where other individuals might come together in the subsequent political stage to form another expression of togetherness.

Only where there is a gap between the status of togetherness and of reprentation can this problem arise; the authority of majority decision and action and its intrinsic limits are an aspect of the problematics of political freedom. It is connected with the gulf that separates men's political aim of crystallizing and shaping their togetherness from the empirical forms which the aim assumes and which may well vary in content and composition alike. Orientation towards togetherness produces a point of enounter uniting many individuals who together aim at togetherness. That point occupies a representative status in relation both to the individuals united and to the togetherness at which they aim. When, however, the end is not collective cohesion to be created by collective endeavor but a given object to be known by individual endeavor, as is the case with intellectual activity, there is neither room nor reason to air the problem of representation, its status and its limits; the knower does not occupy a representative status with respect to the object which he aims at knowing or with respect to other knowing individuals. Because there can be no question of representation in the spheres of such apolitical activities as intellectual inquiry or artistic creation, the individual is able to occupy an autonomous status within limits of these activities.

Originating, as it does, in the political initiative of the individuals by whom it is created, and representing the political initiative of the body-politic for which it stands, a majority can be required to regulate its activities in conformity to the principle of freedom. The authority of majority representation and of majority administration of public or collective affairs is derived from the principle of freedom. This has direct bearing upon one of the problems of present-day political reality, namely, the situation prevailing where political orders have been constituted by a process of national self-liberation from colonial dominion. To justify their anticolonial reaction, these nations argued that there was no other way of making and shaping their togetherness but in a political structure of their own choosing and creation. The crux, however, is this: Only states constituted from below and really reflecting the collective, togetherness-orientated, political initiative of their members concretely express freedom for politics' sake or as political initiative. But many of the states that emerged in self-liberation from colonialism have been constituted, by and large, not from below but from above, and so reflect the political initiative not of the majority but of a minority endowed with that initiative and with leadership. If they were true to their source, to desire to create autonomous expressions of togetherness, if they were loyal to the original end and justification of their act of throwing off an alien yoke, they should have dedicated themselves to the development and encouragement of their members' powers of political initiative. The primary political and human end which ought to be pursued by them is the creation of modes of political life sustained by concerted initiative of individuals. In actual fact, few endeavors in that direction have been made. The leaders of the self-emancipating peoples are not working always to radiate or diffuse political initiative from the center to wider circles. More often than not, political initiative is monopolized by the instigators of the initial anticolonial turn. It will not do to contend that there can be no alternative in view of the population's lack of political initiative. For that, exactly, is the point; the issue is the need to develop the capacity and inculcate the habit of political initiative. Of course, if anticolonial reaction culminates in the establishment of totalitarian regimes, there can be no paving the way to widespread political initiative and majority representation of togetherness; it seems that one of the main causes for the failure to encourage initiative in the political domain, to create political togetherness, is an intent to direct that reaction towards economic development rather than towards the constitution of political togetherness.

The realize the aim of economic development in developing countries, what is apparently required is not diffusion of political initiative and widespread political participation but centralized economic planning under specialized guidance and centralized investment of funds controlled by the central government. But anticolonial reaction was not originally directed towards economic development, simply because, from that point of view, it is very often more profitable to stay within a colonial framework and maintain links with the metropolitan country. This applies especially to areas which have neither the financial means nor the specialized knowledge necessitated by the process of economic advancement and will, therefore, once decolonialized, be driven to seek financial support and specialized guidance elsewhere. A difference ensues, therefore, between anticolonialist trends aiming at self-reliant togetherness and the end of economic development; and it not only blocks the path of possible cultivation of togetherness sustained but actually sponsors a switch in the direction of totalitarian regimes, orientated towards economic development, which, as a matter of fact, are not interested in widespread political initiative.

It might help, at this point, to recall the conclusions of our analysis of the relationship between freedom and property. We found that a profit-economy based upon private property could not absorb far-flung economic enterprise and concluded that the process of economic development ought to be controlled by an ideology of service. Like education or public health, economics is a service provided by society as a whole for the benefit of all its members. There is, however, a discrepancy between economics as a public service and education or health services. In the economic sphere, men serve themselves, so to speak, and share in the creation of the service from which they benefit; in the sphere of public health or education, there is a clear-cut distinction between the public servants (the doctor or the teacher) and the public served (the patients or the pupils). Not every service-economy was necessarily conducive to the cultivation of far-flung economic enterprise, and where economic services are administered by specialists, we still find initiative monopolized by a select few and the many relegated to a position of dependence.

It is possible to launch a process of economic development on the initiative of specialists and under their guidance. But the possibility of widespread lack of economic initiative hardly implies the inevitability of widespread lack of its political counterpart. The argument that economic development necessarily represses widespread economic initiative because it demands specialized knowledge is untenable in the political sphere, because the initiative essential for political life does not do that. Political initiative calls for consciousness of togetherness and orientation towards it, and neither is given automatically; they must be cultivated, encouraged, and fostered. But it does not at all follow from the empirical fact that people are unconscious of their togetherness that the unconsciousness is incurable.

A sense of togetherness can be inculcated and learned, not necessarily by formal education but from political and historical experience. How did the leaders of the anticolonial reaction come to recognize that colonialism was wrong as being a bar to independent expression of their peoples' togetherness, if not from the lesson of the experience of fellow-men in America and Europe? And if they could learn from that experience, their compatriots can benefit from theirs. Negatively, to instill a sense of togetherness, it is essential to remove the fallacious correlation of political initiative with economic initiative in the sense of private enterprise. The need to reveal how mistaken it is to correlate a lack of economic initiative with an irremediable lack of political initiative is one of the most pressing requirements of contemporary politics from the point of view of the principle of freedom.

The number of empirical forms in which the principle of freedom can find legitimate expression is practically unlimited, but the condition of legitimacy is that a form be not empty of that content which is unchanged in all the variety of its expressions. The empirical form must be shaped in the image of the transempirical content, not the other way round. The transempirical content of freedom resists manipulation by the empirical moulds in which it is purportedly cast, just as it refuses to rubber-stamp empirical forms which profess to realize freedom while in actual fact they do not. The theory and practice of Bolshevism are an excuse for deliberate failure to create real human togetherness in the political sphere, that mode of togetherness sustained by real human beings who manifest political initiative. Being based upon the notion tht a prerequisite of political initiative is specialized knowledge of history and its processes, Bolshevist politics permits lip-service to social togetherness where actual togetherness is minimal. By divorcing the end of politics from the end of constituting true togetherness, this way of thinking justifies a deliberate policy of avoiding creation of concrete togetherness in the simple and elementary sense of spontaneous and conscious concert of concrete individuals. Instead, Bolshevism peddles a mystification of togetherness under the guise of an *avant-garde* composed of men who have initiated into the knowledge of good and evil in matters pertaining to social togetherness. As for the men who make up that togetherness, their opinion as to what is and what is not good for their concert need not be consulted or taken into account by the men who know. In the sphere of togetherness, Bolshevism canvasses the belief that the general will of society is represented by a chosen elite, and that there is not need, therefore, to arrange an encounter between the general will and the particular wills of concrete human beings; neither the constitution nor the shaping of the state calls for the encounter.

If this theory and practice are to be rejected, an alternative theory must be formulated and upheld. It would represent the state as owing its very existence to the initiative of its individual members. It would show that initiative can and does orientate itself towards togetherness, and thus lay bare the Bolshevist fallacy of positing a necessary contradiction between individual decision and collective togetherness. It would deny the Bolshevist implicit hypothesis that individual will or desire is innately antisocial and that, therefore, the individual will of the many must be overcome by the powerful prompting of the initiating few whose will embodies the general and who *eo facto* seek that which is good for social togetherness.[5] There can be no true togetherness where voluntary togetherness on the plane of concrete individuals is excluded *ex hypothesi*. The idea of voluntary political togetherness not just with room for freedom but actually sustained by the initiative of real individuals can be vindicated only by a political philosophy which founds its analysis of the problematics of political freedom on a synoptic survey of human reality and on a philosophical exploration of man's position in the world.[6]

NOTES

1. See the present author's *Spirit and Man*, Martinus Nijhoff, The Hague 1963.

2. Encyklopädie der philosophischen Wissenschaften, § 18 (Lasson's edition, Meiner; Leipzig 1920, p. 50).

3. *Metaphysics*, 982 B.

4. Cf. I. Berlin, *Two Concepts of Liberty*, Clarendon Press, Oxford 1958.

5. For a further exposition, see the chapter on "The Political Regime against Human Existence," in the author's book *On the Human Subject—Studies in The Phenomenology of Ethics and Politics*, Charles C. Thomas, Springfield, Ill. 1966.

6. Rawls' theory of justice has its bearing on the principles of freedom and equality as well. This is owing not only to the presence of the Kantian element— mentioned before—in that theory but also to the significance of the aspect of contract and human reasonableness.

CHAPTER NINE

Of Equality

I

Our task now is to analyze the principle of equality and its relation to political reality. In the light of its connection with the principles of sociopolitical conduct, that principle may be characterized as a complement of the principle of justice, which demands that man be taken into consideration; the principle of equality demands that he be taken into consideration as equal to his fellowman. The nexus between equality and freedom is this: The principle of freedom insists that the status of man in general be sustained in political reality; the principle of equality expresses the postulate that concrete human beings in whom freedom is embodied should be considered as each other's equals.

II

We should first point to a difference between the positions of the principles of equality and freedom. The premise of our analysis of freedom was its factuality as the attribute of man. Being a fact, freedom is at the same time an empirical one. Equality, unlike freedom, is not—and cannot be—a given attribute of man. It denotes an evaluative perspective by reference to which men measure each other in their mutual relationships. This implies that its normative status rests on other foundations than freedom's. It would be wrong to maintain that equality is a norm being a source of man's position, in the sense that freedom is. The affirmation that "freedom is an imperative which must be conformed to because men are free" is valid, but substitute "equality" for "freedom", "equal" for "free," and it is not. The most that one can justifiably affirm of equality is that it is a norm and not a given source. The statement that "factual man is equal" is invalid, if only because it is incomplete; for its validity, one must specify, saying that "factual man is equal to his fellow," and this specification necessarily involves an exploration of the nature and norm of interhuman relationships. Again, the statement: "factual man is free" may be considered, to say the least, as a valid statement.

III

There is another point of difference between freedom and equality. Even though, as the revelation of man's distance from his circumstances, freedom can also be conceived as an attribute of interhuman relations insofar as the existence of other human beings comes under the heading of "circumstances." But equality cannot possibly be regarded as pertaining to a single individual, since it is, by definition, a multitermed relationship and, as such, confined to the sphere of interindividual relations. The question of equality does not arise with regard to the relations between tall and short persons, parents and children, adults and minors, and the like; equality pertains to the fundamental—or so considered—relationship of human togetherness or collectiveness, irrespective of people's age, position, or function.

Against the background of the difference, between freedom as an attribute and equality as an evaluative of prescriptive norm, the relationship between the two may be thus described: Upon the factual freedom of every man is founded the evaluation of interhuman relationships which affirms that men are equal; no fact whatever is evaluated by the norm of equality, but the fact of freedom in the primary sense of that concept. Freedom must be taken as the foundation of equality, and not contrariwise, for it is a mode of existence and conduct, whereas equality is a mode of evaluation leading to conduct. In point of historical fact, however, equality has been taken as a warrant of freedom, meaning that freedom has been claimed in the name of equality by men who felt that they deserved to occupy the same status of freedom as was occupied in actual fact by certain other men. The evaluation of men as equal is founded upon the fact that men are, or can be, free, provided that they are granted the prerequisite conditions of freedom. The emancipation of the slaves was, indeed, governed by the principle of equality, but equality was held to be warranted by the preexistent fact of freedom; in actual fact—it was reasoned—even slaves are free, and it is only that their freedom is latent or hidden from view. Similarly, extension of the franchise to all classes was demanded in the name of the principle of equality, but the fundamental argument was that the right to vote, as manifesting the freedom of some men, ought to be granted to others, too. In both instances, the demand for equality was justified by the fact—or grounded in the fact—of freedom either as existing from the outset or as to be brought into existence by the elimination of inequality.

IV

There is still another approach possible. Freedom is but the counterpart of the distance between man and his circumstances; it is, so to speak, this distance in action, and so entails a motion of removal from the circumstances, and of nonsubmergence in them. Movement in the positive direction of regulating, shaping, and intervening in the circumstances complements, and does not eliminate, the negative movement in the reverse direction: Man sustains his distance from his circumstances from the vantage point of belonging to them, and moves towards them from the vantage point of removal. Equality, however, does not imply removal from the circumstances or, for that matter, any kind of removal. If anything, it implies precise relatedness to the other, the vantage point from which man recognizes that between himself and his fellow there is a relationship of equality. If equality is sustained, then it is as a result not of man's reflection upon himself as an individual, or by virtue of the conditions conducive to such reflection, but of men's mutual endeavors to approach one another and their evaluation of one another by reference to the abstract standard of equality. To sustain equality, men must compare themselves to their fellows in terms not of those qualities wherein they differ, but of those which they share.

Empirically, every individual differs from every other. But equality pertains to an appraisal of men not *in terms of* their diversity but *in spite of* it. There are, accordingly, two analytical reasons why freedom had to be considered before the problem of equality could be discussed: one is that equality might be conceived as grounded upon the interindividual diversity which freedom entails; the other—mentioned before—is that freedom is a fact, while equality is a mode of evaluation and a norm of prescription—and fact precedes evaluation and prescription.

It is in the tension between man's given standpoint of removal and the end of sustaining human collectivity that the problems pertaining to equality emerge. Equality is not, and cannot be, a fact that follows from a comparison of human beings to each other. It is a norm, and this can be demonstrated by what we would term a deduction, whose method consists in tracing the links among the principles of equality, freedom, and justice, and whose objective is to show that freedom is the foundation of the norm of equality while justice is the motivation of conduct in conformity to that norm.

To the question of what is implied by asserting that freedom is the foundation of the norm of equality, the answer may be given that freedom characterizes the factual conduct of every man in his individuality. All men being free agents—a fact made manifest in their mutual relations—among other things, they share, as individuals, a certain typical, general characteristic, and from that point of view individuals may be compared to each other. Freedom is thus the common attribute of all individuals and the exclusive attribute of none. In realization, to be sure, it does not go beyond the confines of the individual sphere in which it is realized; the very fact that it is realized in mutually exclusive individual domains introduces diversification into human reality. This diversity cannot nullify the fact that freedom is not the exclusive birthright of any one individual but a right to be shared by all, or can it alter the conclusion that, under comparison from the viewpoint of freedom, men can be evaluated as equal. It is in terms not of the material aspects of the spheres wherein they realize their freedom that they are so appraised, but in terms of their status in relation to the realm of realization. To lay down that on measurement by their relation to their experience and not by its content men emerge as equal is to take the first step in the deduction of the principle of equality. At the same time it is to exclude such specific matters of content as abilities, experiences, activities, professions, and social standings from the universe of discourse.

The connection between freedom and equality can be illuminated in another facet by reverting to the internal and essential relation between freedom and understanding which was discussed previously. Just as understanding is the ultimate fortress of freedom, so understanding is the ultimate characteristic which all human beings share. Hence it may be said that, as beings endowed with understanding, all men are equal. Men do, of course, differ in terms of the content, range, and degree of their understanding. But underlying these differences of content, range, and degree is the typical attribute of understanding whereof all men partake in common.

By affirming a connection between the principle of equality and the attribute of freedom, we underline the importance of this quality and give it priority over the secondary or derivative qualities by whose virtue men differ from each other. The principle of equality demands that we regard certain human characteristics as secondary and others as primary or that we look upon the diversification-breeding course of reality as one that cannot eradicate the traits common to all. Hence it occupies a normative status, which forbids overestimation of empirical diversity or demands regulative authority—one the empirical plane of human reality, diversified though it may be—for the primordial, typical, and collective. The primary direction of the principle of equality is to preclude a division of the human species on the basis of an exaggeration of the empirical differences between men, or, more specifically, to prevent us from setting too high a value upon the hierarchical stratification of humanity. Freedom finds realization at the horizontal pole of human diversification. Equality serves to obviate the translation of vertical diversity of degree into decisive diversity of value or importance at that pole.

Deduction of the principle may be carried a step further here by tracing the link between it and the principle of justice. As we have seen, the principle of justice is integral to the principle of consideration for man as such. Its purpose is to regulate empirical reality in such a way as to engender concrete expressions of the consideration that men show each other because they evaluate themselves and their fellows as men. Thus understood, it is clearly linked with the principle of equality. For both assert the right of all men to be taken into consideration and demand that men's evaluation of themselves and others as men shall find empirical expressions.

Equality, however, specifies the direction to be taken by conduct in conformity to the principle of consideration for man; men's right to be taken into consideration by their fellows is realizable only if there is equal consideration for all. Thus the principle of equality is, at once, activated by the principle of justice and by a further specification of it demanding equal justice for all. Take the concrete example of the formal or juridical demand for equality before the law: this is tantamount to demanding that, in terms of their situation, equals be taken into consideration as equals or nonequals. From the viewpoint of justice and equality alike, it is, therefore, imperative that there be no discrimination among equals, or among nonequals. Hence the ultimate foundation of justice and equality is the awareness that all men are but partial embodiments of the idea of man.

V

Our premise here is that each and every man is but a partial realization of the total reservoir of human potentiality, a reservoir which is "the idea of man." Within the possible range of every man's experience there lies but a limited area of the universe. Many factors make for this limitation— for example, the finite life-span of the individual, the minute fragment of the social and natural panorama open to his view, and so forth. No one man's actual experience can encompass the sum total of that undergone by past generations or, even if he be endowed with the acute sensibilities and highly developed faculties of a great poet, possibly exhaust the opportunities afforded to human beings on the fertile plane of experience. No concrete human position can claim to be adequately representative of the comprehensive experience of mankind.

There are, besides, the bounds of possible understanding and of possible concrete experience. Understanding is bounded both because it is no substitute for experience directly undergone, and because the range of experience open to its contemplation depends upon the data made available to it. Thus there is a gulf between my fellow's actual experience and my understanding of it, and equally it is impossible for me to understand the unborn experiences of future generations. The bounds of possible experience are manifest in, for example, the limited number of relations in which one man can stand towards another or of the economic roles which he can possibly play. Thus if A is B's father, then he is not his child, or, if C is a coal miner, he is not a tailor. Thus man's actual activity in the world is as limited or partial as his cognitive experience of the world. And, in the understanding which accompanies his activity, no man can possibly embrace the sum total of human activities, their import for the agents who sustain them, their repercussions beyond their own spheres, and their relations with other activities. In every man, and through his agency, the reservoir of human capacity is conducted from potentiality into actuality, given determinate form, interlaced in the context of reality, and crystallized in particular human relations. As they are only partial realizations of the idea of man, together with men's actual experiences and activities goes the consciousness of partialness: men are aware of their membership in humanity and of their restricted share in the pool of human potentiality.

The fact that no individual is a complete realization of the universal human capacity is the ultimate source of our acknowledgement of the principle or norm of equality. That norm requires us to disregard the diversification of realization and concentrate upon consciousness of a communion in the comprehensive idea of man. This concept of equality is neither logical nor mathematical. Here, there is no applying Leibniz's definition of equality as a situation in which one variable may be substituted for another without affecting the truth-value of the relationship; for it is a fact that in terms of their experiences, abilities, activities, and so on, men differ from each other. These differences are not denied by the norm of equality; as a norm, equality neither implies the possibility nor entails the necessity of substituting one man for another without affecting the truth-value of the relationship. What it does entail is acknowledgement that men's empirical differences are themselves the product related to a more fundamental fact—that men share in common in the comprehensive potentiality of humanity. That acknowledgement involves an evaluation of men's differences as occupying a secondary status where humankind's comprehensive potentiality is concerned. What is more, the principle of equality expressly sets a higher value upon a common sphere than upon diversity or diversification.

To the assumption that equality is not a fact but a norm, we can now add that, as a norm, it is expressed in demands made by men upon their fellows to be evaluated as equal. No man can make that demand without assuming that equality exists; any demand that I make of my fellow presupposes that he will understand it and will understand me as an understanding creature. No matter, then, how diverse may be the contents, degree, and range of our understanding, the diversity cannot eliminate the fundamental fact that we are all understanding beings, and in that fact the authority of the norm of equality inheres. To present the norm as a demand, to understand the demand (and even rejected demands presuppose understanding) is to recognize the existence of a typical attribute common to all human beings, their empirical diversification not withstanding.

When we say that the principle of equality requires us to refrain from regarding any actual embodiment of the comprehensive human essence as exhaustive, we imply that equality demands that we do not set so high a value upon men's differences as to efface their common essence. In relation to men's empirical diversification, the common human essence occupies the position of an abstraction. In demanding regulative authority for that essence, the principle of equality upholds the bearing of the abstract upon the empirical plane of human relations. When we give that principle the authority of a norm, the abstract is assigned the role of a principle that regulates interhuman encounter on the socio-political plane. The underlying concrete problem of equality, which faces us here, is this: How can the transempirical fact of the participation of each individual man in the common human essence be expressed on the empirical plane where the differences between men are patent? It might be argued—and it was argued—that equality on the transempirical plane is not incompatible with ostensible differences on the empirical, or, in traditional wording, that the cosmic or religious equality enjoyed by men as created in the image of God carries no empirical implications. But once we ordain the normative status of equality, we expressly seek to shape the empirical plane of human reality in the image of the comprehensive human essence, meaning that, as a norm, equality is not a cognitive principle controlling our assessment of things as they are but a practical one orientated towards realizing what ought to be. Equality demands a translation of the abstract into concrete expressions.

VI

How does the principle of equality control the planning and construction of human situations within a sphere characterized by diverse and diversifying ones? The simplest manifestation of the trend towards the typical on the empirical plane is the fact that the diversity of empirical human situations lends itself to classification; examples are such headings as "youth," "laborers," "white-collar workers," "refugees", "emigrants," and "disabled veterans," each denoting a typical situation that calls for a specific mode of conduct on our part. The principle of justice requires us to show such consideration for men as is called for by their concrete situation as one or other of these types. The principle of equality requires us to treat men in conformity to the requirements of their situations, the assumption being that each situation features typical characteristics; such equality might be called relative.

Two modes of diversity must be disregarded in our schematic classification, namely: that of individuals, youngsters, for instance, grouped together under the single heading "youth," and that of additional types exemplified by certain members of the group, which excludes additional types not falling under the given heading. Thus a youngster can be characterized by acute sensitivity to his environment, or musical talent, or the lack of artistic gifts; the principle of equality demands that we disentangle the diverse threads interwoven in the situation of, let us say, a youth who is a candidate for consideration, by seeking further typical groups to which he belongs, the group of musically gifted youngsters, for example.

This dovetailing of divergent types in the situation of a given individual complicates the process of equality-realization: one mode of conduct is called for by the principle of equality when it is applied to the typical situation of youngsters—such as conduct designed to prevent exploitation of child labor or to guarantee universal elementary education—another when it is applied to the typical situation of musically gifted youngsters—such as conduct designed to foster the development of their gifts or grant them facilities not available to other youngsters. In conformity to the principle of equal consideration for all, we try to meet the requirements of a particular typical situation, but it is also in keeping with the principle of equality to grant the individual equal consideration as a member of additional typical groups. As regards each typical group, the principle of justice calls for orientation towards equality, but the dovetailing of which we have just spoken is likely to give a person who belongs to more than one group an advantage over a person who belongs to fewer, as when a musically gifted youngster is given a greater measure of consideration than one not so endowed, implying that, in certain cases, an allotment of special consideration to some can result from the principle of showing equal consideration for all.

Owing to the dialectics of equality-realization, each inroad of this principle into the empirical realm of diversity calls for further endeavors to create typical situations. If we maintain the right of every musical youngster to facilities fostering the development of his talent, then we should give all youngsters an equal opportunity to be examined with a view to determining whether or not they are similarly gifted. The principle of equality forbids us to take the lack of a particular gift for granted and assume that it is unnecessary to give heed to its possible existence when we settle the kind of consideration that a particular person deserves. Our conduct should show all human beings the same consideration as is shown to the members of the diverse typical groups included as subtypes in the comprehensive type of humanity. In somewhat abstract terms, the principle of equality enjoins that we act in such a way as to make mankind at large a diffuse realization of man's comprehensive essence.

VII

The quest for the typical which the principle of equality entails as a norm of the socio-political encounter between men is also manifested in the attempts to establish patterns of human conduct. Just as schematic classification of diverse human beings impels us to disregard diversity and focus on the typical, so schematic classification of human deeds impels us to disregard the diversity of the agents whose actions come under a particular heading. For example, legal procedure, in conformity to the principle of equality, determines the typical distinguishing marks of a criminal offence and not the character and situation of the offender: if a person is brought before the court because he has inflicted an injury upon another person or upon society, consideration is given to the deed done, and not to the doer or his role in society. The legal code calls for abstraction from the empirical situation and concentration upon the typical properties of the deed. Here the quest for the typical is articulated in such rules as equality before the law, or nondiscrimination in execution of the law, or evaluation of equals as equal and of unequals as unequal. In our example, this means that in judging an injury-inflicting deed, our procedure must be controlled by a conception of it as a typical case. But when we pass sentence upon the doer, the principle of equality permits us to take his circumstances into consideration, for, although not covered by the type illustrated by our case, they are covered by other—for example, psychological or social—typical patterns or schemes.

The pursuit of the typical in kinds of human conduct represents a more advanced stage of formalization or abstraction than the quest for the typical group to which individuals belong, for that is a cross-section of concrete human beings, whereas the typical case is a subdivision in the classification of deeds, not of their doers. But, in both instances, the principle of equality calls for nondiscrimination: we must treat the individual members of a specific human group without discrimination, and likewise the cases exemplifying a typical mode of human conduct. The principle holds all discrimination to be unjustified. The only possible justification for unequal judgment passed upon equal cases is the further demand implicit in the principle, namely, that we take into consideration further types, exemplified not by the deed but by the doer. Equality insists that in pronouncing sentence the court take into account not only the type of human conduct exemplified by the deed but also the type of the state of mind exemplified by the doer. In overlooking individual differences, we proceed on the assumption that this essence, as common, cannot be realized in so thoroughgoing a diffusion as to preclude the possibility of establishing types or schematic patterns, whether of men or of their modes of conduct. Asserting that the typical is closer to the essence than is the individual, the principle of equality obliges us to seek codes of conduct within the limits of the typical, understood as representing the common. The principle of justice demands that we take man's concrete situation into consideration because as we encounter him we ought do so, while the principle of equality demands that we never be led by that specific consideration into neglecting the features or characteristics which he shares with other men.

VIII

The quest for the typical in the realization of equality on the plane of empirical diversity may appear at an even more advanced stage of abstraction in such abstract and general ideas as "All men are equal" or "Men were created equal"; it is their name that equality before the law is demanded. This aspect of the norm might be described as deliberately *constituted* equality, pertaining neither to typical groups of human beings nor to typical instances or cases of human conduct, but to typical conditions created by the law itself in keeping with a decision to give all men equal legal consideration. In this sense, the principle of equality lays down the responsibilities, rights, and duties of every man. These designations might be described — in scholastic terms — as *presumptive*, that is, as based upon the presumption that men are equal according to the law which defines them as such. This postulate is patently the expression of a more advanced stage of abstraction than where we abstract from the differences of persons to focus upon their typical situation. Now, we abstract from men's diverse situations to focus upon the abstract relation between them and the abstract law. The status of each and every man in society as the order of men's togetherness finds explicit manifestation in the idea of equality before the law, for that idea underlines the fact that the candidate for equal evaluation is every man;

the typical postulated by the idea is the typical member of society or state, or—in more formal terms—the typical citizen.

IX

Yet another way of seeking the typical and the concomitant process of abstraction from diversity is to assess the wants of man, those, that is, which all men equally share. Thereby, we transcend the particular social or political group in which man is a member. Our standard of measuring men is no longer determined by the particular laws of the particular state of which they are citizens. Here we refer again to mankind in diffusion, and to human wants as they go. True, the wants are satisfied within a socio-political framework, but their nature is not determined by it.

To affirm the equality of human wants is to evaluate men in general on the basis of a theory of human nature, rather than on the basis of the nature of concrete human beings. The theory gives consideration to those needs which are engendered by or are expressions of man's common nature. This implies the possibility of ascertaining his basic wants. One is his need to work nature's resources to sustain himself in existence, and it reflects the fact that, were he not to act upon and intervene in nature, nature would not so sustain him. It is incumbent upon society to create the circumstances conducive to its satisfaction, such as the providing work and hygienic working conditions. Man's wants can also be approached psychologically. He needs to find acceptance in the sight of his fellows, and it is society's task at least to prevent his violent rejection by them, infliction of injury by one man on another, neglect of the aged, and so forth. True, considering the possibilities open to socio-political organization, perhaps society's hardest task is to create conditions conducive to the satisfaction of man's psychological wants. Another possible approach might ascertain what needs arise from man's endowment with more latent abilities than are realized in actual fact. Implicit in his need to develop or actualize his potentialities is his need to learn, to be educated, which society should take into consideration and cater for.

We have cited the different possible approaches only to illustrate a basic trend towards giving equal consideration to the wants which all men, as such, share: it makes no difference whether the wants are conceived in psychological terms or as inseparable from the reservoir of potentiality immanent in the nature of every man. What matters is that the assertion of human equality in terms of the needs that are common to all men. By basing the idea of equality upon an abstraction that exposes his typical needs, we inadvertently discern that equality serves as a principle which regulates the demands made by men upon society in such a way as to prevent the suppression, and guarantee the supply, of men's common wants. It is in this manifestation of the quest for the typical that the dynamic and activating role of the principle is thrown into sharp relief.

X

The idea of equal human wants is subject to what we have called the dialectics of realization. On the empirical plane of human reality, it is the desire to enjoy the same benefits as are enjoyed by other men that prompts the demand for equal satisfaction of wants; the demand is made often not because men entertain a certain idea of human nature but because they observe that some men enjoy hygienic working conditions, or living conditions, which foster their acceptance by their fellows, or an education which conduces to the actualization of their abilities. This means that underlying men's specific demands for equal satisfaction of specific wants is a comparison of some men's situation to that of others, in which case the measure of men's needs is the empirical situation of other men. It is by demands for equality understood in that sense that the egalitarian trend is advanced: egalitarianism interprets the principle of equality as a demand for social levelling, for eliminating the empirical differences between the diverse empirical situations and classes of men, and this accounts for the rancor, anger, and envy which at times accompany the trend.

The general pursuit of products and goods characteristic of the modern era is motivated by the egalitarian trend. But it is far from making for human collectivity; if anything, it spurs human competitiveness. One is reminded, in this connection, of Kant's sketch of two emperors who had a common objective: both wanted Milan, and that was the only "bond" between them. For it often chances that the realization of the principle of equality creates not an empirical human collectivity corresponding to the common human essence upon which the principle rests, but a sort of a racetrack where men compete for the products which equalize their respective achievements. There seems to be only one way of surmounting the difficulty created by the dialectics of equality-realization, and that is to arouse men to an awareness of their fundamental belonging to collectivity as partners in the comprehensive human essence. Since no empirical uniformity of consumption and achievement is involved in adherence to the idea of a universal human essence, the evocation of a general consciousness of fundamental collectiveness might yield a factor capable of curbing the competitive drive quickened by the egalitarian interpretation of the principle of equality.

Owing to the dialectics of equality-realization, it seems to be assumed that only by eliminating men's differences—at least as regards their way of life and their determination by the pursuit of products and achievements—can the universal human essence be ensured on the empirical plane of human reality. The fallacy is this: To realize equality in terms of an absence of diverse degrees of consumption and achievement would be to render the principle superfluous, so to speak, since principle and empirical practice would be indistinguishable if not identical. This implies that egalitarianism, understood as a tendency to level human reality to the empirical plane alone, undermines equality. Nor is it only the existence of the essential community of man that suffers from such levelling. From the viewpoint of the principle of equality, egalitarianism also takes its toll in terms of the concrete manifestations of human community, for men are held equal in terms not of their fundamental value in reality but because of their empirical characteristic and patterns of conduct.

If equal human importance cannot be ensured by uniform ways of life or by uniform orientation towards production and consumption, then collective ownership of the means of production cannot ensure it either. Ensuring the nonexistence of private owners of the major means of production gets rid of only one factor in the nexus of relationships making for human inequality, a factor which might be called organizational, for men are divided even when no particular individuals own the means of production. Division is implicit in the difference between men of economic initiative and others whose place in the process of production they determine, as well as in that between men whose economic role renders others dependent upon them and those economically dependent upon others. Moreover, actual economic activity, in the light of the viewpoint of the opportunities that it affords, diversifies men in terms of income and salary, and, so far as that diversification is concerned, it makes no fundamental difference whether the means of production are public or private property.

The assumption that consciousness of the fundamental community of man's equal importance and equal status represents a transsocial and suprapolitical factor capable of holding social processes in check is strengthened by the fact that not even eliminating private ownership of the means of production can prevent the creation of human differences. By cultivating it, it might be possible to secure, to some extent, the active impact of the transempirical human essence in the empirical conditions and relationships that obtain within society and state.

We do not mean either to maintain a duality between the empirical dimension of human reality and the transempirical dimension of man's common essence or to contend that the two are one. The point is that the transempirical fact of men's participation in their comprehensive essence must not be equated with its expressions in the economic, social, and political relations which exist on the empirical plane of human reality. The proper empirical manifestation of that universal participation cannot be guaranteed by any economic, social, or political relational structure, but only by preventing man's resignation to determination by his circumstances and by encouraging him to evaluate himself by the measure not of the place of the Joneses in the empirical race but of his own fundamental place in the universe. Just as freedom cannot find full realization under any political regime, so neither can equality in any economico-social structure, no matter how "levelled."

To say that man is by nature a creature of distance from the world is to say both that he is at a remove from the physical natural world existing from creation's final day, and that he must be at a remove from the economic and social structures which he himself has superimposed upon that world. A possibility of ensuring the status of freedom and equality is presented by this double removal or distance, which can be sustained on the empirical plane by what might be described as "asceticism of realization and application." Today, the significance of such an "asceticism" is not confined to the problematics of justice, freedom, and equality, but pertains, as well, to the more general human problem created by the perpetual attempts to shape the scientific world pattern in conformity to the technological maxim: "Implement whatever you can."

Perhaps the tendency to slide from the findings of science to the intervention of technology in the world ought to be countered by an ascetic attitude. The rule of asceticism here demands that science be kept in its intellectual place and intellect itself not reduced to being a minion of technology or geared wholly to the enterprise of technological conquest of the cosmos. As for the problematics of principle-realization, the rule implies the somewhat paradoxical postulate that, at times, the mode of realization in keeping with principles such as freedom and equality is the one which is careful not to translate them into empirical terms. The demand is not to permit an excessive encroachment of one realm upon the other and is not a demand for avoidance of the translation of scientific theory into technological practice.

Asceticism implies an awareness that, for example, it is one thing to open the gates of educational institutions to all, and another to encourage competition in the realm of education; or that to guarantee employment for all is one thing, and to incite all to take part in the competitive pursuit of products another. Granting this difference, it follows that certain aspects of the principle of equality call for empirical correlates, and others—namely, its foundation upon and underlining essence of man—are likely to be damaged by empirical translation, at least so far as concerns awareness of, and orientation to, that essence. It is in relation to such matters that the call for "asceticism of realization and application" is sounded.

XI

The incommensurability of the human essence, even with an empirical reality shaped in conformity to the principle of equality, is also mirrored in the fact that the wants of man, by nature typical, are embodied in a diversity of empirical needs. The need to learn or be educated is one typical want, yet, in point of empirical fact, it is refracted through one man's need or desire to learn mathematics and another's to learn history, and so on. Equality requires that all men who want to learn mathematics or history be afforded that possibility; what is called for is not identical contents of empirical wants but equal opportunity to satisfy these diverse empirical wants.

This would apply to the economic as well as to the educational sphere. Although empirical differences of salary and income are not immaterial, their bearing, measured from the standpoint of the common human essence, is only secondary, since they may be regarded as mere expressions of expressions, reflections of the diversity of human occupations which in turn reflect man's need to work. The principle of equality demands not only equal opportunity for all to choose their own occupations, but also equal evaluation of all, whatever their occupations. In respect of equality-realization, the courses open to social decisions concerning the empirical diversity of salary and income seem to be two. One is to adopt the rule of economic compensation inversely proportional to the satisfaction which men derive from their work: the less satisfying the job, the higher the pay, so that, to take an extreme example, street cleaning and garbage collection would be financially more rewarding than scientific research or artistic creation. The other is to adopt a rule of financial compensation directly proportional to the amount and quality of effort expended on the training required by one's chosen occupation: the more effort expended, the higher the earnings. No theoretical analysis of the problematics of equality-realization can afford to overlook these different valid approaches, if only because human wants are not physical forces subject to fixed physical laws but are needs subject to diverse and variable human interpretations. There is, accordingly, no fixed and unique direction in decisions concerning the system of salary and income most in keeping with the demands of the principle of equality, but several optional directions. Which direction a social decision will take depends upon the social influence and power of the men who entertain diverse interpretations of human needs and different ideas as to their practical implications.

XII

It is opportune to reconsider the relation between the principles of equality and justice. The first adds an element of specification or definite direction to the second. Justice postulates the right of every man to be taken into consideration; equality specifies the direction of consideration in terms of the common essence of mankind as a norm of evaluating men as equal. Equality directs justice towards the pursuit of typical groups, situations, cases, wants, and similar manifestations of the common essence. Equality is the more limited principle because it does not entail consideration for men in their unique individuality and in terms of the peculiar circumstances, while justice might very well entail consideration for them by reference not to their typical traits, situation, or conduct, but to their peculiar circumstances. This means that, as a matter of principle, the demands of justice and of equality can collide. For example, a creative individual might stand up for his right to diverge from typical patterns of social conduct on the ground that whatever is typical is stereotyped. In this and like instances, it is in no wise necessary to maintain that the demand for equal freedom for all is right and the demand for equality-defying justice wrong. But here, too, the task of an analysis is not to resolve the conflict of principle in favor of one or the other, but to delineate the position of this conflict and thereby show that, equality being a specified interpretation of it, justice is the more fundamental principle.

If justice occupies a more fundamental position than equality, it is because a man for whom justice demands consideration has a twofold status: empirical and essential. His total status is not adequately accounted for by the interpretation of the essential as typical, which the principle of equality propounds. Each principle entails a different approach to human freedom: justice requires that we take account of man as free man; equality prescribes that consideration for the freedom of one man be not impaired by consideration for the freedom of another, and determines the typical conditions of equal consideration for the freedom of all.

XIII

The principle of equality, then, is a specific interpretation, and not an adequate and exhaustive counterpart, of the principle of justice; it cannot be an exclusive norm of evaluating the worth of human beings and activities. In keeping with its content, men are measured by reference to the human essence embodied, in diffusion, in each. But men's concrete activities and behavior are not exhausted in the essence whereof they partake; they are characterized by specific contents, determinate directions, and particular kinds of contact with our fellows. True, man's conduct is an expression of his essence. But it is not only this, or assessable merely as such; its direction, its conformity to imperatives and standards, and so on, are also criteria—for example, behavior is evaluated in terms of whether it is good or evil, desirable or undesirable, and talk in terms of whether it is true or false, honest or dishonest. For the principle of equality, not only good behavior but bad behavior is an expression of man's essence, and this applies to morally bad behavior, say, dishonesty, and to pragmatically bad behavior, say, sloth. This is not to say that the moral worth of a deed is left unsettled by the principle of equality. That principle is breached by such bad behavior as inflicts injury upon the other or invades his domain, since it betokens one man's arrogation of authority above his fellow's. The principle entails evaluation of men and their deeds in terms of whether they preserve equality in their relations with one another.

But human activities beyond the reach of the principle are subject to evaluation in terms of intrinsic criteria of the sphere in which they are conducted. In the spheres of intellectual and artistic activity, for instance, a man is measured by whether he creates or compiles, or is a skilled or unskilled worker, and by similar yardsticks applicable to these and other spheres of human activity. Before the law, which is the formal expression of equality, all men are equal, be they compilers or creators, skilled or unskilled workers, but not as measured by the material touchstone of professional or creative merit. True, since men participate in the comprehensive human essence, we may affirm that, as a matter of principle, a man has it in his power to be either skilled or unskilled, either creator or compiler. But how this potentiality will be actualized by a particular person does not follow from that essence, and for that reason, the principle of equality cannot be a criterion of man's whole actual endeavor. As regards matters whose merit is reckoned by material criteria, the principle demands that all men be given an equal opportunity to be skilled rather than unskilled, creators rather than compilers, and the rest. Conformity to the principle necessitates an endeavor to eliminate such circumstances as obstruct man's attempt to actualize his potentialities. But the argument is double-edged. For if a man takes advantage of the opportunity granted him in such a way as to make himself unskilled instead of skilled, then he can be held responsible, called to account, and criticized for what he has done with his share of the human potential. If, then, you underline equal opportunity for all, you expose the activity of all to evaluation by material criteria which apply to spheres beyond the range of the principle of equality.

Evaluation of merit by standards can entail consequences that belong to the problematics of the realization of equality. An evaluation which sets higher value upon creators than upon compilers is not far removed from one which sets higher value upon, let us say, intellectual creation than upon artistic; it is not unlikely, then, that criterion of merit will be applied beyond the legitimate limits of its sphere of applicability—say, in the sphere of intellectual creation, where it ranks a genuine creator higher than a mere compiler—and employed to grade diverse occupational spheres in a vertical ladder of preferability—say, to rank intellectual creation above artistic, and so on. It is by no means easy to tell where valid evaluation by intrinsic criteria ends and illegitimate evaluation of the relative human and social merit of diverse occupational spheres begin. Denial of the legitimacy of any hierarchical gradation of human occupations is implicit in the underlying assumption of the principle, namely, that all human beings and occupations are but partial, equally partial, actualizations of the total human potentiality; only within the limited sphere of a single human occupation is a material criterion valid, and, within the respective spheres, material criteria are measures of the level of achievement. There is no measure of the relative merit of diverse occupational spheres. That relativity of merit becomes a social and political problem when the members of diverse spheres are organized in corporations or in classes, and have claims upon the comprehensive society or the state as one class upon another, and call for society or state to settle them. This aspect of the relation between spheres of occupations and the human beings engaged in them may have a general social significance, as when society or state is interested in promoting a certain line of occupation in terms of its economic productivity, and thus encouraging those human beings active in that line, who are hence given preference. A society may, in such a case, express its interest by the rewards that it offers to different occupations in the form, say, of salaries or housing, which can mean the preferential treatment of one group over another. In the many instances of this kind, we may aver that, according to the principle of equality, we must evaluate all human occupations, understood as empirical expressions of the universal human essence, as equal one to the other. Yet the principle is impaired in our actual daily behavior, because we act according to a different maxim or imperative, such as that of developing the state's strategic capacity or economic competitiveness. The fact remains that the principle of equality is blotted out by another principle or maxim of action. Financial rewards have a certain significance in terms of the evaluation of the equality of all the expressions of the universal human essence. Because of that, no empirical expression—and a financial reward is clearly one—can be done away with *a limine*. We cannot claim that, since we stress human essence, we do not care for its empirical expressions. We admit, rather, that a clash occurs between diverse maxims of action and that we do not behave according to the principle of equality, but, out of considerations of efficiency or proficiency, however valid they may be, shelve it. We are not concerned here to examine the reasons of proficiency and efficiency; this is certainly not the only case where one principle of action is restrained by another principle. Our objective is to remind ourselves of a general—or vague—imperative of honesty, namely, that we should not present any action as if it were not a breach of principle, but concede that there may be actions where principles are broken or one is transgressed out of consideration for another. There is no harmony between principles, and also none between actions according to varying principles.

XIV

What is the role of the principle of equality in socio-political reality? The principle pertains to that aspect of the relations among the multiplicity of men which expresses their participation in man's essence; the existence of a manifold human being is the background against which the problem of equality and its regulative function arises. Were it not for the existence of multiplicity of men, the question of their comparative evaluation could not arise. It is not inconceivable, to take an extreme illustration of the difference between equality and freedom in this respect, that a single individual might cut himself off from all other human beings and all institutions and seek seclusion in the wilderness. That does not harm his freedom, at least not his freedom of contemplating the world. But it would be senseless to ask whether he could be equal, since the only context in which that question makes sense, namely, the context of interhuman relations, is lacking. True, he impoverishes his freedom, since, in a wilderness, one cannot sustain freedom within politics, not to speak of freedom for politics' sake. Yet, even though the area of freedom's concrete manifestation will necessarily be contracted in his case, the primary mode of freedom, freedom of understanding will be present. Unlike the principle of freedom, that of equality cannot even be postulated in theory, let alone realized in empirical practice, save in the interpersonal domain. The principle of equality is related to socio-political reality through the mediation of the factual human domain.

The state is a bond between men, which transcends individual differences as implied by the content and duration of their life history, their native abilities, their activities, occupations, and roles. It is not our contention that the state reflects the mode of collectivity represented by men's participation in the common human essence. Man's essence is understanding, the state's is power—but there is a relation between the two. Were it not for the diffuse embodiment of the human essence in their multiplicity, men could not constitute a collective political fabric, abide by its laws, rules, and regulations or conduct themselves in conformity to its patterns. Collectivity cannot exist unless it is understood. Being endowed with understanding, men are able to relate themselves to a wider expanse of the world than is encompassed by their immediate experiences, specific roles, and particular positions. The fact that every man is able to contribute his share to the shaping of the state shows that all men are equally capable of transcending their partial—and hence limited—positions. If this equality is made manifest in participation in political life, then men have a right to demand political expressions of it; they can demand that the state sustain, in and through political practice, that status of equality to which it owes its own existence. The equality of men as participants in the state is at once the starting point and the end of politics. Equality before the law, for example, is both a formal expression of men's initial participation in the state and an instrument for extending the scope of equality by ensuring civil rights or granting civil services, and the like. As the end, as well as the beginning, of collectiveness-orientated politics, equality becomes a regulative principle of political life.

The demand to shape the political domain in the image of human freedom has its inception in the extrapolitical fact of man's status; the demand to sustain equality in the state and through its instrumentality begins in the political domain itself as a collective framework constituted by and for multiplicity of men. Equality's authority to regulate political life is given by its status as an explicit formulation of the conclusions which follow from the fact that the state itself is an embodiment of the equality immanent in men's common constitution of a concrete collective "surround" for their life in concert. The authority of political institutions, then, stems from their instrumentality in the creation of concrete expressions of equality; through them, the state creates, or can aim at creating, such conditions as render equality independent of men's ever-recurring decision, and ensure equality by stable patterns of conduct.

XV

So much for the primary positive aspect of the relation between the political domain and human equality, and between politics and principle of equality. The negative aspect is a particularly troubling element of the dialectics involved in the political realization of equality. Political equality is based upon men's participation in the state. But, empirically, political activity, the positions and roles by which it is sustained, introduce a factor of inequality into interhuman relations: some men administer political affairs, others are subordinated to administration; some manifest political initiative, others submit willy nilly to their guidance. Government through which collective power is refracted in concrete political life, is a cause of divisiveness among the members of the body-politic. This is so even under ideal conditions when judges and executives see themselves as servants of the law or of collectivity. For a judge's relation to the law would still differ from that of an ordinary citizen, and an executive's relation to collective power would differ from that of "the man-in-the-street"—if not to collective power itself, then at least to its shaping.

Division is the price of organization, simply because all organization entails placement. A man is related to the total of an organized relational structure from his allotted place in it; this is as true of a bus line in which A stands after B and before C as it is of the political structure where A is a legislator and C a law-abiding citizen. A man's place in an organized state is determined by his role in the organization. Some men fulfil the role of organizers and so their place is over, or opposite, the organization, and not only in it. There is no panacea for the relative inequality of organizers and organized in the collective state. We say "relative," because it is contingent upon political circumstances and because, outside the state, it is nonexistent; "organizers" and "organized" are not grades implicit in the common human essence. What makes the dialectics of equality-realization all the more vexing is that the more services the state offers to multiply the concrete expressions of equality, the more highly organized it becomes, and, the more areas organized, the more men are cast in the role of organizers. The group or organization-organizers includes not only men elected as administrators by the collective polity, but also others, men legally subordinated to them but nevertheless invested with administrative and political initiative.

If the division is irreparable, is there any way of lowering the price which equality must pay for its organized realization? Indeed, the negative repercussions of organization can be neutralized to some extent by the interaction of several factors. The emphasis is on "to some extent" rather than on "neutralized," for there are no miracle cures, and no complete neutralization can be hoped for.

There is the factor of the "consciousness of collectivity." Let the administrative roles of the state be accompanied by an awareness that their position is measured by, and only by, their contribution to the collective organization. Let the administrators link all their activities to a consciousness of their representative status in relation to the collectivity of the state. Another factor would be limitation of the authority vested in administrators. Let men in organizing jobs be responsible for representing state-collectivity in one sphere and be subordinate to organization, as their fellow citizens are, in all others. This factor already operates in certain arrangements; for example, the separation of the legislative, executive, and judicial branches of the state prevents executives or representatives of government from being judges, and makes them as subordinate as anybody else to the judiciary. Similarly, judges are not legislators but are as subordinate as the commonality to the legislation of the state. What is necessary is to interpret the classical idea of separating the three branches of government in terms not only of government itself but also of the connection between the idea of separation, the status of the men who represent the separate branches and the principle of equality. The factor is at work in the realm of education, too, guaranteeing that subordination of the contents and aims of education to politics will not result from subordination of educators to the arrangements, rules and regulations of the state. The more diffuse and divided are power centers of the state, whether institutional organs of government or outside the sphere of dominion government, the less is equality impaired by organization. The very fissures which, as we have seen, sustain freedom within politics sustain equality at the same time within the state.

A third neutralizing factor is the idea that if the administrators of the state are representatives of the public, then their administrative authority is derived solely from the function assigned to them; in fulfilling their role they are exposed to criticism and obliged to render an account of their doings. This exposure can sustain equality if the state is so organized as to facilitate their replacement by others, but, as regards neutralization, what counts is not the change of personnel in itself, but the legal constitutional and factual possibility of effecting it. Thus criticism, as one mode of freedom for politics' sake, is, *pari passu*, an equalizing factor within the political system.

But the interactive operation of the three factors cannot alone countervail the negative consequences of political organization, unless politics is controlled, in theory and in practice, by the principle of equality. To neutralize the relative inequality which organization produces, equal opportunities must be provided for all men to develop their creative capacities and initiative. The only way of sustaining political equality is to ensure the alertness of all men to human and social issues, as well as their adoption and expression of a critical-regulative standpoint towards society and state. This can only be done by establishing such economico-social and political conditions as minimize men's dependence on each other. One method of enhancing political independence is to lessen the amount of quackery and sham which rob men of their rational initiative by irrational ruses of persuasion. Another is to prevent the state from making men pay, for the economic benefits which it grants them, the price of their political initiative—which is what happens under the Bolshevist regime. The purpose of guaranteeing men economic security and services through the instrumentality of the state is to free them for an active share in political life, not to chain them to a political system and deprive them of their critical and regulative initiative.

Yet, no factor, and no nexus of factors, inside the political domain can counteract the consequences of the dialectics of equality-realization against the background of political organization. Hence, besides the neutralizing factors enumerated, it is essential to cultivate consciousness of the ultimate foundation of the principle of equality: consciousness of the comprehensive essence of man embodied in diffusion in all men. The collectivity of the state must be grasped as but one, partial, expression of men's share in that essence. Without detraction from the importance of the factors analyzed, it must be observed that the most potent force capable of offsetting the consequences of organization is man's self-consciousness—his recognition of his place in the world. There is some reason at least to hope, that this, if it exists, will not fail to express itself in the empirical domain of interhuman encounter in general, and in the political sphere in particular.

No matter how highly organized reality may become, freedom will never be ejected or suppressed; it is a primordial fact, and it endures. Efface its expressions today, and it will find ways of expressing itself tomorrow, or the next day. Not so equality; being only a norm of evaluation, and not a fact, it is not a self-sustaining motive force. It draws sustenance from men's consciousness of equality, which in turn, is fed by their conviction that a common human essence exists and is embodied, in diffusion, in every man. It is to men's considering their participation in that essence more highly than their empirical differences that the principle of equality owes its authority and force on the empirical plane of human reality.

CHAPTER TEN

Of Rights and Duties

I

The foundation of our consideration of human rights and duties has been laid in the preceding chapters, for to determine the principles of sociopolitical life is implicitly to establish man's right to consideration (the principle of justice) as free (the principle of freedom) and equal in respect of the criterion of human essence (the principle of equality). The present exploration need translate to a certain extent the conclusions of the earlier analyses from the context of guiding principles into that of human rights and duties. Man's right to be taken into consideration and his duty to evince consideration are upheld by the principle of justice; his right to occupy a status of his own and the state's duty to sustain it by the principle of freedom; his right to equal consideration and the state's duty to guarantee it for all its members by the principle of equality. Hence the basic content of human rights and duties is defined by those three principles. When emphasis is shifted from them to man's rights and duties, they are endowed with more specific meanings.

II

By the rights of man we mean the justifiable demands made by men for such consideration as will guarantee them a place in human reality, an ensured field of activity, and an opportunity to partake of the possessions which civilization has to offer. By our stress on justification, we exclude from this universe of discourse the demands sponsored by the arbitrary or capricious whims of men or the unwarrantable arrangements of the state, and disclose the essential juncture between man's rightful status and the status of freedom.

The fact that men make demands reveals a fundamental factor or presupposition, namely, that there exists a distance between them and their circumstances. Without it, men would not be able to make demands upon their circumstances. The necessary condition of human rights as demands is the human status of freedom. Even though freedom can be demanded by men and consequently constitute a human right, their freedom is presupposed and made manifest by the demand itself, thus the purpose of man's right to freedom is to guarantee the sustenance and concrete expression of his status of freedom. In the making of demands upon his circumstances, he reveals his freedom from total determination by them. But by expressing his freedom in demands directed towards his circumstances, he endows it with more specific meaning, because, in his acts of demanding, he reveals his freedom not only to make demands but also to interpret his demands according to his circumstances. Freedom to formulate new or diverse demands in relation to new or diverse circumstances is thus a special connotation of the principle of freedom when translated into a context of human rights. In certain circumstances, men might demand, for example, the right to vote for the legislative institutions of the state; in others, the right to partake of the economic possessions which society offers.

We must make two qualifications here. The first was glanced at in the definition of human rights as the justified demands of men. In point of fact, we become aware of the problem of human rights in our confrontation with men in their capacity as makers of demands. But, the range of human rights being narrower than the compass of human demands, we qualify our correlation of rights and demands by limiting the demands to *justified* ones. Under the qualification, human rights are defined as demands based upon, and justified by, principles. The problem of rights is raised by the existence of principles such as justice, freedom, and equality, in whose light man emerges as occupying a status of right, that is, as posing legitimate demands and interpreting them accordingly.

The second qualification is needed becasue the compass of the concept of "circumstances" is wider than that of the circumstances to which men address their legitimate demands. Within the universe of discourse of legitimate demands or of rights and duties, the term 'circumstances' does not mean any physical, geographical, or other circumstances confronting men, but those capable of responding to their demands; namely, their fellows, and along with that, the social order. We enter this reservation not only because, as a matter of fact, men come in contact with, and address demands to, one another, but also because, as a matter of principle, the human status of rights is sustained by the principle of consideration for man, and that principle is binding upon all men. The context of legitimate human demands, of human rights and duties, is created by the interplay of human interrelations, for that alone affords the grounds of meaningful legitimate demands.

III

We can now clarify the connection between the principles of rights and of justice. Defining human rights as justified demands implies that man's status as a maker of such demands is implanted in the principle of consideration for him as formulated in the principle of justice. Although the foundation of his status of rights is his status of freedom, freedom itself presents a demand for consideration by the circumstances, that is, by one's fellow or by the organization of society. The purpose of the idea of rights is to guarantee that the status of freedom will be recognized not only as a primordial fact but also as a principle endowed with binding authority. In the language of human rights, the obligation to take freedom into consideration is man's right to occupy a status of freedom; the principle of rights not only expresses but also demands consideration for him as free. If the foundation of human rights is freedom, then the germinal content of the principle of rights is a demand for justice. Insofar as the principle of equality is a certain interpretation of the principle of justice, a demand for equality can also be implicit in the idea of rights. Finally, a demand to create conditions conducive to the regulation of socio-political life by freedom is implicit in the idea of rights, since the fact of freedom to which man's status of rights is bound presupposes certain concrete conditions for the discharge of its function in society and state.

It follows that, though the formulation of human rights is sociopolitical, their foundation is transsocial and transpolitical. It may be said that the modes of contact between man and political reality are formulated in the idea of his rights and duties; why in the duties, we shall see presently. In this sense, the idea of human rights can be related to the traditional concept of natural law; it is by natural law, and not by the positive law of the state, that man is free. Although the traditional concept of natural law is endowed with multiple meanings, its primary one is the essential law in its relation to man as a law dwelling in his essence as an understanding being and in the demand for consideration which, as such, he makes. This implies that, by natural law, a particular man expects his fellow to behave towards him as an understanding creature just as he behaves towards his fellow as one. If natural law is based upon the fact that men are endowed with understanding, then it presupposes—among other things—the activation of that understanding in an interpretation of human rights that will distinguish between rights in which man's essence as an understanding creature is reflected—for example, the right to freedom—and those which guarantee his power of preserving his essence as an understanding creature, such as the right not to be subjected to overwhelming propaganda and improper coercion. Since the particular formulations of the rights of man reflect the way in which actual men understand themselves, their circumstances and their relation to them, formulation will vary according to variable historical, cultural, and socio-political conditions. The connection between the principle of rights and natural law permits historical-cultural and relative diversification of mankind from the aspect of the specific rights or legitimate demands of men. The verbal distinction drawn in several Western languages between Right and rights (*Recht, Rechte; droit, droits*) mirrors the two sides—universal-absolute and particular-relative—of the principle of justice in its relation to rights.[1] The positive laws of a state do not establish man's rights, but only give them political sanction and expression by translating them into such political rights as the right to protection of life, to freedom from interference, to housing. The purpose of the state is to provide political sanction for man's natural rights and guarantee that the legitimate demands which they embody will be satisfied in the diverse spheres of activity and organization.

IV

The idea of human rights cannot be understood unless one correlates it with the idea of human duties. The relation between the concepts of right and duty is closer than is suggested by the common-sense notion that if a person enjoys political rights, then he has political duties to fulfil. It seems that the two concepts have one and the same content, namely, the legitimate demands of men, except that right signifies *my* demand and duty a demand addressed *to me*. If it is my right to claim a response to my legitimate demands, it is also my duty to respond to legitimate demands addressed to me; right bespeaks a legitimate demand addressed by a particular man to his fellow or society at large, duty one addressed to a particular man by his fellow, or by society, or even by himself.

Neither the matter-of-fact correlation of political rights with political duties, nor the placement of the concepts of right and duty to a common origin implies that there is a preestablished harmony between man's rights and duties. For example, a man's right to object to certain state regulations— say, his right of conscientious objection to military service—may clash with his duty to observe state regulations, in this case, to serve in the army. So far from implying the impossibility of legitimate conflict between man's rights and duties, the common origin of both in legitimate demands implies the possibility of it. It is because there are legitimate conflicts between the legitimate claims embodied in rights and duties that we face the problem of a guiding rule whereby the conflicts can be resolved. There is no easy answer; the decision may rest with tribunals created for the purpose by society and state, or be left to moral conscience, which need not necessarily find formal expression, or, at worst, a conflict may explode in criticism and open struggle, as when men resort to resistance, passive and peaceful or active and violent, to defend what they conceive to be their rights.

The interrelation between the concepts of right and duty can be further clarified by reconsidering the implications of human rights as embodiments of legitimate demands. The primary content of human rights as legitimate demands is the principle of consideration for man as such. This means that when a particular person makes a legitimate claim for consideration, he demands that he be taken into consideration not only as a particular person but also as man; thereby he upholds the right of every man to consideration and consequently acknowledges his fellow's right to it. Therefore, we can say that if it is man's right to be taken into consideration, it is his duty to take his fellow into consideration. In affirming my right to consideration, I give the principle of consideration priority over the fact that it is *I* who demand it. Anchored in that principle, man's status of rights permits us to distinguish between a man's egotism and his individuality. Egotism involves lack of consideration for one's fellow, or an illegitimate claim for consideration; an egotist claims exclusive consideration for himself alone. An individualist claims universal consideration for the unique individuality of every man, including himself; he affirms that his fellow may be, and is, as much of an individual as himself, and the right to consideration as an individual man, therefore, belongs to all men without exception.

Nor is this the only implication of the concept of right. For by claiming consideration for ourselves, we assume the duty of taking ourselves into consideration. If I demand that others respect my individuality, I myself am in duty bound to sustain it as the sponsor of my demand for consideration. There is, thus, a double dovetailing of rights and duties; man's right to be taken into consideration being at once his duty to take both his fellow and himself into consideration as considerate creatures, capable of claiming and showing consideration for man or men.

As concerns the status of rights, the function of understanding is to define and formulate his wants in terms of his rights, and all that the state need do is ratify them or facilitate the satisfaction of the legitimate demand which they embody. It is, therefore, impossible to accept the notion that individuals endowed with consciousness and self-consciousness are mere accidents of the sweeping substantiality of the state. Likewise, it is impossible to accept the line of reasoning which argues from the judicial aspect of the concept of right to the twofold conclusion that the concept owes its meaning to the judicial system of the state, and that men owe to the state not only the actual expressions but even the ontological possibility of their status of rights. Where this argument errs is in identifying the judicial formulation of human rights with their ontological foundation because they are founded upon man's status in, and in relation to, the state. Men's legal rights are no more than interpretations and expressions of that status, which, logically and ontologically, is prior to its particular and variable legal formulations.

V

It is this difference between the transpolitical foundation of the human status of rights and the relative political expressions given to it that is reflected in the wide diversity of spheres where man's rights find determinate and variable presentation.

The idea of rights is realized on several planes of human reality, from that of individual inwardness to that of the individual's relations with his fellow and to the state, and man's relation to civilization.

1. On the plane of individual inwardness, man has a right to abide by the imperatives of his conscience, to evaluate phenomena by his own standards, and, in general, to sustain an inner dimension of individuality. Here, the status of rights is made manifest in the consciousness of the individual; in speaking of individual consciousness as the primary manifestation of man's status of rights, we have in mind not any particular contents but the authority of consciousness as an inner tribunal. As only individuals are endowed with consciousness, this is the plane of individual rights, as demands for acknowledgement of man's authority to obey his conscience and judge his environment independently, demands addressed by individuals to other individuals as well as to society and state. Although such demands are obviously directed at someone, their starting point is the factual existence not of a multiplicity of human beings but of individuals endowed with consciousness, possessing the right to sustain their status as such.

Duties being the reverse side of rights and both being embodiments of legitimate demands, a man's duty to obey the behests of his conscience is implied by his right to conscience. What differentiates an individual's duties towards himself from his duties towards society and state is that the first are not accompanied by coercion whereas the second are; founded on consciousness, a man's duty towards himself cannot be coercive, for consciousness and coercion are mutually exclusive.

2. The second plane of human reality on which the status of rights is reflected is bounded by the relations of the individual to his fellows, to the individuals with whom he comes in contact, or society, or the state. In any or all of these areas of contact, it is man's right to give free expression to his opinions of that other. The difference between a man's right to abide by his conscience on the plane of individual inwardness and to freedom of expression on the plane of his "other-relationship" is clear. Whether or not a man sustains his inner tribunal is the direct concern of no one but himself; but whether or not he is free to give outward expression to the decisions of that tribunal concerning his fellow turns on his consideration of that fellow, especially since speech can inflict injury or provoke action. Once more, rights and duties go hand in hand. By demanding acknowledgement of his conscience, a man not only claims his own right to conscience but also takes upon himself the duty of respecting his fellow's right to it, and, similarly, in defending his right to freedom of speech, he accepts the duty of acknowledging his fellow's right to it, and, similarly, in defending his right to freedom of speech, he accepts the duty of acknowledging his fellow's right to it.

On the plane of the "other-contact" of man, the right of the individual to consideration as one carries the right to self-expression in a more general sense than freedom of speech. It is not only with his tongue that he expresses himself, but also in the direction and form that he gives to his life; the right to self-expression accordingly means his demand to be allowed to lead his life in such a way as to make it a realization of his individual capacities and a reflection of his personality. This right signifies a demand to sustain islets of privacy free from the pressures of the public domain. Since men express themselves in deeds as well as in words, it is a legitimate demand to do what one wills within limits set by the duty of respecting one's fellow's similar right. These limits cut both ways: there are many islets of privacy in the sea of the public domain, and they inevitably—at least sometimes—collide.

Governing human rights and duties, as it does, the principle of consideration can also be made a norm of education, which, so controlled, would be simultaneously political and moral: political, because it would orientate man towards the other in the triple sense of individual, society, and state; moral, because that orientation would be guided by acknowledgement of his fellow's right to consideration not only as a fellow-citizen of the state, but also as a fellow-man. The duty of respecting our fellow-man's right to self-expression, as laid upon us by the principle of consideration, is not at all contingent upon his standpoint agreeing with our own. The demand for consideration does not get its authority from general agreement upon, let us say, the thoughts which find verbal expression; the contrary is true—acknowledgement of our fellow's right to disagree with us is what the principle of consideration requires.

3. Thirdly, the idea of human rights is expressed on the plane of the political order in its capacity as a field of activity open to the individual members of the body-politic. There, the status of rights is reflected in men's demand to take active part in the state. Man's membership in the body-politic validates his demand to express it by making decisions affecting the direction and content of political life. The starting point of the right to take part in politics is the factual existence not of consciousness-endowed individuals but of the body-politic. Respecting the existing body-politic, man's status of rights is articulated as the right to make it the content of his activity. His right to share in the life of the body-politic finds detailed externalization in such positive laws as concern, for example, the procedures of voting for legislative institutions, or political parties, or the existence of the press and other channels of public opinion. Another demand of the individual on this plane is to be given an equal opportunity to take part in public affairs from his private standpoint, refracting his right to active membership in the body-politic through the concrete and partial prism of his own experience. If, as members in the body-politic, all men have equal rights, then a particular man's right to shape the state lays upon him the duty of acknowledging his fellow-citizen's right to do likewise. This right of all men to active membership in the body-politic is, at the same time, the state's duty to respond to their demands to sustain it in existence. The right to be taken into consideration is at the same time its duty to create and sustain conditions conducive to men's active realization of their right.

4. From the plane of man, as a member of the existing body-politic, we reach the plane on which, as an active member of the body-politic, he expresses his status of rights in specific demands for legal protection, equality before the law, and political protection and realization of his rights, for example. The difference between the third and fourth planes becomes clear in the light of the distinction between the projection of crystallized power and the investing of that power with determinate contents. That makes it possible to differentiate between man's right to take part in the projection of power and his right to invest power with contents orientated towards the protection of those rights. He thus has a right to turn the state into an instrument for protecting his rights; as active members of the body-politic, men demand that the state formulate and institutionalize that duty of protection in its laws, judicial and legislative organs, and economic system.

Once emphasis swings to the contents of power, such as housing or employment, the state becomes an instrument at man's disposal. On the plane circumscribed by the instrumental relation of the state to its members, the purpose of politics is twofold: to set up an instrumental state and to determine the ends for whose sake the instrument will be wielded. Here again, rights and duties go hand in hand. For men's rights cannot be protected, or satisfied by the state through its legal machinery and economic services unless they submit to the duty of obeying the law or paying their taxes. Implicit in their right to political realization of their rights is a double duty: that of the body-politic to sustain the status of its members, and that of its members to enable it to fulfil that duty.

Man's political duties may be conceived as directly proportional to his political rights: the more legitimate demands men make upon the state for services, the more duties the state lays upon them. The state does not, however, necessarily shrink as the result of its transformation into an instrument. It is not the status of instrumentality but its content that determines the state's expansion or contraction; it all depends on whether the instrument serves just as a nightwatchman or as a provider and legal guardian whose task it is to provide you with economic and educational services, employment and old-age insurance. Man's right to an education will illustrate the point: It is not because he is a member of the body-politic, but because he is a creature endowed with consciousness, that this right is his. As such he makes the demand to activate it and to turn it towards contents, and only by a process of learning, training, and cultivation can the demand be satisfied. That satisfaction is within the political domain though its foundation is transpolitical, as man owes the realization of his right to an education to the educational services, arrangements, and institutions of the state. The realization of this, and of similar rights whose foundation is transpolitical, through the instrumentality of the state adds to the tasks of the state and consequently to the duties of the individual. Greater dependence upon the state is the price which men must pay for its services. Therefore, no delineation of the state's authority is implied by the status of instrumentality; that delineation hinges upon the contents with which the instrumental status is filled or the determinate ends to which the state, as instrument, will be directed. These consideration may help us to understand the turn taken by the political process in modern times: far from minimizing the authority and activities of the state, the emergence of politics for the sake of human rights has, if anything, amplified them.

5. The fifth plane of expression of the rights of man owes its existence to the fact that the state, as instrument, can be directed to the realization of rights that are not at once political. On this plane, men's demands are addressed to the historical process or to the march of civilization and couched in terms of demands to partake of the goods which civilization has in its gift. It is here that men claim the right to a high standard of living, to economic development, to technological advancement. This plane of man's right transcends that of his right to the services and protection of the state, where it is the anonymous historical process that is called upon to satisfy

his demands. But, for all practical purposes, his demands to have civilization and its possessions brought to his very door is addressed to the body-politic. Only a state has the power of action and the international connections with other states that are the conditions of bringing the individual into contact with civilization or bringing civilization to him.

It is possible that an individual's duty to sustain the body-politic will oblige him to defend its physical existence against aggression or attack. In that event, the right to sustain islets of privacy can obviously be subordinated to the state's right to demand of its members that they sacrifice their lives for its sake; a man's duty to respond to the state's demands is put before his right to self-preservation. In extreme instances such as this, one duty is given precedence over all others. The origin of this order of priority seems to be men's belief that, of all courses of conduct, sustenance of the body-politic's very existence comes first. It is a belief warranted by two considerations. One is that, from the point of view of the multiplicity of individuals and the succession of generations which it encompasses, the sphere of the state is wider than that of any of its individual members, present and future; the other, that the individual could not possibly sustain even his own islet of privacy were it not for his membership in a body with the power and means of self-defence. This body is an ordered structure, and its order allots each individual a place of his own. Rather than lose the body upon which the survival of his islet of privacy depends, the individual renounces his right to sustain the islet, and even to live, for the sake of saving the existence of the body-politic; men pay with their lives for the conditions of life, on the assumption that, where those conditions are lacking, life itself is impossible. It might be argued that life itself seems preferable to its conditions, and validly—validly so long as they exist; but, once threatened with extinction, they are given precedence over life itself.

VI

What conclusions are we to draw from the analysis of the multilayered structure in which the status of human rights finds expression? A negative one is that it would be a mistake to assume that the ladder which we have limned—from the plane of his rights as a creature endowed with consciousness, through the plane of his rights as an active member of an existing body-politic, to his right to partake of the possessions of civilization—is mirrored in the concrete consciousness of men. For men do not array their demands in that order; for example, they do not place their demand for conscience, or an education, or an active part in political life first, and for a share of the possessions of civilization last. If anything, the opposite is the case. For, in the modern era, men's notion of their rightful deserts is not one of many strata controlled by the logic of the idea; their demands are governed by an empirical guiding rule, namely, by the benefits which their environment has to offer, with the consequence that priority is given to the demand for a share of the possessions of civilization.

We do not deny that the principle of consideration is realized in the process. In fact, we would claim that the principle gives man the right to decide on which planes of human reality he prefers to be taken into concrete consideration; it is his right to prefer consideration as a high standard of living to consideration as acknowledgement of his right to abide by his conscience and evaluate his surroundings by his own standards. Danger of such a turn towards fragmentary realization lurks in the principle. But when it takes in manifold planes on which human rights are realized, it is incompatible with exclusive preference for any one plane at the expense of all the others, and affords ground to criticize the modern man and society for their outlook on civilization.

VII

A second conclusion concerns the position and destination of the modern state. Its transformation into the handmaiden of men's demands marked its birth, and it was born of their demand to take part in the administration and government of the body-politic. When men became conscious of themselves as occupying a status of rights, they set out to destroy the political order in which it had found no reflection, and to create a new one, wherein they could realize their rights. This is the significance of the notion "from status to contract."

The birth of the idea of rights was, at the same time, the birth of man's fear lest he be devoured by the state, and recognition of his rights was accompanied by an attitude of reservation towards it. As crystallization of order and a concentration of coercive power, the state was regarded with suspicion, and men claimed the right to defend themselves against it. In setting out to fashion a new political order, they believed that they would be able to transform the state into an expression of their active participation in the projection and shaping of power. They hoped thereby to prevent the possibility of a breach or duality between their rightful position of an active part in politics and the aggrandizement of power.

Looking at it from the historical perspective of the second half of the twentieth century, one can say that the modern state, based on the idea of human rights, has run its course. Its fate was sealed the moment that man began to apply this instrument of his to the project not alone of facilitating his active participation in the political domain but also of providing him with the possessions of civilization. Birth of the idea that the state is a vehicle for transporting civilization to the individual's doorstep marked the decline of the modern state as a scene of operations open to the active performance of its members.

A reversal of values is involved in man's conception of the instrumental state not as an arena for the shaping of an order of human togetherness controlled by the principles of justice, freedom, and equality, but as a ferry to civilization. What men want most today is civilization, which is, for them, the record of technological and scientific achievement set by the countries most highly developed in that respect. For the prerogative of keeping abreast of the march of civilization, men are willing to devolve more and more authority upon the state and enlarge its sphere of activity; possessions of civilization are worth more now in their eyes than a part in the creative shaping of the state, more even than the preservation of their islets of privacy. Because the right to partake of the possessions of civilization is on the topmost rung of the ladder of human rights, the problem facing twentieth-century man is not how to defend his rights against the state but how to defend his essential self against his empirical self, himself as a pursuer of those impersonal possessions or as their consumer. The Leviathan of the twentieth century is not the state but civilization. Curiously enough, men do not fear the new Leviathan of civilization as much as they did the old. Seventeenth-century man saw the dangers of a crystallized concentration of coercive power; his twentieth-century counterpart, attracted by the delights of civilization, will do anything for the sake of enjoying them, even if it means submitting to a totalitarian regime.

But why is it that men are oblivious to the peril of pursuing the new Leviathan? It is because the right to partake of the possessions of civilization entails no submission to extra duties. Civilization makes no demands of them and men are willing to make fewer demands in return for the benefits which it bestows. They deem the privilege of passive consumption of material goods a bargain at the price of renouncing the privileges which involve activity, the privileges of upholding an inner tribunal, of self-expression, of sustaining and shaping the state.

But one should not press the parable of the new Leviathan too far, lest, by personifying the antagonist in the drama of human rights, we shift the blame for the turn it has taken from men to a hypostasized entity. For it is to modern man's conception of himself, his place in reality, and his destination that civilization owes its elevation to the rank of man's highest end. It might be contended that, just as in times of crisis, preservation of life is a demand which takes precedence over all others, so, in the race for the benefits of civilization, the demand to meet or beat the record set by highly developed countries has absolute priority. But the fallacy is that the end of preserving life follows from the nature of the state; more than that, it is the reason of the state's being. By contrast, neither the desire for a share of the spoils of civilization nor the transformation of the state into a means of satisfying it follows from the nature and status of the state; both are consequences of men's moral and historical views and of the duties laid upon the state as a result of them.

If he gives any thought to the time-honored question of what is the good life, twentieth-century man finds that life is good if it encompassses the enjoyment of tools. In his eyes, the nature of the highest good is defined by the highest possible, or actual, level of tool production and consumption rather than by the principles of justice, freedom, and equality. Originally, the idea of human rights reflected man's demand to shape reality in his image; nowadays, the idea that consumption of civilization is the epitome of right-realization reflects his relinquishment of his active role as a shaper of reality and his submission to being shaped by his own products. The tables have been turned, the creator is shaped in the image of a reality which he has himself fashioned.

The foregoing considerations should not be construed as a denunciation of the direction taken by the course of history or as implying that man has no right to partake of the possessions of civilization. Man deserves a share of the spoils of civilization, because civilization is the collective creation of mankind. Its possessions owe their existence to the inventive powers and creative efforts of generations of men, to the division of labor among them, to the endeavors of the body-politic, its organization and institutions, to bring into being conditions conducive to the success of these collective efforts. The technological advances of recent ages are an outstanding manifestation—perhaps overestimated, but a manifestation no less—of man's dynamic role in reality, his active intervention in nature, and his mobilizing of its processes for his ends and needs. Precisely because it is his creation, civilization must be regarded by man as a creation and no more; and, at that, as merely one, partial, creation among many. As such, then, civilization has no right to engulf or suppress other creations of mankind, namely, society as the order of human togetherness, and the state. It is true that principles of human conduct entitle man to partake of the possessions of civilization. But it is not true that civilization is a principle. It is imperative to draw a distinction between principles and the planes on which they find realization. For every plane of principle-realization is necessarily partial, and, as such, occupies a secondary position in relation to principles which are partly realized on all planes and exhaustively realized on none.

Failure to keep principles and their partial realizations apart characterizes the life span of the state based on the idea of rights from its birth as a sphere and instrument for shaping reality in the image of unrealized principles to its demise as an instrument for shaping man in the image of realized possessions. Ushered on to the stage of history as the champion of human rights, its exit was heralded by the very success of its mission. The mission accomplished, and men's right to sustain and shape it realized, the state transcended itself in the effort to transport them to civilization; the effort meant collapse of the multilayered or stratified structure in which human rights had found their realization.

The dialectical turn taken by the rise and fall of the state founded on human rights should be an object lesson to present-day political philosophy. A new approach to that philosophy is called for by the reversal of man's evaluation of himself and his relation to society, state, and civilization. The trend of the new approach ought to be classical, that is, it ought to explore the nature of the state against the background of human reality, understood as the total sphere created and shaped by human activity. The subject matter of the new political philosophy should, of course, be modern; the task of contemporary political philosophy is to characterize the changes wrought by modern processes in human life and self-evaluation, and to grapple with the problems raised by those changes. A classical approach to the problematics of modern political life is the only way to revive the idea of human rights; a synoptic view of the stratified or multilayered structure of human reality is the indispensable prerequisite of preserving man's status, who upholds and expresses his essence by shaping all planes of his reality in its image. To protect his status of rights from submergence in any one of its multiple and diversified expressions, there must be insistence upon the duties which his rights lay upon him. To remind him of his duty to protect and preserve the human essence which he embodies, and of his obligation to sustain the state as an instrument of shaping society in conformity to the principles of justice, freedom, and equality, is a primary and preeminent task of the classically inclined philosophy of modern political reality.[1]

NOTE

1. See R.M. Hutchins, *Two Faces of Federalism*, An Outline of an Argument about Pluralism, Unity and Law. Center for the Study of Democratic Institution, Santa Barbara, Calif. 1961.

Alasdair MacIntyre in his book: *After Virtue: A Study in Moral Theory* (London: Duckworth 1981) questions the validity of the conception of human rights. In the present analysis we point to the changes in the realization of the idea of rights and do not question its justification. On this the present author's: Background and Justification, *The Journal of Value Inquiry* 1986, pp. 169ff.

Chapter Eleven

Presuppositions and Some Consequences

I

We may conclude the preceding analysis with an attempt to formulate some of the presuppositions of the socio-political realm, the task of a philosophical approach being to articulate these presuppositions and to place them in a systematic context.

In the first place, it has to be said that the socio-political sphere was not created by a deliberate act or set of acts—whether in the historical or hypothetical sense of a contract. The coexistence of human beings is a primordial fact, a result of their ontogenetic nature, receiving their common acknowledgement, however muted. The socio-political sphere, in particular its political dimension, is an exposition and extrapolation of this primary aspect of human reality. Being an exposition of human coexistence it becomes visible in and through the state. As extrapolation, it is endorsed by the very trend towards making coexistence prominent, while at the same time the extrapolated sphere turns into an instrument for the given coexistence. The conjunction of the inherent aspect with the instrumental one is a characteristic of coexistence, as we find it, for instance, in the various aspects of the division of labor—the other side of which is collaboration. The socio-political sphere creates itself continuously, yet at no stage is it, or has ever been, created *ex nihilo*. The normative aspect of that sphere is based on its dependence on human actions, while in turn they are expressions of man's transempirical essence. The instrumental aspect of the political sphere can be summed up by saying that it derived from the transempirical essence of human existence and therefore aims at maintaining that essence; maintaining it is impossible without continuous cultivation and promotion.

II

The empirical aspect comes to the fore not only in the instrumental elements of the political reality but also in the impact of historical situations on the shaping of that reality. The empirical interpretation of the normative as well as of the instrumental aspects of the political order—and the two are interrelated—becomes more prominent under the impact of historical conditions on the direction of the political reality, in terms of socio-economic situations or in terms of the expectations that concrete human beings direct towards the political instruments. One contemporary aspect of the instrumental quality of political reality is the welfare state and the concurrent interpretation of human rights related to that structure. Yet the previously explored "dialectic of realization" leads us to the conclusion that no specific interpretation of the instrumentality of the state can be exhaustive. The immersion of that instrumentality in the historical process brings about a continuously problematic situation: not only do deficiencies in realizations give rise to difficulties, but so also do successes. Placing realized goals within concrete situations causes the goal to be immersed into the process within which the realization takes place; thus a "pure" realization is impossible.

III

A structural or phenomenological analysis of the domain of the state and of political activity brings us face to face with a basic feature of this sphere: its *raison d'etre* is its being the manifestation of the order inherent in human coexistence—and hence collaboration—by rendering that order explicit and thus organized, or more precisely, ordered. In this sense, law and order become the face of this domain. Order, in turn, can be considered as instrumental for the infrastructure of human existence. But by the same token, it may be turned into an instrument of its own existence—*raison d'etat* thus becoming the *raison d'etre* of the domain. It seems likely that, due to the structural elements of the domain, no built-in remedy exists for these shifts from self-concern to monopolistic concern. The only way to arrest the process is to revert to the position of man as a being not totally immersed in the circumstances of his existence, thus enabling the application of norms which are not identical with institutions.

IV

The question whether man is a social being by nature or whether his social existence is the outcome of an agreement is irrelevant. Man is a being living with other human beings, whether that mode of existence is the outcome of his limitations and his resulting search for reinforcement, or whether he is born into a given situation which he, as a descendant, did not create. Hence the involvement with other human beings is his primary situation, which can thus be viewed as belonging both to his essence and to his existence. As regards his essence, its most prominent aspect is that of maintaining an attitude towards other human beings (or, on a higher plane, towards togetherness in a more abstract sense), and planning vis-a-vis himself and his fellow-men, not only in terms of particular acts but also in terms of structures, including that of order. Order is an abstract concept, and as such calls for an attitude that entertains abstract meanings, representing the precondition for creating order as an abstract structure. A created order is imbued with a status, and can thus potentially become estranged from the factors that created it—just as any product of creativity gains an independent position. A created work, such as a work of art, may or may not have an impact on the ongoing creativity of the artist or of his environment. But the socio-political order, precisely because it is an abstract product, cannot be maintained except in and through the continuous intentionality of the human beings involved. They refer to the order, and they absorb it as a meaningful entity in thier intentionality. If taking an attitude is a precondition of the existence and the functioning of the order, this is because intentionality is the essential quality of human existence; the social attitude and order as its "noema" are among the manifestations of that basic quality. Intentionality as present in some contents may change, and the involvement of one content in another, including the absorption of a content as a "noema" of a preceding intentionality—all these are possibilities inherent in the nature and status of intentionality. One of the consequences of that analysis is that there is no way for a total separation or alienation of the political order from the intentionality of human beings towards it. A political order cannot be a mere "landscape." Here again, from a structural point of view, we may refer to the phenomenon of totalitarianism founded on an ideology.

V

The totalitarian state is based on the alleged full identity of the instrumental element of order with the aspect of a goal. The regime is to serve total adherence either to the determining element of race, that is, biological belonging, or, with all the differences, to the overriding aspect of the shape of society, grounded in the deterministic direction of the historical process, as in the case of Soviet communism. Hence totalitarianism is based on several assumptions: the isolation of one element of social existence, which is made to predominate, resulting in the deterministic shaping of human existence, since involvement in the process is a basic fact anywhere; the possibility of separating one element out of the multiplicity of elements of the social context, thus making the other elements nonexistent or secondary; and the justification of the instrument of the regime by the determining element, turning the instrument into a determining factor or goal vis-a-vis the population. The outcome is totalitarianism, that is to say, the complete subordination of the people to the regime, which presents itself as embodying goals that are above or beyond human decisions.

Yet those who control the regime become a social class whose position is not based on agreement but on the determining factor. Hence the authoritarian character of the regime is the corollary of its totalitarian structure. That part of the population which does not accept the order laid down by the regime is considered as whimsical, if not outright psychotic. Totalitarianism thus prescribes behavior without obtaining the consent of the population itself.

In this context, an additional element relating to Soviet totalitarianism has to be mentioned. The way to relate political activity to a predetermined goal is to interpret freedom as the acceptance of necessity; the goal is inherent in necessity, and affirmation of the goal, and even subjugation to it, is considered a freedom. Hence freedom is not interpreted as founded on the distance between man and his circumstances, but as a synthesis between man and his goal, where necessity sublates the circumstances. That kind of totalitarianism, though claiming to be related to the historical process, actually disregards the prevailing circumstances of that process and emphasizes the goal placed at the end of the process, leaping from the circumstances to the goal. Since circumstances cannot be eliminated, the totalitarian regime adopts the totalitarian attitude and behavior towards the circumstances, subordinating the population to its mode of regime. The conjuction between the instrumental aspect of the order and its teleological aspect leads to the suppression of factual human reality and of coexistence.

One could suggest that, on the face of it, the totalitarian state is based on the duties it imposes upon its citizens and not on their rights. Yet, as we have seen, duties and rights interact, both being forms of demand. Thus if a political order extricates, as it were, duties from the total context, duties cease to be what we suppose them to be. Duties become orders, that is to say, they become demands addressed to men by the regime; they are basically calls. Man's position cannot be disregarded, and his existence does not consist in following the orders imposed. The difference between demands in the context of justification and calls based on power is an essential one and must be maintained.

VI

Coexistence is the factual basis of the social and political realm, providing the foundation on which the structure of the state is created. To be sure, coexistence as a factual basis can be interpreted as containing ingredients and factors which may lead to the socio-political structure. Yet this interpretation is a retrospective attitude, entertained from the point of view of the socio-political structure.

Coexistence is not only the basis but also an essential element in the structure related to it and to some extent superimposed on it. The institutional character of a state is therefore both an interpretation and an imposition. A special ingredient in that two-way relationship between the basis and the superstructure can be discerned in the partialness of the political or institutional character of the state.

Coexistence can be understood as pertaining to the factual basis of the situation of human beings in itself, and thus it is not limited to particular individuals or to any limited area, in the various meanings of that term, of their existing next to each other. Hence coexistence can be understood as an essential feature of human reality, preceding the suprastructure, since essence can be seen as given, while a suprastructure must be conceived as brought in. A corollary of the created character of the suprastructure is the partialness of the social political realm. There is no structure which can be seen as coequal to coexistence as a universal feature of human reality. It is a historical fact, at least, that states are partial entities, and a universal state has not been erected to become a structure expressing the universality of mankind. We should probably and cautiously not derive definitive conclusions from historical reality; a universal state may indeed be envisaged, although it is not a fact. We may perhaps suggest as a tentative conclusion that this putative future universal state will still embrace partial structures, since organizational universality will probably be supplemented by various sorts of partial semistructures. However, as things stand, the organizational exposition and extrapolation of coexistence are embodied in partial state organizations.

VII

The structure, on the other hand, carries within itself not only a descriptive attitude to itself as it is but also an attitude in terms of the norm to be applied to it. This has to be said with reference to the principles of political activity as explored, such as freedom, equality, and justice. The position of a state as a structure created out of coexistence and for the sake of it, makes the state a secondary product of human intentionalities. As such, it is never safe or secure. Both the created aspect of the state and its partialness lay it open to the assumption that it is always exposed to the danger of annihilation, either as an artifact or at the hands of another partial structure, that is to say, another state. This double-faceted fragility can and has been interpreted as forcing the structure of the state to be perpetually concerned with the attempt to safeguard its very existence. It is probably in terms of this fragile position that, historically speaking (as in the case of individual life), the *raison d'etat* consideration has been cited as a principle—or sometimes as the supreme principle—of political activity, after the built-in imperative of maintaining existence. Hence the *raison d'etat* principle may be considered to represent the secondary position of coexistence. *Raison d'etat* is a kind of political equivalent of "primum vivere." The clash between the principle related to existence as such, compared with the principle related to the "good life," is probably built into this position of the state. An additional aspect of this consideration will be discussed presently.[1]

VIII

As we move within the tension between the factual character of coexistence and the created position of the state structure, we find within the social and political domain the continuous effort to introduce into the interaction between the two aspects some factual ingredients of coexistence that may become both factual and created components of the structure of the state. We refer here to the various attempts to discern affinities between human beings, created and not natural, but still belonging to the factual sphere and not to the normative one. The most striking case in point is the linguistic component of the coexistence of human beings, who, while coexisting, communicate, and their communication is an expression proper, that is to say, one embodied in language. The partialness of historical languages as against the inherent capacity to speak, which is characteristic of human beings in general, is a fact incorporated in the socio-political structure and is taken to be both a basis for that structure and a fact of enhancing its reality, and thus, at least internally, safeguarding it. Once the aspect of historical component comes into the picture, the historical continuity of people—for instance, in the sense of nation—is understood to be an additional factor which can be placed on the border line between that which is given and that which is created. It is obvious that the notion of a nation-state is precisely one of the manifestations of the built-in attempt to combine the two factors, that which is given and that which is created.

To be sure, this linguistic aspect is not always unequivocal. This is evident in a state embracing a population which is linguistically divided. In such a case, there is no simple correlation between the community in terms of language and the structure in terms of political extrapolation of the factual basis. Yet there is one component in the structure of the state which seems to be more dominant even than that of language, namely, what is called the territorial basis of a political entity. Coexistence between human beings takes place in space. Though historical consciousness in terms of the continuity between generations is present in social structures and is even deliberately brought into it, the spatial component is related to intergenerational coexistence. The political structure is related to a deliberate attempt to bring the given spatial dimension of coexistence into the framework of the political structure. The notion of sovereignty relates at least partially to authority vis-a-vis the territorial basis. That notion is a juridical or legal interpretation and is thus an interpretation introduced into the existent dimension of spatial coexistence between human beings.

We can sum up this part of our phenomenological analysis by showing that it indicates a norm inherent in the structure of the socio-political realm. If we look at the attempts prevailing in that realm to relate the structure to a factual basis, we come to the conclusion that the factual basis cannot be simply transposed to the structure. It has to be interpreted, and as much as it contains in itself a normative aspect which combines the justification of the structure in terms of coexistence and safeguarding the structure because of its inherent deficiency in terms of its factual character. The normative attitude contains in itself a twofold justification: the state as a continuation of coexistence and the state as an instrument for the sake of this continuation.

Moreover, though there is a difference between the factual and normative aspects, the discernment of the factual may lead to a formulation of the normative. At this juncture it is proper to refer to the ethical consideration as a whole, and not only to its partial presence in the political structure. The ethical consideration refers to the same factual basis as the political structure, that is to say, to human coexistence. Yet the direction of the ethical consideration proper differs from the political perspective, since the ethical norm does not lead towards an organization but toward the mutual acknowledgement of the human beings involved in coexistence. The ethical standpoint is in this sense horizontal, while the political activity is vertical. The ethical consideration contributes a dimension to the factual encounter between human beings. Acknowledgement of their mutuality may be manifested in the affirmation of the respective rights of the individuals involved to exist, but it may also evoke the attitudes of help, of care, of entertaining common goals, and so forth. In this sense, the ethical attitude is, to say the least, more universal than the political structure, since it refers to human individuals in general and not only to those encountered, as it were, within the scope of one's empirical visibility. In terms of institutional considerations, it might be said that the ethical attitude in the pure sense of the term does not create structures. It is an attitude with all the strengths and weaknesses of an attitude only. We may consider the position of an attitude as corollary to the position of universality. The ethical attitude pays, as it were, a toll for its universality. The political attitude related to the political structure is partial, and as such it finds its manifestation within institutions.

The difference between the respective directions of the two interpretations of coexistence does not imply that they do not intermingle. For instance, within the political structure we find the extrapolation or interpretation of the impact of the ethical structure in the principles of political activity: freedom implies the acceptance of individuals as such, coexisting but with a status of their own; equality implies the recognition of human individuals as basically equal, though they may differ functionally; justice implies the duty of the state to respond to the individuals whose position is primary and cannot be, that is to say ought not to be, disregarded. This interaction between political and ethical concerns is in a sense a response of the political realm to the ethical consideration, and that response in turn can be seen as an exposition of the given coexistence which is differently, though not necessarily contradictorily, interpreted by the two attitudes.

Still, it must be said that the interaction between the attitudes does not provide a basis for assuming a primary harmony between them. It opens the way for the interpretation of the fact of coexistence as the broad scope of human reality and, as such, exposed to different interpretations, which in turn demonstrate the fact that there is no necessary preestablished harmony between those interpretations. The political realm may try to find its justification in ethical considerations, while the ethical realm may try to find in the political realm an instrument for the realization of its principles. To be sure, the complexity of these relations manifests the fact that since the political realm is in its very structure, at least partially, instrumental, it can serve as an instrument not only for the sake of its survival but also for the sake of the implementation of principles in the normative sense of the term. These, because of the structure of the political realm, are partially implemented—partial in terms of the scope as well as in terms of the transitory character of any implementation or realization.

The distinction between the basis and the structure within the political realm leads us again to some comments on totalitarian regimes. It can be said in epitome that totalitarianism turns the *raison d'etat* of the state into *ratio* or *reason*. It takes the instrumental aspects of the political reality—whether in terms of direction towards the population inside the state or towards other states within the context of international relations—as expressing the goal of history and thus as the realization of reason, at least in as much as the historical process is concerned. This process can be seen as explicit or implicit, since the totalitarian regime disregards the awareness of the various layers of the socio-political reality. It presents itself as a structure of identity on the basis coexistence. In this sense, the manifestation of coexistence entails a built-in presupposition that the manifestation replaces that which it manifests.

To sum up, one may say that the totalitarian interpretation of the political realm, precisely because it is oblivious of the multidimensional character of social reality, is inherently connected with what goes by the term "false consciousness." It goes without saying that the identification of the needs of the state with reason leads to a built-in neglect of some of the moral problems related to coexistence and to the normative dimension to be applied to it.

We come back to our previously formulated conclusion that the phenomenological analysis of the socio-political realm, by leading to the discernment of ethical aspects, leads also to a critical approach to political regimes, and, in the first place, to totalitarian regimes. The positive and the negative aspects of a political reality are correlated.

NOTE

1. On the history of the notion of *raison d'etat*, consult Friedrich Meinecke, *Die Idee der Staatsrüson in der neueren Geschichte*, R. Oldenbourg, München/Berlin 1924.

Index of Proper Names

Althusius, Johannes, 60, 62, 69
Aristotle, 8, 13, 14, 15, 17, 37, 66, 87, 88, 102, 110, 183

Berlin, Isiah, 183

Gehlen, Arnold, 54

Hart, H.L.A., 134
Hegel, George F.W., 33, 34, 47, 92, 94, 100, 104, 112f., 137f., 151, 170, 183
Hobbes, Thomas, 8, 13, 30
Hutchins, Robert M., 22

Kant, Immanuel, 12, 33, 34, 99, 112, 124, 183, 196

Leibniz, Gottfried W., 190
Locke, John, 30

Machiavelli, Niccolo, 31, 57, 85, 92
MacIntyre, Alastair, 222
McKeon, Richard, 104
Marx, Karl, 10, 50f., 151
Meinecke, Friedrich, 231

Nozick, Robert, 35
Nadel, S.F., 34

Oakeshott, Michael, 62f., 69

Parsons, Talcott, 35
Perelman, Chaim, 134
Plato, 10, 50f., 77f., 83f., 102, 108f., 112f.

Rawls, John, 134, 183
Rousseau, Jean Jacques, 39
Russell, Bertrand, 33, 35

Schmitt, Carl, 41
Smend, R., 20
Strauss, Leo, 100, 104

Tillich, Paul, 35

Weber, Max, 98f.
Weiss, Paul, 134
Whitehead, Alfred North, 53

Subject Index

absolute, 99, 212
abstraction, 25f.
achievement, 220
adjustment, 127f.
acknowledgment, 7, 25f., 62, 229
actuality, 190f.
advancement, 217
Afrika, 174
agreement, 61
aggressiveness, 13
allocation, 8f.
America, 181
anarchism, 169
anticolonialism, 160, 179
apolitical activities, 149f.
arbitrary, 6
art, 74, 84, 119, 147, 175, 225
artificial, 13
asceticism, 123, 167
Asia, 80, 120, 174
authority, 54

balance, 163f.
balancing, 128f.
biography, 74f.
biological existence, 34
biology, 97
Bolshevism, 152, 182, 200, 225f.
brute force, 44

cardinal numbers, 8
causality, 136
cause and effect, 136

choice, 143f., 151f.
Christian theology, 8
church, 23
circumstances, 40, 43, 57f., 71f., 116f., 146f., 186f., 210f.
civilization, 118f., 217f.
climate, 72
coercion, passim
coexistence, 223f.
collectivity, passim
collective ownership, 197f.
compulsory education, 165f.
compulsion, passim
confidence, 94
conscience, 214f.
conscientious objection, 155, 212
consciousness, passim
consequences, 99f.
consideration, 87f., 110f.
contemplation, 120, 150f.
contract, 12f.
cosmos, 67
"cosmic imperialism," 52
creative potentiality, 52, 115f.
criminal offence, 193
criticism, 97, 160f.

demands, 191, 209f.
democracy, 61, 149
depersonalization, 59f., 95, 149, 151
detachment, 137
determinism, 135f., 225f.
dialectics, 58f., 85, 95f., 111f., 137f., 164f.

"dialectics of realization," 97f., 119, 159f., 192f., 196f., 224
dictatorship, 164f.
discord, 109f.
distance, 135f.
diversity, 10, 185f.
division, 205f.
division of labor, 10, 229
droit, 212
duty, 94f., 109, 209

economics, 74f., 181f., 197f.
education, 49, 165f., 181f., 195, 198f., 206, 215, 217
egalitarianism, 196f.
egoism, 85
egotism, 213
emancipation, 128, 131, 180
emergency, 41, 66
empirical,
employment, 69
ends, 95f.
epistemology, 3
equality, 10, 30, 46, 48, 66, 90f., 185f., 200
essence, 12f.
ethics, 3f., 220
Europe, 181
evaluation, 185f.
experience, passim
expression, 5f.
extrapolation, 233f.

family, 4, 9, 21, 22
fellow-man, 29f., 86, 164f., 185f., 211f.
fiction, 5f.
folklore, 5f.
foreign relations, 65
form(s), 4f., 37, 67
formalization, 24f.
franchise, 186
freedom, 135f., 185, 206, 207
friendship, 5
"from status to contract," 219
future, 72f.

government, 25f., 50f., 64f., 205f.
gradation, 202

harmonization, 167
harmony, 113
health service, 181
hierarchy, 40
hindrances, 33f., 141f.
historical criticism, 161
history, 18f., 19, 24, 34, 46, 62f., 71f., 113, 137f., 228
horizontal diversity, 189f.
humanity, 50

"the idea of man," 189f.
identification, 138f.
ideology(ies), 23
image of God, 191
imperative, 99
indetermination, 143
individual(s), 9, 16f., 25f., 50, 89f., 145f., 185f.
individuality, 213
industrial advancement, 152
inequality, 90f.
initiative, 158f.
institution, passim
instrument, 223f.
integration, passim
intention(s), 98f.
intentionality, 8, 26f., 225
inwardness, 102f.
irrationality, 99f.

Jews, 128, 163, 169f.

judges, 205
just, 44
justice, 8, 9, 30, 66, 107f., 140, 153, 185, 200, 209, 211f.
justice, commutative, 130f.
justice, distributive, 130f.
justification, 209f.

Kingdom of Heaven, 8

language, 14f., 145, 228
law(s), 22, 41f., 87f., 189, 194, 194f.
legal form, 5

Subject Index

legal procedure, 193
legislation, 176
"lesser evil," 94
"Leviathan," 220
Liberty, 66, 131
love, 94

maintenance, 67
majority, 178
mankind, 19, 227
man's essence, 114f.
Mars, 142
means, 25f.
Millenium, 73
modernity, 222
modes, 4f.
monopolization, 165
moral principles, 31
morality, 83f., 107f.
motives, 99f.

nation, 228
nation-state, 228
national independence, 79
national movements, 160
nationalization, 61
natural, 6
natural law, 211f.
nature, 12f., 23f., 42f.
necessity, 6f., 140f.
Nazi regime, Nazism, 161f., 169f.
nondiscrimination, 193f.
norm, 18f., 23f., 46f., 66, 107f., 185f., 223f.
normativity, 11

objectivity, 18, 117f., 149f.
objectivization, 46
occupation, 109
order, passim
organism, 42
organization, passim

partial, 18, 22, 58f.
partial embodiment, 189f.
partialness, 227f.
participation, 39f.

past, 71f.
penalty, 20
philosopher-king, 51
philosophers, philosophy, 51, 77, 223
physical reality, 16f.
plebiscit, 161f.
possession, 118f.
politics, 48, 57f.
potentiality, 139f., 158f., 175, 190f.
power, 7, 25f.
predictability, 43f.
preference, 84
presumption, 194f.
principle, 99
privacy, 218
private properties, 16f.
profit-economy, 137f.
progress, 100f.
projection, passim
proletariat, 50
property, 66, 77
psychological needs, 195f.
public, passim
publicity, 22f.
purpose(s), 63f., 71f.

race, 225
racial theory, 169f.
raison d'etat, 227f.
rationality, 17, 45, 47, 101f., 143f.
reason, 47f.
Recht, 110, 212
reciprocity, 87f.
recognition, 109
reflexion, passim
relative, relativity, 99, 153, 192, 202, 205, 212
regressive analysis, 3f.
regulation, 12
religion, 168
religious organization, 156
religious thought, 160
responsibility, 98f.
restraint, 7f., 109f.
results, 99f.
revolution, 48, 88
rewards, 202
right, 44, 110
rights, 155f., 209f., 224
retribution, 111

sanction, 46f.
science, 5f., 7, 59, 67, 74, 84, 119, 147, 160, 198
self-alienation, 118
self-consciousness, 16f.
self-expression, 215
self-origination, 143f.
self-preservation, 41, 218
self-realization, 151
service-economy, 179f.
society, passim
soul, 169
sovereignty, 41f., 175
Soviet Union, 163
species, 9, 18, 19, 22, 49, 60
spontaneity, 87, 137, 143, 157
state, passim
Stoics, 53
stratification, 189f.
structure, passim
subject, 91, 135f.
subjective, 99f.
submission, 17
subordination, 39f., 90f., 149
Supreme Court of the United States, 46
synopsis, 51, 222

technology, 198
teleological activity, 59f.
telos, 13, 37
territory, 11, 23f., 52, 77, 229
time, 19
togetherness, passim
toleration, 86f., 124, 167f.
totalitarianism, 49, 68, 151f., 178, 180, 225f.
totality, passim
transempirical, 116f., 223
truth, 118, 122, 153
typical, 188f.

understanding, 14f., 79f., 116f., 190f.
unity, 22f.
unjust, 44
universal, 9, 22f.
universality, 227
utility, 100f.
utilization, 171f.
utopia(s), 47

validity, 120
vertical diversity, 189f.
violation, 20
vidence, 195
virtue(s), 109f.
voting, 176, 210, 216

war, 41, 66, 96, 98
welfare state, 224
West, 174
will, 47, 61
wrong, 44